THE PRIVATE LIFE OF
JAMES II

THE PRIVATE LIFE OF JAMES II

JUSTINE BROWN

PEN & SWORD HISTORY

AN IMPRINT OF PEN & SWORD BOOKS LTD.
YORKSHIRE – PHILADELPHIA

First published in Great Britain in 2024 by
PEN AND SWORD HISTORY
An imprint of
Pen & Sword Books Ltd
Yorkshire – Philadelphia

Copyright © Justine Brown, 2024

ISBN 978 1 39905 077 7

The right of Justine Brown to be identified as Author of this work has been asserted by her in accordance with the Copyright, Designs and Patents Act 1988.

A CIP catalogue record for this book is available from the British Library.

All rights reserved. No part of this book may be reproduced or transmitted in any form or by any means, electronic or mechanical including photocopying, recording or by any information storage and retrieval system, without permission from the Publisher in writing.

Typeset in Times New Roman 11/14.5 by
SJmagic DESIGN SERVICES, India.
Printed and bound in the UK by CPI Group (UK) Ltd.

Pen & Sword Books Limited incorporates the imprints of Atlas, Archaeology, Aviation, Discovery, Family History, Fiction, History, Maritime, Military, Military Classics, Politics, Select, Transport, True Crime, Air World, Frontline Publishing, Leo Cooper, Remember When, Seaforth Publishing, The Praetorian Press, Wharncliffe Local History, Wharncliffe Transport, Wharncliffe True Crime and White Owl.

For a complete list of Pen & Sword titles please contact
PEN & SWORD BOOKS LIMITED
George House, Units 12 & 13, Beevor Street, Off Pontefract Road,
Barnsley, South Yorkshire, S71 1HN, England
E-mail: enquiries@pen-and-sword.co.uk
Website: www.pen-and-sword.co.uk

or

PEN AND SWORD BOOKS
1950 Lawrence Rd, Havertown, PA 19083, USA
E-mail: uspen-and-sword@casematepublishers.com
Website: www.penandswordbooks.com

Contents

Acknowledgements vi
Prologue Hide-and-Seek vii

Chapter 1   From Gold into Iron 1
Chapter 2   A Mirror World 13
Chapter 3   The True Eaglet 26
Chapter 4   The Rover 41
Chapter 5   The Garland King 53
Chapter 6   The Best Revenge 64
Chapter 7   Apocalypse 77
Chapter 8   Reconciliation 86
Chapter 9   Numerous Charms 97
Chapter 10 The Duke's Company 106
Chapter 11 Fountain of Impudence 117
Chapter 12 The High Road 129
Chapter 13 A King of England Too 140
Chapter 14 Another Exile 153
Chapter 15 The Jacobite Peerage 166

Select Bibliography 176
Notes 179
Index 196

Acknowledgements

Thank you to my loving husband, Hugh Brown; my mother, Joan Haggerty, for writerly encouragement; Stelios Rigopoulos, Christoph Mahler, Sarah-Beth Watkins and Michelle Higgs.

Prologue

Hide-and-Seek

The time had come for young James, Duke of York, to flee his homeland. The English Civil Wars were all but lost. His adored father, Charles I, was Parliament's prisoner. His older brother, Charles, Prince of Wales, had escaped to the Scilly Isles and beyond. The Royalist stronghold of Oxford had fallen to Parliamentary troops in June 1646. The 14-year-old James, whose father had left him to hold down the city, then formally surrendered to Sir Thomas Fairfax. The general did not kiss his hand – though the other Roundhead officers did. Stripped of loyal servants, denied even the court dwarf companion 'whom his Royall Highnesse was desirous to have retain'd with him', James was sent to join two fellow hostages: his little brother Henry and sister Elizabeth.[1] The queen's loyal lady-in-waiting had defied Parliament and spirited the tiny Princess Henrietta, dressed as a peasant boy, to her mother in France. For eighteen long months the young duke chafed under the governorship of the Earl of Northumberland, first at Syon House and then, for additional security in the face of rumoured plots, at St James's Palace. Knowing that he could be used to his father's disadvantage, James constantly daydreamed of breaking free. More than once, secret escape plans were revealed to Parliament. At one stage he was interviewed by a committee of both houses and promised 'upon his honour and faith' to stop trying to flee. Knowing he was being watched closely, he declined to accept a smuggled letter from his mother. When Charles I was informed of a New Model Army proposal to upend the succession and crown James king, he sent a cipher ordering his second son to slip away and make for the Continent. An order from his father overruled any promise made to enemies. Upon hearing the king had escaped to the Isle of Wight and Carisbrooke Castle, James exulted; learning of Charles's eventual imprisonment in that place, he sobbed out bitterly, 'How durst any rogues to use his father like that?'[2] When a servant shook a finger at him, threatening to report these hot words to Northumberland, James tried to slay the man with a longbow.

Now, in April 1648, the young spark grasped his chance. Nothing his captors 'could say or do was capable of hindering him from endeavouring his escape.'[3] The 13-year-old Princess Elizabeth whispered encouragement: her big brother had to break free. King Charles had put him in touch with a Presbyterian spy, Colonel Joseph Bampfield, currently pledged to the Royalist cause. Charles enlisted Bampfield to help James, writing: 'I believe it will be difficult, and if he miscarry in the attempt it will be the greatest affliction that can arrive to me; but I look upon James's escape as Charles's preservation, and nothing can content me more. Therefore be careful what you do.[4]' The scheme was to disguise James as a woman. A handsome boy with a cleft chin, light-brown hair and dark blue eyes, he was slender and had not yet shot up to his full height. Bampfield asked his mistress, Lady Anne Halkett, to have a dress specially tailored to James's measurements. Lady Anne's mother had served the royal family in the past, so she was proud to be of use, and would be waiting to magic the Duke of York into a maiden if only he could get away from St James's Palace.

For several weeks James had been playing hide-and-seek with the children every night after supper, staying concealed a little longer each time, up to half an hour, to get Northumberland's servants used to his absence. But this evening was different. He had to move swiftly. Princess Elizabeth's friendly little black dog trotted behind him, so he shut it up in her bedroom. Elizabeth and Henry played along, looking in all the wrong places, stretching out the game. James knew that he had a half an hour before Northumberland's servants would raise the alarm in earnest. He crept down the back stairs and out into St James's Park, locking the doors behind him with a key he had charmed out of the gardener. Colonel Bampfield was waiting at the garden gate with an extra cloak and periwig for his charge. The two took a coach and boat to a house in London Bridge, where Lady Anne was waiting. 'The first that came in was the Duke, who with much joy I took in my arms,' she related, 'and gave God thanks for his safe arrival.'[5] James called out, 'Quickly, quickly, dress me,' and took off his clothes. The outfit – of mixed mohair, with a red petticoat – fit perfectly, 'and he was very pretty in it,' she added. Lady Anne dressed his hair and added a cap. She fed the boy and sent for a City of London specialty called Wood Street cake, with rosewater icing. She knew how much he loved it.

Saying their fond and hurried farewells to Lady Anne, Colonel Bampfield and his companion boarded a barge to get them out of the port of London. By now the alarm had been raised; there was no telling when the fugitives could be arrested. The barge-master grew suspicious when he spied James unceremoniously expose his leg and ask Bampfield to adjust his garter. Seeing his passenger behave 'in so unwomanish a manner', he began asking blunt questions, for these were tense times. James decided that his best chance was to make 'a clean breast of the matter' and reveal his true identity. To his great relief, the man turned out to be no Roundhead sympathiser, but willing to risk his life for the brave young prince. Now the barge-master took the helm, dimming the lights so they could pass through the harbour unnoticed. The craft moved steadily out of danger.

At Tilbury, James and Bampfield boarded a Dutch ship bound for the Low Countries, posing as siblings. Once they reached the Hague, James was joyously reunited with his actual sister, the dark-haired Mary, now Princess of Orange. He had not seen her for six years. He remembered the day he and Charles, aged 7 and 10, had escorted her to the altar. She had been a vision in cloth of silver, her train carried by sixteen ladies in white satin. Their mother, Queen Henrietta Maria, had taken Mary to Holland to begin her role as wife to the Prince of Orange. At long last, he had joined her. Full of excitement at having escaped, he jested that the men on board the ship had hoped he was a woman of easy virtue.

James stayed for nine months with the lovely Mary. Charles I, leery of the republicanism inherent in the Dutch project, had hesitated to give the hand of his eldest daughter to a mere Stadtholder. Instead, he had offered his younger daughter, Elizabeth. But Dutch financial support was crucial during the English Civil War, so they were in a position to insist on the Princess Royal. It had to be admitted that Mary's marriage to William II of Orange had created a haven for the imperilled Stuart royal family.

Now the 17-year-old Prince Charles arrived to congratulate his brother on his daring feat. He also came to greet nine shiploads of English sailors, who had declared for the imprisoned king as part of a larger rising in Kent, and pitched up in James's wake at the Dutch port of Helvoetsluys in June. Charles, James and Mary conferred about what was to be done with them.[6] James was, in fact, destined to serve as Lord High Admiral once he came of age. Charles put their older cousins, Princes Rupert of the Rhine and Maurice, in charge of these ships – the *Constant Reformation*, the *Roebuck*, *Hind*, *Pelican*, *Satisfaction*, *Convertine*, *Antelope* and *Crescent* – and the two set off on a privateering mission targeting Parliament's West Indian trade routes to raise money for the Royalist cause.

The Prince of Wales's court-in-exile grew as followers crossed the Channel, among them a young Welshwoman whom the polymath diarist John Evelyn would describe as 'that browne, bold, beautiful and insipid creature'.[7] The ravishing Lucy Walter had come from a broken home to seek her fortune at court, and met Charles in the month of May 1648. Meanwhile, Queen Henrietta Maria was eager to see James again. She summoned him to Paris after that year's Christmas festivities. As civil war was also raging in France, this one between the monarchy and a portion of the aristocracy, James was obliged to stop en route. Archduke Leopold of Flanders ensured that the gallant young man was invited to stay with the Benedictines of the Abbaye of St. Amand 'where the Monks entertain'd him very nobly'.[8] There he could admire the high altar, completed in 1617 by Rubens, a painter much employed by the Stuarts. Taking his leave of the Benedictines, James journeyed on to Paris and was reunited with his mother. They were happy and relieved to see one another again after so long. Their pleasure was short-lived, however. They received unimaginably bitter news: 'A day or two after his arrival in Paris, he heard of the horrid murder of the King his Father, and what impression that made upon the Queen and the Duke, may more easily be imagined than expressed.'[9] Young James had the air knocked out of him: his father had been executed. Charles I had been marched to the Banqueting House in Whitehall, with its treasured Rubens ceiling memorialising his own father, James I and VI. He was led through the place where he and his court had enjoyed many enchanting candlelit masques, and outside to an improvised scaffold. There, on 30 January 1649, a dark parody of the masque form had unfolded before a hushed London multitude. The anointed king had been beheaded, along with the traditional order.

John Evelyn refused to attend the execution. He wrote broken-heartedly of 'the Villainie of the Rebells in proceeding so far as to trie, condemn & murder our excellent King, the 30 of this Moneth, struck me with such horror that I decided to keepe the day of his Martyrdom as a faste, & would not be present, at this execrable wickednesse.'[10] Many struggled to grasp that Roundheads had gone so far as to kill the king. All of Europe was reeling – none more than James, who held his father and kingship sacred next to God. He now consecrated his life to restoring a lost world.

Chapter 1

From Gold into Iron

> Ask me no more whither do stray,
> The golden atoms of the day ...
>
> Thomas Carew, 'A Song'

Church bells pealed and the common people lit bonfires when Queen Henrietta Maria, after a difficult pregnancy, was delivered of a healthy son at St James's Palace. It was 14 October 1633. The birth of a second prince secured the Stuart dynasty, promising stability for the Three Kingdoms. The child was christened James by Archbishop William Laud in honour of his grandfather, James I and VI. His godparents were his aunt, Elizabeth of Bohemia, and Frederick Henry, Prince of Orange. He received the titles Duke of York and Albany. After an early babyhood illness which had the gossips whispering that his nurse, being Catholic, was surely a poisoner, James thrived. Most of his early childhood years were spent in the royal nursery in Richmond Palace. He was a comely and energetic child who 'cared not to plod upon his games' but 'delighted with quick and nimble recreations'.[1] The boy adored his brother Charles, two years older and dark as he was fair, and his pretty sister Mary. By 1641 there were five surviving royal children: Charles, Mary, James, Elizabeth and Henry. Charles I was over the moon with happiness. His wife received precious gifts each time their family grew. The king commissioned court painter Sir Anthony Van Dyck to do their portraits, which he displayed in his rooms so he could gaze upon them. The sight of James's glowing pink-cheeked likeness filled his father with pride. He was 'a good, lusty child, God be thanked', wrote the naval captain John Penington of the boy who would be named honorary Lord High Admiral as soon as he was 5 years old. Out of his infant's cap and gown and into his first pair of breeches, James looked forward to commanding England's fleet once he reached manhood. As his father greatly prized the Royal Navy, he wanted to do the role justice.

All his life, James would cherish his memories of childhood, with England at peace and a Golden Age at the Caroline court. From the Royalist perspective, it was the best of times. As Edward Hyde, 1st Earl of Clarendon, famously wrote in his *History of the Rebellion*: 'This kingdom ... enjoyed the greatest calm and fullest measure of felicity that any people in any age for so long time together have been blessed with.'[2] The Cavalier poet Thomas Carew summed up the era as 'our Halcyon days'. The peace was thrown into greater relief by the Thirty Years War raging on the Continent. Charles I had banished the crudity and licentiousness of the Jacobean court, celebrating instead an ethos of pleasure tempered by virtuous married love. Admittedly, the king's own union had a rocky start. Charles sent most of his new wife's French courtiers packing because they were complicating matters between the two. Court favourite the Duke of Buckingham stirred up trouble as well. Ultimately, however, lilies and roses intertwined: James's mother and father fell deeply in love.

Religious differences were another hurdle for the couple. Henrietta Maria was an ardent Catholic on an explicit mission to intercede for the Catholics of her three new realms. Before she left for England, Pope Urban VIII had conferred a special honour, known as the Golden Rose, upon her in order to bless the undertaking. So the queen's traditional intercessory role became specialised in this case. When she built a spectacular friary at Denmark House, mass was celebrated in public for the first time since the death of Mary I.[3] It was a signal to English Catholics that a new era had dawned for them. They had a sincere advocate in Queen Henrietta Maria – and the 'godly men' (Puritans) had a fresh source of outrage.

James's father, for his part, took his role as the Head of the Anglican Church very much to heart. According to Edward Hyde, the king believed 'in his soul the church of England to be nearest to the practice of the Apostles'.[4] Though Charles and Henrietta differed on religion, there was considerable common ground between them. The preservation of bishops in Anglicanism provided a potential bridge back to Catholicism. Charles corresponded with the Pope; he also welcomed a papal legate, Father George Conn. Although the king had no reunification plans, he did keep that avenue open, much to the Puritans' chagrin. He and Archbishop William Laud embraced the twin doctrines of 'the beauty of holiness' and 'Thorough', a plan for enforcing religious conformity throughout the

British Isles. Puritans saw these policies as crypto-Catholic. Moreover, the royal couple shared an intoxicating aesthetic vision. Through the arts, they projected the Stuart philosophy of Personal Monarchy. Both Charles and Henrietta adored paintings, and closely tracked the Baroque movement so bound up with the Catholic Counter-Reformation. Of all the kings of England, Charles had the most refined sensibility and was the greatest collector of art. He employed numerous painters, and had at least one household servant who doubled as a painter – Richard Gibson, a court dwarf and Page of the Back Stairs, who became a remarkable portrait miniaturist. Charles, a passionate aesthete who found inspiration in paintings and sculpture, commissioned one splendid work after another. An example by Van Dyck shows the king seated *en famille.* The queen is dressed in yellow satin. She holds baby Mary, while a toddler Prince of Wales in cap and gown grasps his father's knee. A little spaniel, emblem of fidelity, sits at his master's foot. The effect is warm and inviting. At once regal and intimate, the painting communicates the idea that Charles's benevolent reign over his family extends to his people. And if Charles could husband his Catholic queen successfully, the emblem suggested, he could rule the Catholic minority in his realms as well.

James's mother particularly delighted in staging masques for the pleasure of the court – candlelit entertainments interweaving dance, chamber music, allegory, poetry and fantastical costumes and sets – that gave rise to ballet and opera. Typically they began with an 'anti-masque' representing chaotic elements, which would then be brought to heel in the masque proper. Much like a Renaissance comedy, the masque passed from disorder through to a renewed order. Henrietta Maria had performed in such court theatrics since she was a young girl; in fact, the dark-eyed and delicate princess had first flickered past Charles, then Prince of Wales, while performing in one at the Louvre Palace. (At that time Charles was on his way to Spain, accompanied by George Villiers, 1st Duke of Buckingham, as part of a heady scheme to marry the Spanish Infanta.) Royal family members, including James, regularly joined in these enchanting spectacles, and members of the court did as well. Henrietta Maria tried to cast her valiant court dwarf, Sir Jeffrey Hudson, in every entertainment. Court masque pageantry radiates through one of King Charles's greatest commissions, the mural *Apollo and Diana* by Gerrit van Honthorst. It displays the king and queen enthroned in triumph as god and goddess, gazing at an idealised assemblage of costumed courtiers below. Poets such as Ben Jonson created masques in co-operation with the great set designer and architect Inigo Jones. Each royal palace was adapted for the staging of masques and plays.

These high-flown entertainments underlined to young Prince James that the royal court set the tone for the realm. James, who danced gracefully and mastered the guitar, understood that he was to embody the highest ideals. He learned that each subject played a part in the harmonious whole; each was sworn to serve and strive together for the greater good. There was no place for discord; *rebellion* was a dirty word. Loyalty and service were all. James was educated much in the same way as the brother he looked up to, Charles, Prince of Wales. They were brave boys, full of energy. Both moved rapidly. Charles, nicknamed 'Black Boy' for his inky hair and eyes, was thought to take after the children's Medici grandmother, while fair-haired James resembled his paternal grandmother, Anne of Denmark. Their temperaments differed along with their colouring. While James was sincere and serious, Charles was wry and playful. With them at Richmond Palace were George and Francis Villiers, sons of the slain royal favourite, the 1st Duke of Buckingham. Charles I made them his wards when their father was murdered in 1628, and they were welcomed into the royal nursery. Five years older than James, blond and sparkling George would be a frequent, if unreliable, presence in his life.

Another key figure at court was the princes' gallant teenage cousin Rupert of the Rhine, who first arrived at court when James was a toddler, seeking help in restoring his parents to the Bohemian throne. (But raising money for war meant recalling Parliament, something Charles I was in no hurry to do.) Nicknamed *Robert le diable* for his alluringly fiery spirit, Prince Rupert was already a seasoned warrior at 14. He shone as a lodestar for the boys as, aged about 4, they began martial training exercises, such as fencing, wrestling, vaulting and archery, as well as hawking and hunting. It was all part of belonging to the ruling warrior caste. James did not expect to become king, but he fully expected to become a great leader of men, a great patron. In addition to war games, James came to excel at tennis, as Rupert did. Outfitted in a costume of satin and lace, little James would ply his racquet before a crowded stand of courtiers. Although, by the standards of the era, Charles I and Henrietta Maria were intimately involved in their children's lives, each prince would have his own governor and form his own loyal household, or 'family'. The princes were trained to rule. James embraced it, later reporting that he 'had been bred in business from his infancy,' adding that 'it would be an uneasiness to him ... to live an idle life.'[5] He was 5 when the great Renaissance man and famed equestrian William Cavendish, Earl of Newcastle, became Charles's governor; Newcastle taught riding, dancing and the savouring of literature. He would later write Prince Charles a Machiavellian manual on the governance of the Three Kingdoms. James would have studied Latin, still widely used in diplomacy. By the time he was a young man, he had mastered French, had considerable Spanish and could read Italian. He would also have had some Greek. Sir William Harvey, the great physician who pioneered the theory of blood circulation, was another of the boys' tutors. Then there was King Charles's chaplain, Bishop Brian Duppa. A follower of Archbishop Laud, Bishop Duppa schooled the princelings in the form of Anglicanism that seemed to dovetail most closely with monarchy in general and Charles's vision of Personal Rule in particular. (King Charles had dismissed Parliament in response to the Petition of Right of 1628, relying instead on informal consultation to govern.) Thus, religion was an essential form of statecraft. Bishop Duppa emphasised the very features that Puritans were zealously striving to expunge from the national church – bishops, sacraments, figurative art, communion rails, candles, incense and other appeals to the senses: ritual in general. What Laudians called 'the beauty of holiness,' Puritan divines denounced as vestigial Catholicism, precisely what they meant to root out. This radical pruning was the *raison d'être* of Puritanism. Remnants of Catholicism could lead Englishmen back to the Old Faith, they reasoned. Because traditionalist Anglicanism sanctified kingship – as James I had summed it up, 'bishops crown kings' – the Stuarts embraced it. It was the form of worship that had buttressed the reigns of Elizabeth I and her successor. As a child, James accepted Anglicanism unquestioningly. After all, thanks to Henry VIII's move to break with Rome, his father was head of the Church. And James revered his father. At the same time, he grew up aware that his loving mother never attended services with his father, but made her devotions separately, with her own brown-cassocked priests, at an ornate chapel specially designed by Inigo Jones. It had all been agreed as part of her marriage settlement.

The very existence of this chapel grated terribly upon the Puritans. Because of their visceral loathing of Catholicism, that growing faction were blind to the considerable virtues of the Caroline court. They perceived James's mother, Henrietta Maria, as a malignant and corrupting force. It did not matter that the queen was a devoted wife and mother, and a graceful addition to the country: she was a papist, a papist who had made a very public visit to the scaffold called Tyburn Tree to pray for the many English Catholics martyred there. It made Protestants bristle. Various members of the Caroline milieu reverted to the Old Faith. Two examples close to the queen were Sir Jeffrey Hudson and Walter 'Wat' Montagu, who went on to become a Benedictine abbot in France. And as for the queen's splendid court masques themselves, they were a scandal. Puritans opposed public theatre and court entertainment alike. Acting was prostitution; theatres were dens of vice. Drama itself they identified with the drama of the mass. Without access to Parliament, highly-placed 'godly men' relied on the pulpit and on generating pamphlet storms.

In 1632 the hot-eyed Presbyterian William Prynne had published his lengthy polemic against the theatre. Prynne's targeting of festive folk customs, as well as drama, is typical of the Puritan thought: 'Our Christmas lords of misrule, together with dancing, masks, mummeries, and other such Christmas disorders ... were derived from Roman Saturnalia and Bacchanalian festivals, which should cause all pious Christians eternally to abominate them.' *Histriomastix* included a denunciation of actresses as 'notorious whores' that was felt to be an attack upon the queen, who had recently appeared with her ladies-in-waiting and in a lengthy speaking role. The masque was Wat Montagu's tribute to Platonic love, *The Shepherd's Paradise*. The queen played Bellessa, 'beauty', who rules this pastoral idyll. The masque was staged at a time when female roles in the public theatre were played by boys, so court extravaganzas featuring noblewomen – painted and even bare-breasted, in keeping with a bold masquing fashion of the era – upped the ante. The king, who was pleased with his wife's efforts, especially her recent mastery of poetic English, did not take kindly to William Prynne's critique. Prynne denied attacking the queen, but stood by his book. Charged with seditious libel, he stood before the Star Chamber and endured a series of severe punishments. He was pilloried, fined, jailed and his ears were shorn off. Prynne kept right on publishing. He peppered Anglican divines with angry pamphlets from his prison cell as the 1630s unfolded. And what Charles dubbed Personal Rule, Puritans labelled 'The Eleven-Year Tyranny.' Throughout the blissful years of James's early childhood, then, the gulf between the royal party and the Puritans kept steadily widening. Soon the whole polity would be swallowed up in it.

James was 8 years old when he was invested with the Order of the Garter. The Garter Feast was held in York rather than St George's Chapel at Windsor that year, and sparsely attended: it was April 1642, and the whole country murmured of civil war. But James was proud when his father made him a knight, swearing him to chivalric service. The boy donned his cloak and pinned his blue sash and star badge enamelled with the shield of St George – innovations of his father's – on the left. Loyalty was James's guiding principle. His earnest devotion touched the king's heart. Both knew that great tests were in store. Charles had ordered James's governor, William Seymour, 1st Marquess of Hertford, to send the boy to him. Parliament opposed this – they had already moved to detain Princess Elizabeth and Prince Henry – but Hertford obeyed the king. The Scots had rioted against the king's 'Thorough' policy, which entailed introducing the Book of Common Prayer into every parish church and bringing them into line in other respects as part of an effort to create religious – and therefore political – conformity in the Three Kingdoms. Religious policy had direct political implications.

Unfortunately for Charles, the powerful Puritan faction in the English Parliament had rallied round the rebel Scots. They had issued him with a thick list of grievances entitled the Grand Remonstrance, and had grown more and more defiant, blocking his efforts to raise money at every turn. Trying to gain some breathing space, Charles had agreed with Parliament's plan to execute a loyal minister, the Earl of Strafford. It was something he always regretted. James felt the sting of this betrayal of a devoted servant sharply, crying bitter tears when he learned of it. He grasped that a leader could not stave off the mob by making concessions – at least, not for long. James shared his father's view that the sacrifice of Strafford was a colossal error.

Meanwhile, his mother, the queen, had departed for Holland, taking Princess Mary and the Crown jewels along with her. Ostensibly she was getting Mary settled into her new home. Using this as cover, at her husband's behest, she pawned some of the jewels to buy weapons. Having 'got his George' – won the privilege of wearing the blue silk sash of the Order of the Garter, and therefore becoming a knight – James was quickly pressed into the king's service as well. Charles I needed his son's help in capturing Hull, a fortified city boasting a huge arsenal, second only to the Tower of London. A worrying situation had developed: after failing to arrest five MPs, the king of England had been forced to take his family out of London for fear that *he* would be arrested. Edward Hyde was among the key Royalist MPs who joined him at York. Charles had gone to set up a mint and a printing press there so the Royalists could engage in the pamphlet battle. Now he found himself locked out of this key town with its immense weapons cache.

Firstly, the king sent the extravagant figure of William Cavendish, Earl of Newcastle. Newcastle decided to ask admittance under a pseudonym, Sir John Savage; he was instantly recognised and blocked by Hull's governor, a touchy fellow called Sir John Hotham who had defected to Parliament when he lost a coveted royal post. It was then that the king 'made use of [James] (as young as he was) to get possession of the town of Hull'.[6] If James could get in, Charles could follow. Surely Hotham would admit an inoffensive child who also happened to be the Duke of York?

It was 22 April when James arrived at Hull city gates. Affecting a casual air, 'as if out of curiosity to see the place',[7] he asked for admittance. The young duke was accompanied by his 25-year-old cousin Charles Louis, Prince Elector Palatine, and a group of about fifty noblemen. Charles Louis was another of Prince Rupert's brothers; like Rupert, he was an unwavering Calvinist. Unlike Rupert, Charles Louis also happened to be something of a Parliament sympathiser. He believed this faction would be better able to help him win back his father's Bohemian throne. His inclusion in the party may have been calculated to appeal to Sir John Hotham, a veteran of the Palatinate wars. Another Royalist present was Hotham's cousin, the handsome and accomplished George Digby, 2nd Earl of Bristol. At first the charm offensive appeared to work: Hotham opened the gates, treating the little duke with 'every demonstration of respect'.[8]

The mayor and aldermen invited the visitors to feast. At the same time the country was beginning to grasp that King Charles was no longer truly sovereign over England, James, for his part, was wishing his father would send someone to arrest the knave Hotham and have done with the charade. James mentioned to Hotham that the king would join them for dinner the following evening, 'At which news Hotham suddenly turned very pale, struck himself on the breast, and returned no answer to him' – except to shut the gates.[9]

The Duke of York was now a hostage. He might be well fed and comfortable, but he was trapped. His father arrived to find the entrances to Hull blocked. Hotham's defiance was incredible to father and son alike. Charles told the man that denying the king access to his own town was 'open rebellion'. This had no effect. He tried persuasion, using 'the moderation of a Prince who has no other means' at his disposal. Hotham, immoveable, fell back on routine talk of the king's 'evil counsellors'.[10] Charles retreated in humiliation. At first Hotham held onto his hostages, but eventually began releasing them one by one. James was finally permitted to rejoin his shaken father.

The Earl of Bristol reasoned with his cousin, who agreed to admit the king. But when Charles returned to Hull city gates in July, Hotham once again refused to let him in. It was treasonable conduct. Making good use of the printing press, Charles called the Yorkshire gentry to his side: 'You see that my magazine is going to be taken from me (being my own goods) directly against my will ... I have thought it fit to have a guard that I may be able to protect you, the laws, and the true Protestant profession.'[11] Charles, like his predecessors Elizabeth I and James I and VI, cast himself as steering a middle way between the burgeoning number of radical Protestant sects on the one hand, and Catholics on the other. Although Catholics overwhelmingly supported the king in this fight, Charles still had to be seen to denounce them, or risk playing into the hands of Puritans who labelled him a crypto-Catholic. Sometimes this meant having priests hanged, drawn and quartered as a form of appeasement.

The strategy worked. Royalist numbers swelled as members of the local nobility and gentry flocked to the monarch's side. James rode with his brother and father to Nottingham, where Charles raised the royal standard on the rainy evening of 22 August. 'Give Caesar His Due', it read. A thousand supporters shouted 'God save the king!'[12] The Cavaliers, as they were nicknamed for their ideal of elegant equestrian nonchalance, embraced peacocking court fashions: roomy blouses; satin and lace suits; single pearl-drop earrings; tall, cuffed riding boots; and, above all, long curling hair worn with a lovelock, a longer piece typically tied with a bow. Lovelocks came under fierce fire from the 'godly men', increasingly known as Roundheads for their comparatively short hair. The Puritans preferred a plain aesthetic. Prynne devoted two pamphlets to denouncing Cavalier hairstyles: *The Unloveliness of Lovelocks* (1628) and *A Gagge for Long-haired Rattle-heads Who Revile All Civil Round-heads* (1646). Among the most archetypal of Cavaliers was Prince Rupert of the Rhine, now a Royalist commander given to swearing and swagger, a big white hunting poodle named Boy at his side. (Rupert loved Boy so much that he commissioned his talented sister, Princess Louise Hollandine of the Palatinate, to paint the dog's portrait. For their part Parliamentarians denounced the intrepid Royalist mascot as a 'dog-witch'.)

Rupert was the chief cavalry commander at the Battle of Edgehill, which took place in Warwickshire on 23 September 1642. The fight kicked off with the Soldier's Prayer from Sir Jacob Astley, commander of the Royalist infantry: 'Lord, Thou knowest how busy I must be this day, so if I forget Thee, do not Thou forget me.' Prince Charles and Prince James were at their father's side in the midst of the action. James was impressed by 'the naturall courage of English men, which prompted them to maintain their ground'. Worried that his sons would be killed or captured, the king had trouble finding an officer willing to abandon the field and lead them to the hilltop so they could watch from a safe distance.[13] 'The Earle of Dorset answer'd him with an oath, That he would not be thought a Coward for the sake of any King's Sons in Christendom.' Edward Hyde oversaw the boys' protection. Eventually they were left with their tutor, Sir William Harvey. Aubrey relates that Harvey got absorbed in his reading, even as bullets whizzed overhead: 'during the fight, the Prince and Duke of Yorke were committed to his care: he told me that he withdrew with them under a hedge, and tooke out of his pockett a booke and read; but he had not read very long before a bullet of a great gun grazed on the ground neare him, which made him remove his station.'[14] Harvey had clean forgotten his charges. Luckily for all concerned, Charles and James were still lying flat close by, glued to the battle scene.

The action ended without a clear win for either side. The Royalists had the advantage, but they tended to become unruly and break ranks to loot when they had the enemy on the run. A certain Oliver Cromwell, who had arrived late to the action, was unhappy with the state of the Parliamentary army. As he wrote to his cousin and fellow soldier John Hampden, 'Your troopers are most of them old decayed serving-men and tapsters.' The Royalists, on the other hand, he described as 'gentlemen's sons, younger sons and persons of quality ... to cope with men of honour we must have men of religion'.[15] Cromwell typified the class of men who now challenged the old order. The dissolution of the monasteries in the sixteenth century, overseen by his great-uncle Thomas Cromwell, had redistributed church lands to the gentry as a way of buying loyalty for Henry VIII's break with Rome and self-appointment as Head of the English Church. Land produced political power, since suffrage was tethered to land ownership. Oliver Cromwell was an MP because his family had been elevated in this way. Having benefitted materially from old church lands, this new class was now in a position to oppose the monarch. As G.K. Chesterton puts it, the Puritans 'were but one wing of the new wealthy class which had despoiled the Church and were proceeding to despoil the crown.'[16] The irony was that the Crown itself had provided the internal enemy with the resources they needed to do so. In the midst of the Civil War, Oliver Cromwell envisioned a reform of the military which, in some sense, paralleled the reform of religion. He would go on to realise it in the New Model Army.

London was in the hands of Parliament. It was now the Roundhead capital. The rich, layered world of the royal court had vanished from the palaces of Whitehall, Greenwich and St James's. An anonymous 1642 pamphlet, *A Deep Sigh Breathd Through the Lodgings at Whitehall*, laments a lost hubbub:[17] 'A Pallace without a Presence! A Court without a Court! These are misteries, and miseries, which the silken ages of this peacefull Island has not beene acquainted with.' Charles I, meanwhile, knew that he could not mount a challenge to this rapidly strengthening rival elite, or hope to win the war, without at least establishing a worthy capital of his own. It must offer a refuge for his family and be a source of inspiration for all who followed him. There had been improvised travelling courts at York and

Nottingham, but these were too unstable for his purposes. The 'she-Majesty Generalissima', as Henrietta Maria playfully called herself in letters to the king, rejoined her family at Edgehill after a dangerous voyage from the Continent. Parliamentary forces had tried hard to intercept her. 'I carry with me 3,000 foot, thirty company of horse and dragoons, six pieces of cannon, and two mortars,' she wrote.[18] She also brought the indefatigable dwarf courtier Sir Jeffrey Hudson, a close companion. A skilled swordfighter, Sir Jeffrey had converted to the queen's faith and was keen to fight for the king. Prince Rupert rode out to meet his aunt, accompanying the queen's party through dangerous country. Seventeen months had passed since Henrietta Maria's departure. After a rapturous reunion, the king and queen scooped up James and Charles, and rode for Oxford, arriving on 29 October. Little did James suppose, as he beheld the teeming spires and gargoyles of the ancient university city, that it would be his home for the next four years.

Chapter 2

A Mirror World

> Tell me not, sweet, I am unkinde,
> That from the nunnerie
> Of thy chaste breaste and quiet minde
> To warre and armes I flie.
>
> Sir Richard Lovelace,
> 'To Lucasta, Going to the Wars'

The royal court vanished from Whitehall and resurfaced at Oxford, where they were greeted by the vice chancellor. Church bells rang out, and crowds cheered the king and the two young princes as they rode through the streets with their huge company of dashing Cavaliers. It was 29 October 1642. James, who had just turned 10, watched his father and mother set about recreating their sparkling milieu in a kind of internal exile. It was not, of course, unknown for the court to move about, but voluntarily; indeed, it had long been common for English kings to go 'on progress' with their huge entourages. They would pay extended visits to various noble seats in the country, obliging powerful hosts to display their fealty and expend their wealth in rich entertainments; meal after meal, night after night. Oxford was different, and not only because it was a university, and a university in a time of civil war, but because Charles went on to establish a rival Parliament there in a bid to drain off the Westminster Parliament's legitimacy. What we call the 'Parliament side' in English Civil War history was only ever a portion of that body – it was the faction that came to dominate the ancient chambers, but nearly half of MPs in the House of Commons supported the monarch, together with a majority of the House of Lords. A large group of these members had joined the king in Oxfordshire and, in 1644, formed a new formal institution, the Oxford Parliament (or Mongrel Parliament, as the Roundheads dubbed it). The Commons met in Convocation House, while the Lords convened in the Upper Schools. This splitting in government had grave consequences for the English populace. The division could be felt in Oxford itself, in a break between Gown and Town: while the university supported the king, many of the middling-sort townsfolk did not. On the other hand, the common people were for the monarchy.

Oxford served the Royalists as second capital, refuge and military base from October 1642 onwards. For leaders in the making such as Prince James and, of course, Prince Charles, the reconstituting of the capital was a crucial lesson in the elements of governance. It was a key part of their education. The king established his household at Christ Church College, which had been converted from a monastery by Cardinal Wolsey in 1524. Wolsey had, in fact, designed it with the monarch in mind.[1] Moving into the Dean's Residence, King Charles ordered that the arrangements should mimic those at Whitehall, designating a Presence Chamber, a Privy Chamber and a Withdrawing Chamber. There would be Grooms of the Guard, Gentlemen Ushers and pages to control movement, regulate access and shape court life through ceremony. (A herd of cows bawling in the quad undercut the effect somewhat, but the Cavaliers had to be ready for siege conditions.) The Christ Church Great Hall would be perfect for accommodating the Oxford Parliament. The king attended services at Christ Church Cathedral, sitting in the Vice Chancellor's throne. He disported himself hunting to hounds and playing tennis with Charles, James and Rupert. The queen arrived in 1643, bringing her Catholic retinue, and settled into nearby Merton College, where servants unpacked her collection of Mortlake tapestries, Turkish carpets and plate. The king would retreat from the tight ship of his own court to relax with his wife at Merton.[2] Prince Charles and Prince James each kept a royal household. The Privy Council assembled at the cathedral chapter house, while the French ambassador and the two of the Palatine princes most loyal to their uncle, swashbuckling Rupert and strapping Maurice, were ensconced at St John's College.

All the remaining functions of government were housed by various other colleges. The royal arsenal was established at All Souls, while New College was home to a powder magazine. The gibbet stood outside St Mary's as a warning to spies. The mint, which was set up at New Inn Hall (where St Peter's College now stands), produced King Charles's new Oxford currency in silver and gold. One side of the coins asserted the Crown's defence of the Protestant religion, English law and the liberty of Parliament; according to the Stuart ideal, liberty arises from order. Similarly-themed commemorative medals were also struck. One depicted the king and queen as St George and his damsel with the dragon of Rebellion lying prone at their feet. Crucially, the Royalists adapted a printing press to their purposes in a period when wars were increasingly waged by propaganda as much as arms; they had to answer the blizzards of pamphlets being churned out by Parliament. The official Royalist gazette *Mercurius Aulicus,* edited at Oriel College and smuggled into London, offered suitably witty Cavalier perspectives on wartime. The king's proclamations could be printed there as well. In addition to serving these functions, the colleges accommodated courtiers and soldiers on a grand scale, packing them in tightly. Conditions were crowded and people were tense. A lot of rowdiness spilled out onto the street, where soldiers courted and cavorted. The students, meanwhile, set aside time from reading for building fortifications and arms training.[3] Eventually most students were sent home to make space in the colleges for soldiers. Oxford grew by thousands into a very different city, one repurposed for projecting monarchical power – a power that was fighting for its survival.

James knew how fortunate he and Charles were to be with their beloved parents in the new capital. Princess Mary was safe in Holland, out of the war zone, but 6-year-old Elizabeth and 2-year-old Henry were less fortunate. They had been taken hostage by Parliament in August 1642, just after the Civil War had broken out in earnest. Forbidden to join their family when the royal court settled in Oxford in October, the children were being held at St James's Palace under Northumberland's governorship. The Westminster Parliament specified that they were to be raised as strict Protestants, committed to ongoing reform. Parliament sought to cultivate a Calvinist counter-elite sympathetic to the emergent model of government by an 'elect'. This is how the Puritan MPs envisioned themselves. Because the Stuarts were the legitimate kings of England, Scotland and Ireland, Parliament's best course was to foster a Stuart monarch they could control. As King Charles was queasily aware, tiny Henry, Duke of Gloucester, was to be moulded in their image and raised as a 'pocket-king' (and, indeed, he did grow to become somewhat inclined towards constitutional monarchy).

The Duke of York, another such candidate as far as Parliament was concerned, was permitted to pay Elizabeth and Henry a visit that year. James arrived to find that his clever auburn-haired sister, whose gentle spirit had won her the nickname 'Temperance', had impressed her captors. The French ambassador described her as a budding beauty, able to appreciate varied points of view. Attentive to brown-haired little Henry, the studious Elizabeth had a talent for devotional writing. With help from her governess, Bathsua Makin, a remarkable lady who was permitted to remain with her charge until 1644, the princess had become conversant in Hebrew, Latin, Greek, French and Italian. A perceptive girl, Princess Elizabeth understood how valuable her older brother was to the Royalist cause. The royal children were at once a source of strength and a vulnerability for the king. Lonely as she would be when he rejoined their father at Oxford, she urged James not to tarry long for fear that he would be detained as well. They said goodbye, promising letters which they knew would be pored over by a Parliamentary committee.

Wartime Oxford life shaped James's imagination and understanding as he developed into a youth. In the summer the men went fighting, while in winter, traditional court activities played out. At the age of 11 he began attending the Royalist House of Lords with his father. The university awarded the young Duke of York an honorary Master of Arts. Ambitious young noblemen flocked to the new centre, which offered the mutual benefit of patronage and loyalty, as well as marriage prospects, as royal courts had always done. Large numbers of Royalist noblewomen were sent to the king's new capital for safety's sake.[4] As the princes and other noble boys grew older, they would seek mates from among their ranks. For example, a bookish 19-year-old lady named Margaret Lucas moved from Colchester, where she was in danger, to serve as maid of honour to Henrietta Maria. From a stoutly Cavalier family, she eventually caught the eye of the princes' tutor, the Earl of Newcastle. (She would one day be famed as the philosopher-Duchess of Newcastle, aka 'Mad Madge'.)

People like Margaret had already willingly suffered for the Royalist side. Her brothers served in the king's army. The Lucases were united behind the king. From their perspective, the monarchy underpinned the proper order of things. Margaret later wrote: 'As it was natural for one body to have but one head, so it was also natural for a politic body to have but one governor ... monarchy is a divine form of government.'[5] Another such noblewoman, Anne Harrison, came to Oxford with her Royalist family, whose estates had been sequestered by Parliament. She became Lady Fanshawe when

A Mirror World

she married Prince Charles's war secretary, Richard Fanshawe, in 1644. As we shall see, James would always feel most at ease among these women – loyalists who had known privation for the Stuart cause.

Certain families were bitterly divided by the war. Feelings ran high, rivalry was intense, and tempers frayed in Oxford. Conditions were competitive. Many duels were fought between Cavaliers. One such duellist was James's elegant 21-year-old cousin, Lord John Stuart, freshly returned from the Grand Tour to support the king's cause. The seasonal cycle of plays, masques and balls unfurled in this politically intense atmosphere. Musicians and gifted painters like William Dobson flocked to join the court. Official portraitist Van Dyck had died in 1641, and Dobson hoped to fill the vacancy. Dobson's painting of James aged about 12 shows a graceful boy with a determined set to his chin, touching his blue Garter sash proudly. Cavalier poets who had graced the palace were now in Oxford fighting for the king. Now more than ever, these artistic forms confirmed the Cavalier sensibility summed up in Richard Lovelace's verse: 'I could not love thee, dear, so much/Lov'd I not honour more.' Pleasure and virtue, properly ranked, combined.

But it was all under threat. The cultural destruction that followed was hugely disturbing to James's family and friends. One of the Puritans' first acts of iconoclasm after they took the helm in London was to shutter the theatres that had made the poetry of Marlowe, Shakespeare and Jonson famous beyond court circles. In 1642 Parliament issued an order declaring that the 'times of humiliation' could not be reconciled with the 'lascivious Mirth and Levity' of 'public stage-plays'. Another such act resulted in the destruction of the Queen's Chapel in London. When Parliament ordained that all royal chapels be 'cleansed from all Popish Reliques and superstitions', a mob obliged, ripping out the Rubens altar and heaving it into the Thames. The authorities then used the chapel as a stable. Anglican churches received similar treatment from Puritans – St Paul's Cathedral was repurposed to house over 800 horses. Its choir stalls, organ and bishop's chair were destroyed.[6] Statues of Charles I met a similar fate. Clearly, these attacks added up to burning the king and queen in effigy. The result was that every artistic gesture – as well as every observation of tradition, every rite and ceremony – among the Cavaliers was imbued with added emphasis. Their entire mode of being was slated for destruction – and that made it all the more precious. For his part, James relished dancing – he and Charles had a new dancing master in Oxford – as well as music, masques and, in particular, plays. He would one day attend 'more plays proportionately than any other monarch'.[7] The Stuarts' guardianship of communal art forms, festivals and customs was one of their great strengths from the point of view of the common people. The Puritans' jettisoning of folk ways made them a lot of enemies.

The First English Civil War proceeded apace, with each side accusing the other of making dangerous departures from tradition in governance. (In a similar fashion, warring religious denominations charged one another with 'innovation' and claimed to be in line with 'Primitive Christianity'.) Prince James understood that everything good and natural, as guaranteed by a father he adored, was at stake. There were peace talks at Oxford, with safe passage guaranteed for the chief negotiators. Parliament issued a list of demands almost identical to their last such list. Charles was resolute. He would not reward rebellion with concessions, for it was his authority that guaranteed the social order. As he wrote to his cousin and Scottish adviser, James Hamilton, later 1st Duke of Hamilton, in December 1642: 'I have set up my rest upon the goodness of my cause, being resolved that no extremity or misfortune shall make me yield; for I will be either a Glorious King or a Patient Martyr.'[8] His position was strengthened by arms and money arriving, not just via the queen but also from the Prince of Orange and the kings of France and Denmark. The Royalist army enjoyed a spate of successes under Prince Rupert's command. After victory at the Battle of Camp Hill, near Birmingham, in April 1643, Rupert and company spent the night at Birmingham. Charles had directed him to subdue the citizens of Birmingham as a punishment for their insults to the king at the Battle of Edgehill. In response, the Roundheads generated a pamphlet entitled *A True Relation of Prince Ruperts Barbarous Cruelty against the Towne of Brumingham* featuring a woodcut of Rupert and Boy looking fearsome.

The next mission was to lay siege to Lichfield, Staffordshire, which held a valuable arsenal. The princes' childhood companion, 15-year-old George Villiers, 2nd Duke of Buckingham joined the Cavaliers there, as did his brother Francis. The previous year Buckingham had received an M.A. from Trinity College, Cambridge, a university which leaned more Parliamentarian than did Oxford. For the moment at least, Buckingham had decided to support his king, the man who had protected him and Francis when they were orphaned. Parliament reacted swiftly, sequestering the Villiers lands and moveable goods. While appreciating his presence, James had learned to be a little on his guard when it came to Buckingham. Compelling, adventurous and witty, Buckingham was also mercurial. One could easily find oneself at the pointed end of that rapier wit. He liked to remark, for instance, that while Charles 'could see things if he would,' James 'would see things if he could.' Charles found it difficult to resist the acerbic Buckingham, who was to be a most consequential person in the two princes' lives. If someone could put a wedge between James and Charles, it was him.

It soon emerged that the princes were to have a new brother or sister: Henrietta Maria was with child again, having conceived at Oxford aged 34. It was a difficult pregnancy, made worse by fears that Parliament, who had impeached the queen, would soon attack the city. Another concern was that disease was rife in that overcrowded city. As Henrietta Maria wrote to her sister, Christine of Savoy, 'I am the only one who is miserable, because I am pregnant, and do not know where to go for safety.'[9] Deciding that she would be a distraction to her husband and sons if she remained with them at Oxford, she left the city, bound for the West Country. James, now aged 10, bid his courageous little mother farewell. The king accompanied her as far as Abingdon, where the two embraced for what was to be the last time.

The latest hostage to fortune arrived on 16 June 1643. Charles wrote to congratulate his wife. 'As for the christening of my younger, and, as they say, prettiest daughter', he directed her to have the child baptised Protestant, as all the royal children had been.[10] The new baby was duly christened Henrietta at Exeter Cathedral and placed in the care of her godmother, Lady Dalkeith. It was too dangerous to remain together. Henrietta Maria set off with her motley band of supporters – little Sir Jeffrey Hudson, who had earned the nickname 'Strenuous Jeffrey' for his wartime efforts; the aged doctor Theodore Mayerne, and the sleek Henry Jermyn among them. This crew managed to elude the Roundhead commander who had been tasked with hunting the queen down, and made it across the warship-infested Channel to France. If the royal family were ever to be happy together again, they would have to struggle on fragmented.

The Battle of Naseby on 14 June 1645 ended the First English Civil War with defeat for the Royalists. They now faced a radically reordered and emboldened enemy. Only six months before, Parliament had executed the second of the king's so-called 'evil counsellors', Archbishop William Laud. The man who embodied 'the beauty of holiness' doctrine and had baptised the royal children was decapitated on Tower Hill. Meanwhile, Oliver Cromwell's critique of the Parliamentary military forces had led to a total restructuring to form the New Model Army. England's first modern fighting force – uniformed, centralised and professional – was peopled by uniformed zealots who, when let off their chains, went about smashing religious art and rebuking the errant instead of drinking and wenching. In addition to Cromwell, the New Model Army at Naseby was led by Sir Thomas Fairfax, Henry Ireton and Philip Skippon. Their opposite numbers were Charles I, Prince Rupert, Lord Astley and Marmaduke Langdale. Though his men were greatly outnumbered and outflanked, the king was determined to fight on. When they finally retreated, they did so in disarray. Charles was forced to leave his lengthy personal baggage train behind in the rush to elude Parliament's advance. Along with everything else, the Roundheads took possession of the king's letters, finding among them missives to and from the queen. What the letters revealed, apart from passionate intimacies ('Deare Heart', 'eternally yours', 'I am yours after death if it be possible') and Henrietta Maria's persistent rallying cries, was that the king was considering bringing in Irish Catholic regiments to support his efforts and might in return consider giving Catholics of the Three Kingdoms freedom to practise. The letters most offensive to Puritans were then published in a pamphlet luridly entitled *The King's Cabinet Opened, or, Certain Packets of Secret Letters and Papers, Written in the King's Own Hand.* With its carefully framed introduction, the pamphlet made a dramatic impression upon many Englishmen and women, already terrified by previous accounts of massacres of Protestant settlers by 'the bloody Tygers of Ireland'. The writer associated the king with a threatening foreign element, 'a combination of all the Papists in Europe almost,' as opposed to 'the Protestant subjects of England and Scotland.' (Anglicans were now portrayed as nothing more than crypto-Catholics. As for English Catholics, they had long been redefined as foreigners for adhering to the Old Faith.) The people of England and Scotland were further invited to disdain and mock the royal couple, to see the king as a weakling ridden by a harpy. From James's perspective, the enemy had weaponised something that had been a constant source of strength for him and his brothers and sisters – his parents' marriage. That his parents loved one another, that his mother urged his father on, that his father trusted and confided in his mother – all these things were presented as disastrous for the nation. Inevitably, the patriotic James found all this disturbing. Sometimes he could not help wondering if his mother had sunk his father. One day, however, he would seek to do both his parents justice.

The Cavaliers limped on for some months, but the die was cast. The royal family made plans to fan out anew. They could ill afford to be captured together. For 12-year-old James, the goodbye embraces continued one by one until he was left in charge of negotiating the surrender of their doomed Oxford stronghold. 'It was James's fate, as a boy, to endure that agony to the end.'[11] 15-year-old Prince Charles left the city to rally Royalist forces in the West Country. The king slipped away on 27 April 1646, before Oxford could be fully surrounded. Servants had disguised him as a groom, shearing the distinctively pointed beard and curled lovelock, removing the pearl droplet earring, and adding a peaked cap to obscure his face.[12]. King Charles decided to give himself up to the Scots Presbyterians at their camp near Newark-on-Trent, reasoning that theirs was the most attractive offer on the table. The Scots were in touch with the French chief minister, Cardinal Mazarin. (James's first cousin Louis XIV was still in his minority at this time.) On 19 May the king ordered his men to lay down their arms.

In Oxford, Prince James was negotiating his surrender to Sir Thomas Fairfax. 'Black Tom' Fairfax, aware that James and his company were on half-rations, sent in 'a brace of bucks, two muttons, two veals, two lamb and six capon' as a means of persuasion.[13] They were hungry, and so was the city. James made no reply to this gift, but it was only a matter of time before the Royalists would fold. The surrender came on St John the Baptist's Day (24 June). Fairfax received the keys to the city, and he and his men made straight for Christ Church College, where they entered the Presence Chamber to find the 12-year-old Prince James waiting for them, sitting on the chair of estate. James recalled that the Roundheads 'had not yet banish'd all appearances of respect to the royal family.' Everyone apart from Fairfax kissed his hand, and one officer, by the name of Oliver Cromwell, kneeled before him. Whereas Prince Rupert and Prince Maurice were given 'liberty to go beyond the seas', James was taken into custody. Fairfax ordered one of his Gentlemen of the Bedchamber, Sir George Radcliffe, to remain at his master's side for the time being (later dismissed in favour of Northumberland). Radcliffe, an Irishman, had been close to the martyred

Earl of Strafford. Having said farewell to his family members, James had to part with every other member of his household. The boy protested when his captors tore away even his court dwarf companion. There would be a new regime to watch over him. It was a blessing that James was not to be 'a close prisoner', confined to a single room, for that would have been torture for the high-spirited prince who so loved to be outdoors, hunting and hawking with his family and friends. But now when he took exercise – as he chafed to do every day of his life – he had to be accompanied by men on horseback lest he try to flee.

Meanwhile, the New Model Army poured into Oxford. Roundhead soldiers rousted and replaced the Cavaliers, and the city came in for considerable punishment. For having supported the king's cause, Oxford was 'slighted'(its defences were removed). The triumphant new troops shot up statues on the church of St Mary Virgin, where the royal family and courtiers had attended services (Charles I's devotion to the Virgin Mary horrified the Puritans). Roundheads also burned the records of the Oxford Parliament: no trace would remain of the parallel assembly that had challenged the Westminster Parliament's newfound sovereignty. Shortly after this, that all-powerful assembly abolished episcopacy. This meant that the princes' long-time tutor, Bishop Brian Duppa, lost his bishopric, along with all the other bishops. Having followed the king to Oxford, where he had a home at All Souls College, Bishop Duppa was now cast adrift. It was the end of the Church of England as the English knew it. It also meant that there would be no more bishops to support the Royalists in the House of Lords. As the 1640s progressed, the Puritan party ensured its dominance of Parliament by excluding its enemies from voting.

James was now placed in the care of the highest-ranking rebel, Algernon Percy, 10th Earl of Northumberland. The son of the storied 'Wizard Earl', Northumberland had abandoned the court party for the Roundheads. He had risen to prominence in the House of Lords by going after one royal servant after another – first the Duke of Buckingham, then the Earl of Strafford, against whom he had given damaging testimony. Northumberland had acted as Lord High Admiral until King Charles, considering him untrustworthy, had dismissed him in 1642. Betrayal seemed to run in the family: Northumberland's sister was double agent Lucy Hay, Countess of Carlisle. She had used her position as lady-in-waiting to the queen to spy on the king and betray his plans to Parliament. James once more found himself among enemies – high-born, wealthy and gracious ones, but enemies nonetheless. And there was little likelihood of deliverance this time. The one bright spot was that he got to see Elizabeth and Henry once more. He would be able to aid and encourage his sister and brother, now aged 11 and 6 respectively.[14]

At first the royal children lived at Syon House, Northumberland's West London home. A Bridgettine nunnery until the dissolution of the monasteries, it had been Katherine Howard's prison while she awaited execution. Now it was prison to James, Elizabeth and Henry. The Duke of York suffered a serious 'ague' (fever); he took months to recover. He exchanged frequent letters with his father, who at one point had urged his son to 'ply his book more, and his gun less'.[15] James was distressed to learn that the Scots had handed the king over to Parliament. On the other hand, he was elated to hear that Henrietta's governess had defied Parliament's orders and smuggled the tiny princess out of England in disguise. Anne Villiers, Lady Dalkeith, had feared discovery because little Henrietta insisted on telling people that she was no boy, but a princess. Thanks to the courage of this Royalist heroine, Henrietta had been reunited with her grateful mother at the palace of St Germain-en-Laye. Defying her husband, Queen Henrietta Maria brought her daughter up Catholic. There the name 'Anne' was added to her name as a compliment to Anne of Austria, and perhaps to her courageous governess also. She was thereafter known as 'Henriette Anne'. Prince Charles would later nickname her 'Minette'.

After a spell in Jersey, where Prince Charles disported himself while his governor concentrated on writing his *History of the Rebellion*, he made it to France as well. Now a tall 16-year-old, Charles was easily distracted by women. He had first been seduced, aged 15, by his own governess. There were rumours that he had got a girl pregnant in Jersey. Now Charles was making efforts to romance Madame de Montpensier. Meanwhile, Edward Hyde was trying to arrange a marriage for him. Because of the Stuarts' dim prospects, this was proving difficult.

Finally, just before Christmas 1646, James was permitted to see his father in detention at Maidenhead, where the Scots were in the process of handing him over to the English. It was distressing and humiliating for James to see his father so impotent, the very inverse of a king. Although Charles I's dignified carriage was some reassurance, James hated to see his father hesitate or make any concessions to the rebels. He supported the king's rejection of their terms, which would have involved declaring episcopacy inherently wrong and surrendering fifty-six of his followers to almost certain execution.

Meanwhile, a split had developed among the Royalists between the king's main adviser, Edward Hyde, and the queen's Lord Chamberlain, Henry Jermyn, which James would have perceived as a division between father and mother. The latter faction was known as 'the Louvre'. The Hyde camp wished to see the Church of England preserved at all costs, while the Louvre held that making a deal with the Presbyterians was the best way forward. The queen apparently saw no distinction between Protestants: one was as bad as the next, so the king had better ally with the most powerful one, at least for the time being. James respected his father's principled position, his goal of preserving the Anglican Church within the constitution. As for the more cynical Prince Charles, he was temperamentally opposed to hard-line Protestantism, but by the same token he appreciated Jermyn's case for practicality. Both young men longed to see their father crush the rebels.

The carefully guarded James kept in close contact with his imprisoned father. James thought often of escape, perhaps with little Henry, Duke of Gloucester, at his side. One of Elizabeth's servants, a Mrs Kilvert, gave him some encouragement. She and a barber named Hill were engaged to help him, but the plans fell through when a letter in cipher was discovered. 'I received Yours of the 1st February by Mr. Fox, who is a very honest Man, and will do his Endeavour to the utmost of his Power,' James had written, adding in code 'in conveying me away.' He signed the letter 'Your friend, J. Darly'. Interrogated by Parliament, he admitted that the handwriting was his own, but declined to expose his co-conspirators. Asked why he had hidden it, he explained, as it was summed up at the time, that 'it was out of obedience to the king's command and out of kindness to his father', adding that 'he had so many obligations from a loving father as to command secrecy from him.'[16] Some MPs called for the young duke to be sent to the Tower of London. Cooler heads prevailed, however. James promised his enemies 'upon his faith and honour' to stay put. He later related that 'even in the heat of this affair while his Royal Highness was yet under examination, he began to form a new design for his liberty'.[17] His duty to his father came first. Northumberland, intuiting this, told Parliament he would not be held responsible if the duke got away. Meanwhile, Charles I had got wind of an army plan to capture and crown his second son. The king got in touch with Colonel Joseph Bampfield: 'It has been deliberated by some of the army to possess themselves of the duke of Yorke,' he wrote. 'Consider whether you cannot find means to convey him out of England.' The plan was under way.[18]

In summer 1647, Cromwell and Fairfax permitted the three royal children to visit their father, bringing the king to the Greyhound Tavern in Caversham for the meeting. Henry, now aged 7, had not seen him for five years. 'Do you know me, child?' asked the king. The little boy said no. 'I am your father, child,' Charles told him, 'and it is not the least of my misfortunes that I have brought you and your brothers and sisters into this world to share my miseries.' James and Elizabeth burst into tears. Charles pulled them close to him. Cromwell, who was watching, called it 'the tenderest sight that eyes ever beheld'.[19] During that summer, James, Elizabeth and Henry were permitted to wait upon the king at Hampton Court Palace frequently. The children would spend long hours in the garden with their father, running and playing. Charles was affectionate, kissing and embracing them, counselling them to be true to one another and to their brother, the Prince of Wales. He kept James close at his side. They played tennis and chess. Charles, himself a second son, had a strong appreciation for the serious, resolute and courageous youth. They were joined by the Dutch portraitist who had succeeded Van Dyck, Peter Lely, whom Northumberland commissioned to paint the imprisoned king and the devoted James together. The future Sir Peter Lely depicted the son looking piercingly across at his father, whose troubled gaze is slightly downcast. This painting inspired verses from Cavalier poet Richard Lovelace. 'See! What a clouded Majesty! and eyes,/whose glory through their mist doth brighter rise.' The Duke of York stands attentive, poised to carry out his father's orders: 'Whilst the true Eaglet this quick lustre spies/And by his *Sun's* enlightens his own eyes.' And, indeed, James was at the ready. He had his orders: foil Parliament's plans for him and fly to Mary in Holland at the first opportunity.

Chapter 3

The True Eaglet

> By Turenne form'd, and stamp'd with Turenne's praise,
> O'er sea and lands (as seas and lands
> have seen/Thee greatly brave) ...
>
> Anne Finch, 'Elegy for James II'

As Fortune's wheel carried the Royalists ever downward, James now found himself staggering with pain and rootless on the Continent. This patriotic prince no longer had a home in England.[1] Now he knew true exile. It was 1649, and the Rump Parliament had stolen his father's life. The young man's mind was crowded with memories, impressions and worries. His mother was devastated. He had left his little sister and brother on their own. Their familiar caretaker back in England, Northumberland, opposed executing the king; as a result, Parliament took the royal children away from him. Elizabeth and Henry had been the last family members to see the doomed King Charles. The 13-year-old princess wrote a heartrending account of this meeting, which took place on 29 January, the eve of the execution. Princess Elizabeth was crying so hard that she worried she would not be able to remember all her father told her. He sent his eternal love to the queen. He reminded his daughter to be steadfast in the Protestant religion, recommended works by Hooker and Laud, and gave her a Bible which became her prized possession. She described Charles taking Henry upon his knee and counselling him: '"Sweetheart, now they will cut off thy father's head." And Gloucester looking very intently upon him, he said again, '"Heed, child, what I say; they will cut off my head and perhaps make thee a king. But mark what I say: thou must not be a king as long as thy brothers Charles and James do live, for they will cut off thy brothers' heads when they can catch them, and cut off thy head too at last, so I charge thee, do not be made a king by them." At which my brother sighed deeply, and made answer, "I will be torn in pieces first!"'[2]

Little Henry's fierce reply delighted his family members. It was a bright spot in an otherwise bleak scene. England was now declared a republic for the first time in its history. Many Royalists treasured the king's final speech, in which he argued that there could be no liberty without order. He left them with the words 'I go from a corruptible to an incorruptible crown.' Charles was widely regarded as a martyr, his book *Eikon Basilike* was selling rapidly, and miniature portraits of the king and other such mementoes were in great demand. A dissident cult developed around the king's memory, but the royal oak was severed. It is difficult to overstate the disruption this represented. English kings had been dethroned in the past, but by rival kings rather than an oligarchy claiming to stand for the populace. The Church of England had been abolished along with the monarchy, carrying along countless links to the old ways, to the cyclic festive calendar of communal life stretching back more than a thousand years. The Commonwealth government sold off the royal regalia, including much of the king's beloved art collection.

This new republic was powerful, but less than loveable. A popular ballad captures the sentiment: 'To conclude, I'll tell you the news that's right/ Christmas was killed at Naseby fight:/Charity was slain at that same time,/ Jack-Truth too, a friend of mine,/ Likewise then did die, roast beef and shred pie,/Pig, Goose, and Capon, no quarter found;/Yet let's be content, the times lament, You see the world turned upside-down.' Now more than ever, the Stuarts were the custodians of a suppressed Merry Old England. Charles's old tutor William Cavendish, now Marquess of Newcastle, was in exile on the Continent. He counselled the Stuarts to guard that flame carefully, for it could be the key to their renewal. He now wrote for the new King Charles II his handbook of English governance, as if to anchor him mentally in his lost homeland. In it he evokes the very dimension of English life that Puritanism eroded. Newcastle's chapter on 'sports' amounts to a list of banned customs. He advises reopening the playhouses 'for all sorts of diversion and pleasure', adding that the king should reinstate 'daily feasting in merry England ... May games, Morris dances, the Lords and Ladies of the May, the fool and the hobby horse must not be forgotten ... carols and wassails at Christmas, with good plum porridge and pies which are now forbidden as profane, ungodly things.'[3] Newcastle's evocations of an England faraway in time and space would have filled his fellow exiles with longing: 'After evening prayer every Sunday and holiday, the country people with their fresher lasses will trip on the town green about the

May Pole, to the loudest bagpipes, there to be refreshed with ale and cakes.' For now, the common people squirmed under Malvolio's thumb. But their carnivalesque spirit might yet be harnessed in service of the Stuarts. One good sign was that there were occasional rowdy outbursts of Christmas cheer in defiance of the ban.

James had been robbed of his father, but he had three people to turn to on the Continent – his sister Mary, his brother Charles and his mother. All were laid low by the dreadful news. When it reached Paris, two weeks after the execution, the queen's confessor, Father Cyprien, had been warned to stay with her because a profound shock was in store. It fell to Henry Jermyn to tell the queen, who, upon learning the truth, stood still as a statue for over an hour before finally collapsing in sobs. Henrietta Maria clutched the hand of Madame de Motteville, saying 'I have lost a king, a husband and a father, whose loss I can never sufficiently mourn.'[4] It was difficult for the family and their followers to grasp what had happened, so great was the import. In the words of one: 'This sad and execrable murder of our blessed master hath so disordered me that I shall hardly ever recover true quiet of mind. My soul abhors the thought of it which no age ever heard the like. Yet, through all distractions, I must force myself to action when it may conduce to avenge the blood of that royal and glorious martyr upon those base inhuman murderers.'[5]

James knew that getting revenge upon his father's killers meant giving Charles II his full support. As spring 1649 wore on, and James remained at the Louvre with his mother, he began to chafe at her bridle. James recalled that his father had always urged him to obey his mother – except in matters of religion – but he was bored and frustrated, and could not help quarrelling with her. He and Charles were firmly in the Edward Hyde camp, and 15-year-old James for one resented Henrietta Maria's reliance upon Henry Jermyn. His camp was known as 'the Louvre'. In some way, he blamed Jermyn for the Royalists' troubles. At one point he accused the queen of loving her rotund favourite more than any of her children.[6] Against Henrietta Maria's preferences, James accompanied his brother to Jersey, where Charles had been proclaimed king publicly on 17 February. Apart from Scotland, it was the only part of the British Isles still officially loyal to the monarchy.

Another navy ship, the *Hart*, preceded them, the crew having defected in protest after the execution of Charles I. In mid-September the young king and duke arrived to joyful acclaim. They brought about 300 men, among them James's new court dwarf, Monsieur Becquers. Guns blasted, church bells rang out and bonfires were lit. So noisy were the celebrations that they tipped off Cromwell's forces anchored nearby. Nonetheless, the brothers and their friends enjoyed several pleasure-filled months on the island, where they lived at the solidly fortified Elizabeth Castle, once occupied by Sir Walter Raleigh. James was appointed Governor of Jersey. The island was a Royalist microcosm where they could roam freely, yachting, hunting and hawking, and then feasting contentedly. Having brought the royal furnishings along, Charles decorated the governor's house and chapel in rich tapestries and gold plate. The king marked James's sixteenth birthday with a grand party. He held receptions for the local gentry.[7] Now that he was monarch, Charles could follow custom and 'touch for the King's Evil' (scrofula). Sufferers would flock to the royal chapel, eager to feel the monarch's hand and receive a healing gold coin to wear close to the body. He brought a troupe of English players to entertain his followers. But as money was growing tight, the court with all its ceremony was more difficult to sustain.

The brothers' flamboyant old companion George Villiers, 2nd Duke of Buckingham, arrived in early January, bringing a message from Henrietta Maria which interrupted their idyll. Charles had to meet her at Rouen. The unpleasant news arrived from Ireland that the Royalist Irish Confederates under James Butler, then Marquis of Ormond, had been crushed. The news from Drogheda of Roundhead massacres was chilling. Soon after this, Charles II travelled to Scotland, arriving in June 1650. Although the Scots had had a key role in starting the civil wars, most were horrified when the Rump Parliament tried and executed Charles I, who had been born in Fife and crowned King of Scotland in a separate ceremony. 'Ever since the murder of his father ... the best part of them ... protested against and opposed the wicked and violent proceedings in England.'[8] It was one thing to oppose the king's policies, but quite another for the English to murder him and abolish the monarchy. And there were shades of an earlier decapitation of a Stuart monarch at the hands of the English government: Elizabeth I had cheapened the lives of crowned heads everywhere when she executed Charles's grandmother, Mary, Queen of Scots. Scotland pushed back, proclaiming Charles II in Edinburgh. Soon he would be crowned.

The English responded to Charles's arrival in Scotland by punishing Princess Elizabeth and Prince Henry. Sister and brother were sent to the Isle of Wight to be confined in Carisbrooke Castle, a place where their father had been imprisoned. Elizabeth had pleaded with Parliament, saying she was too unwell to travel, but her worries were ignored. She grew more and more melancholy. On the way to the Isle of Wight, the princess caught a cold that rapidly developed into pneumonia. Elizabeth died at Carisbrooke Castle on 8 September 1650, reportedly clutching the Bible the king had given her at their final meeting. Her gravestone was marked only 'E.S.' for Elizabeth Stuart, titles having been abolished along with the monarchy in 1649. James was visiting Mary when he received the heart-breaking news that his kind and thoughtful sister was dead. He had left her in England to fend for herself, and now she had perished. Prince Henry, now entirely alone, applied to Parliament to join his family on the Continent, but the request was denied. Parliament were still thinking about how best to use the last Stuart child still in their grasp.

Meanwhile, in Scotland, Charles stole Parliament's thunder by being crowned King of Scotland, England, Ireland and France at Scone Palace – after which he could turn his attention to Cromwell down south. To reach this point, Charles had to make the very compromises that his father had rejected. The playful, pleasure-loving new king had embraced French court life. He disliked the austere Covenanter ethos under which, he said, 'There was not a woman to talk to, and the barbarism was such that the men thought it a sin to play the violin.'9 He once remarked to a friend that Presbyterianism 'was no religion for gentlemen.' Though Charles II submitted to the Scots, having few other options, he confided in the Dean King of Tuam that he remained 'a true child of the Church of England' and 'a true Cavalier'. In truth he much preferred the flippant grace of the Duke of Buckingham to the Covenanter David Leslie, but he had to promote the Scot over his old comrade-in-arms. (Buckingham took it as a snub.) Charles II was a practical, rather cynical man and a skilled politician, willing to bend the truth and suffer certain indignities in order to cultivate power. In his view Presbyterians were preferable to Roundheads because they were monarchists of a sort. So he made his peace with them.

Bishops having been abolished, Charles was crowned by the Scots chancellor, assisted by four other lords. In keeping with tradition, the herald recited the new monarch's ancestry all the way back to Fergus. After hearing a lengthy sermon, Charles made a coronation speech, pledging to uphold Presbyterianism in Scotland. (He did stop short of taking the National Covenant, however, and this alienated a portion of the nation.) The crucial point was that he had promised the Scots that, if restored, he would impose it in England as well. This would mean installing a comparatively egalitarian system of church elders – presbyters – as opposed to the traditional episcopate. The Scots' part of the bargain was to fight beside their king against the even more strictly Protestant government of England. (Oliver Cromwell, an Independent, was in turn facing challenges from an even *more* hard-line splinter group, the Fifth Monarchy Men.)

James would be able to mark the first anniversary of their father's death in the knowledge that his brother had been affirmed by the Scots. He voyaged back to Holland to meet Mary, who was pregnant, in time for 30 January. She applied to the Estates General for permission to commemorate the occasion publicly, only to be denied. The Duke of York had arrived at a tricky moment for the States General, who had just welcomed Cromwell's ambassadors for the first time since the execution of Charles I, an act that the Dutch assembly had deplored. The English diplomats were in town with a proposal designed to mollify them: England and Holland should ally to drive the Spanish out of the West Indies. Meanwhile, James and company were prancing loudly past the residence of the English ambassadors trailed by enthusiastic crowds of Dutch citizens who had been taught to chant 'Cromwell's bastards! Cromwell's bastards!'[10] The States General worked hard keeping the proud young warrior separate from his father's murderers so that he did not 'take that revenge on them which they so well deserved'.[11] The fact that the Prince and Princess of Orange had to defer to the States General showed James what constitutional monarchy looked like, and he heartily disapproved of it. On the other hand, Mary and her husband were able to provide her family members with much-needed money and shelter. Nothing was so rare as money in those days, he later recalled. The duke made another visit to the Hague when the Princess of Orange gave birth to a son on 4 November 1650, a few scant days after smallpox carried off her husband. Mary had wanted to name the newborn Charles in honour of her father, but she was overruled by her mother-in-law. James's new nephew was baptised William after his father. Because his father had just died, he was born the Prince of Orange.

The Stuarts had fled their home country, only to find that France was caught up in its own civil war. A portion of the aristocracy rebelled against the monarch. The conflict was between Louis XIV advised by Cardinal Mazarin on the one side, and challengers led by the Prince de Condé on the other. The civil unrest was dubbed the Fronde in reference to the slingshots used to break the cardinal's windows. A frightened Henrietta Maria wrote to her sister, Christine of Savoy: 'Nobody dares go outside the gates of Paris without risking their life, whether from soldiers, robbers or peasants, who are ruined ... God wants to humiliate kings and princes. He began with us in England. I pray that France is not going to follow.'[12] Taking advantage of the division, Spain backed the rebels. Condé, an uncle of the boy-king, blared out the age-old pretence that the monarch needed rescuing from 'evil counsellors'. James and Charles had heard this cry from the Roundheads.[13] The two necessarily threw their weight behind their first cousin, Louis XIV. John Evelyn noted that when the Battle of Worcester dashed all Royalist hopes, 'the sweet duke of Yorke' thought to make his way as a professional soldier.[14] James was responsible not only for himself but also for his household and a large number of increasingly rag-tag followers in search of honour and position. Charles had left him under his mother's command, so he applied to her for permission to serve in the French army. She agreed, and so did Cardinal Mazarin. James was 18, old enough and sufficiently hardy to bear the strains of war. The youth had to borrow money for the training, and his equipage was poor, 'yet,' he noted, he 'chose to go this way rather than not at all.'[15] James now entered upon a happier time. As one observer wrote, 'He ventures himself and chargeth gallantly where anything is to be done.'[16] Born and bred a warrior, he was honing his craft; his talents were put to good use; and his loyal entourage, whose fortunes rose and fell with their master's, could be formed into regiments and employed in turn. He received a pension, enough to enable him and his household to live decently until King Charles had need of his services again. Some sense of order returned to life.

Meanwhile, Charles faced off with Cromwell at the Battle of Worcester. It was 3 September 1651. The king had the support of Scottish troops. He hoped that the Midlands would rise for the king as it was historically a Royalist area, but Cromwell's side managed to stir widespread fear of the Scots. National tensions jockeyed with religious and political preferences in the Wars of the Three Kingdoms, sometimes overriding them. Ultimately, the New Model Army won the day. James and his family feared that the king was dead. Finally, word came that Charles was alive, but on the run.

James prayed fervently that he would elude his enemies. He was serving under a widely respected general, Henri de la Tour d'Auvergne, Vicomte de Turenne and Marshal of France. Among other feats, Turenne had saved Louis from being captured by rebels. A Protestant in a strongly Catholic circle, the general had so far held out against political incentives to convert. He took James under his wing and schooled him. He had a high opinion of 'the young prince whose father had perished on the scaffold'. The general was 'not a little delighted in having so illustrious a person as his Schollar in the discipline of warr'.[17] James, for his part, came to believe that Turenne was the 'the greatest Captain of this and perhaps of any age'. This was high praise coming from a warrior through and through. This apprenticeship came at a crucial time for James, who had lost his father just as he was entering manhood. Turenne considered that 'in the matter of courage in a man, he desired to see nothing better than the Duke of York.' He also commended 'his quick knowledge of what to do'.[18] The French general would be a great source of strength for the younger man in the testing years to come. He hosted the prince in his tents when they were on campaign, and James accompanied him everywhere, serving as the older man's eyes, since he was short-sighted. 'For James proved an excellent lieutenant – brave, enduring, eager to learn and amenable to discipline. Phlegmatic, except when his deepest emotions were aroused,' and he had 'a passion for order and routine, yet bold'.[19] He was highly observant of military matters, as his detailed memoirs would demonstrate.

James was intensely English, and always inclined to cheer for Englishmen, but he developed a great deal of respect for the French by fighting alongside them. The French language that he had learned from his mother and tutors became excellent. He had a high opinion of French officers, remarking that he only ever saw one drunk. They conducted themselves impeccably, in his experience. 'In these countries they make war not so brutally,' he wrote, adding that he never saw such an officer commit 'any unhuman act'. Also, he saw them as guided by faith: 'There were public prayers at the head of each Battalion or Squadron, and as many as could, confessed and received the Blessed Sacrament ... no army ever showed more marks of true devotion.'[20] He was among those who could not receive the Catholic Eucharist, but this devotion made a strong impression upon James. The French crowd seemed a different story, cruel and unreasoning. He felt horror at seeing a mob set fire to a house and cut down the occupants as they fled the flames. The Parisian mob, it seemed to him, was every bit as dangerous as the London one. A rabble, fired up against Cardinal Mazarin, used slingshots to break his windows and generally rioted at the behest of the rebel princes. Eventually, though, the fickle crowd tired of the chaos they had engendered. 'Despite their seducers,' the people 'began to see how much they had been deluded, and had thoughts of returning to their duty,' James wrote. He believed that they came to realise that they 'had been made the stalking horses of some ambitious spirits'.[21]

War was a study in contrasts. He saw men perish in battle and suffer on campaign. His friend Harry Jermyn had his horse shot out from under him. One of his Grooms of the Bedchamber, Colonel Worden, was wounded. He himself broke a leg. He saw soldiers freeze to death. Food was scarce and so was forage for the horses. Sometimes they had to eat horse-flesh and cabbage-stalks nicknamed 'the Cardinal's bread'. But the seasoned young prince was alert to beauty as well, such as when he observed 'a still very fair night' with a bright moon. 'As the moon went down,' he recalled, 'it began to blow very fresh and exceedingly dark ... lighted matches ... made a glorious show ... the wind ... kindled them and made them blaze through the darkness of the night ... the sparkles were carried about by the wind to increase the light.'[22]

James was back in Paris after one campaign when he heard that Charles had reached France after two long months of silence. He had feared for his brother's life, writing that Royalists 'were in dreadfull apprehension for the King, and continu'd in fearfull amazement'.[23] England was littered with wanted posters after the Battle of Worcester. Parliament issued a proclamation 'for the Discovery and Apprehending of CHARLES STUART, and other Traytors his Adherants and Abettors'. English people were warned to be on the lookout for this 'malicious and dangerous Traytor to the Peace of this Commonwealth'. They were offered a large reward to turn in their fugitive king. Nobody claimed it. James eagerly rode out to meet Charles on the road and to escort him to Henrietta Maria. When he found him at Magny, his brother was scarcely recognisable. Thin, tired, penniless and dressed in peasant's clothes, Charles II had only one companion left. But the king was alive and in one piece. James, overjoyed to see him at last, embraced him with relief and escorted him back to Paris. The whole court were elated.

Charles regaled the company with the story of the last two months. It was an unforgettable episode, one that would reshape the king's outlook.

He would never forget those who had helped him along the way. Despite the reward and the fact that hiding the outlaw monarch was punishable by 'death without mercy' – which meant hanging, drawing and quartering for the men, and probable burning for the women – many ordinary people risked everything for him. After their disastrous routing at the Battle of Worcester on 3 September 1651, Charles fled for his life on horseback. He was accompanied by several lords, including Buckingham and Henry Wilmot, 1st Earl of Rochester. Unlike James at 14, the king could not pass unnoticed in women's weeds. His companions cut his long curling black hair and dressed him as a farm labourer in a leather doublet, green breeches and ill-fitting coarse leather shoes. He soon found shelter at Boscobel House, home of an old recusant family. Learning that government troops were coming to search the house, Charles and a companion, Colonel William Carliss, ventured into the grounds and climbed into the branches of an ancient oak tree. They spent the whole day there, picnicking on bread, cheese and beer. The king's friend held him while he slept to prevent him from falling. At one point, New Model Army troops passed below. Charles won his nickname 'the oak apple' on that occasion. Once the troops had searched the house, the two returned to spend the night in a priest-hide, built in the time of Elizabeth I to conceal Catholic clerics who risked torture and execution if caught.

Moving on to the home of another Catholic family, Moseley Hall, Charles met Father John Huddleston. The king was given a hot meal, fresh clothes and a bed. Before he turned in, the Benedictine bathed and tended to his sore and bleeding feet. Charles was touched, saying, 'If it please God I come to my crown, you and any of your persuasion shall have as much liberty as any of my subjects.' He read the priest's manuscript, *A Short and Plain Way to the Faith and Church*. The whole encounter with Father Huddleston planted a seed in Charles. Two days later, Roundhead troops arrived, and the king was quickly hidden in another priest-hide.[24]

The young king had been crushed militarily, but he drew consolation from the kindness of ordinary Englishmen who risked their own lives to help him. Englishwomen played their part as well: at the next haven, Charles met a quick-witted Catholic supporter named Jane Lane. He travelled on with her, pretending to be her servant. Later, he and another brave gentlewoman, Juliana Coningsby, posed as an eloping couple. For eight weeks Charles travelled through England, dodging soldiers who had orders to look for 'a tall, black [haired] man, six foot two inches in height'. Finally, he and Wilmot struck a deal with the captain of a coal-boat, the *Surprise*, to take them from Shoreham to Le Havre. Jane Lane fled the country dressed in peasant's garb. It would be a long time before either Charles or James would see their homeland again. Once the young king had been back for a few days, melancholy overtook him. Never had his prospects seemed so dim.

The possibility of marriage between Charles and France's greatest heiress, the buxom Anne-Marie Louise d'Orléans ('La Grande Mademoiselle') was floated and abandoned: with the prospect of restoration seemingly vanishingly small, Charles was at a disadvantage. She was pleased to let her tall, dark, fine figure of a cousin sit at her feet. His French was poor, so he had to rely on Prince Rupert to romance Anne-Marie. 'Since at that time I thought of marrying the Emperor,' she wrote, 'I looked on the Prince of Wales merely as an object of pity.'[25] Meanwhile, James's governor proposed marrying his charge to another tempting lady, Marie d'Orléans-Longueville, daughter of the Duke of Longueville. Mademoiselle de Longueville was eight years older than James, but wealthy and well connected. She wore her blond hair fashionably curled. She was attractive and observant, a familiar face at the French court. The youth was agreeable, but negotiations stalled. Charles hesitated to let James marry before he did.

James was pleased to see Prince Rupert when he dragged himself back from his seafaring adventures. Privateering brought the Cavaliers a trickle of money. Like Charles, Rupert was in a desolate mood. Prince Maurice had perished in a Caribbean tempest. They had lost yet another family member. On the bright side, in 1652, Oliver Cromwell finally decided to free the last royal captive, Henry, Duke of Gloucester. In James's view, the Lord Protector let the 12-year-old loose, 'not out of any principle of humanity, but merely to save the charges of maintaining him any longer'.[26] Now that Cromwell was king in all but name, any idea of crowning Henry was forgotten. Like James before him, the boy went first to the Princess of Orange. After a few months, Henrietta Maria asked Henry to come to Paris. Mary was hesitant to let him go to the Louvre; she worried about their mother's influence. When he arrived, Charles and James were there to greet him and introduce him to the woman who had given him life. He did not remember his mother, and he had been educated to despise her religion. Moreover, France was totally new to him. So when his mother doggedly went to work trying to convert her long-lost son to Catholicism, he resisted. Her eldest son she left alone, but her other children she considered fair game.[27] When Charles left France, he tasked James with making sure Henrietta Maria left Henry alone. The king agreed with Edward Hyde that the Stuarts had to think of the effect a high-level conversion would have on the English people back home. They had to consider the Anglicans, driven underground when Parliament abolished the national church, and clinging to mementoes of the martyred king. His cult was growing steadily. This large group of Royalists needed to be sustained. They would feel betrayed if any of the Stuarts turned Roman Catholic. The queen, undaunted, dismissed Henry's Protestant tutor and assigned him her old friend and new chaplain, Father 'Wat' Montagu, as catechist. She and Jermyn maintained that only Catholic powers could help the Stuarts regain their throne.[28] James would sneak Henry to Anglican services at the house of Sir Richard Browne on their way to riding and dancing lessons.[29] Henry defied the queen, and she disowned him – at least for the present. Abbé Montagu also took a run at James, but failed to convert him. The fact that he enjoyed attending mass, transported by the music, and that there were a number of Catholic converts in his household, led to rumours. However, the Duke of York remained Protestant.[30] James watched over Henry as Charles had asked. As things stood, the queen's only firmly Catholic child was Henriette Anne, who grew up in the French court. A pretty little girl who loved poetry and music, playing guitar and harpsichord, she won hearts in all quarters.

Over the next few years, James went on several more campaigns with Turenne in defence of Louis XIV. In 1654 he won the commission of lieutenant general. In between times, he led a hectic social life in the capital, dancing in glittering masques at the Palais Royal and 'attending so many balls, dinners and "divertissements" that he seldom got to bed before four in the morning.'[31] On one occasion he and Henry, gorgeously costumed, joined other members of the court in dancing a ballet entitled *The Nuptials of Thetis and Pelis,* with music by a young Lully.[32] The 9-year-old Henriette Anne performed a debut dance as well. It was the kind of production that their cousin Louis XIV, learning to project majesty through art, adored dancing in himself. James had found a home among the French. Among many others who noticed him was the genial and amusing Philibert, Count de Gramont. Another courtier noted that the duke won favour through his 'comeliness and personal dexterity in his behaviour'.[33] He was tall now (at least 'two yards high'), and with his lantern jaw and well-shaped features, the very picture of a Christian knight: strong, faithful and brave. The French king, five years his junior, was very fond of him. Also, James overcame his jealousy of Henry Jermyn and the two grew close. Jermyn's charming nephew Harry found a place in James's entourage.

Late in 1655, however, the duke received unwelcome news. Cardinal Mazarin had been forced to come to terms with Cromwell. Under attack from wayward nobility, the French monarchy could not afford to be at odds with England as well. There was too great a danger that England would support the rebels, or that the Spanish would ally with England. And here was the rub: the treaty specified that James leave the French army. Charles II and his loyal band of Cavaliers, with the exception of Jermyn, had to leave the country. The itinerant English king was sent off to Cologne in summer 1654. Charles had embraced life at the French court, finally mastering its language and absorbing its etiquette; now he was to depart. It was a sort of exile within an exile. Queen Henrietta Maria took the recognition of her husband's murderer hard. As she wrote to James, 'Since my great trouble, I have felt nothing equal to this. God take us under His protection and give us patience to await His time.'[34] Cardinal Mazarin was apologetic. He interceded with Cromwell for James, arguing that the nephew of Henri IV and first cousin to King Louis should be permitted to fight in the French army. The Lord Protector relented, but specified that James must not serve in Flanders. Henrietta Maria, meanwhile, wanted her second son to promise that he would not fight against France.

Around this time, a conflict broke out over James's personal household. The episode is typical of the infighting of the court-in-exile, where true influence was in short supply, along with money and every other commodity. Courtiers squabbled incessantly over thin shards of power. The Hyde camp had poisoned Charles against his brother's current governor, Sir John Berkeley, because he had been appointed by the queen and Jermyn, a kinsman. Berkeley had served Charles I as ambassador to that extravagant Baroque pearl, Queen Christina of Sweden. He had fought in the English Civil Wars and helped Charles I to escape from Hampton Court when the king learned he might be assassinated there. Berkeley had been present at Exeter Cathedral when Henriette Anne was baptised, at which point he seems to have fallen in love with the child's protectress, Anne Morton, née Villiers, Lady Dalkeith. Following the Stuarts into exile, Berkeley accompanied James on campaign. His lively nephew, Charles Berkeley, was a close companion; James, Charles and young Harry Jermyn formed an inseparable trio. The duke respected Sir John Berkeley as a soldier and loved him for his loyalty. One problem was the jealousy of Joseph Bampfield, the Presbyterian colonel who helped the Duke of York escape England. He whispered against Sir John Berkeley because he wished to replace him as governor. Another source of enmity between Berkeley and the Hyde faction was this: Hyde had taken pains to discourage Berkeley and Lady Dalkeith from marrying. Berkeley 'fell out with him upon it ... being ever afterwards on all occasions his bitter Enemy.'[35]

Because of this animosity, Charles came to believe that Berkeley was trying to divide the royal brothers. There were rumours that Berkeley was an intriguer, cultivating contacts in England on the Duke of York's behalf. James sent his personal secretary, Sir Henry Bennet, Earl of Arlington, to Flanders to stamp out 'strange stories' which had reached his brother's ears, provoking 'groundless jealousies'.[36] A particularly incendiary rumour had Berkeley planning to marry James to one of the Lord Protector's daughters for a potent mix of royalism and republicanism. Mary and Frances Cromwell were still unmarried in 1656. The ambitious Buckingham, back in England since falling out of favour with King Charles, now made a bold play to become Cromwell's son-in-law. The Protector rejected his suit. James commented thus: 'That Usurper at least had so much honour in him to say, he could never give his Daughter to one who had been so ungrateful to his King.'[37] Having failed to obtain a Cromwell girl, Buckingham settled for the offspring of General Fairfax instead. Black-haired Mary Fairfax impetuously threw over her fiancé for him, even after the banns had been read. She was madly infatuated. As for Buckingham, it so happened that Thomas Fairfax had been granted Buckingham's confiscated properties. Marriage to Mary meant he could retrieve them.

The hot-headed Colonel Bampfield made accusations, and yet it was he himself whose resentment would prompt collusion with the enemy. He had long coveted the post of governor to James. At one point he had expressed the opinion that Charles ought to have tried harder to save his father from execution. The young king angrily dismissed the colonel from the court-in-exile. Bampfield returned to England and eventually offered his services to Cromwell's grim spymaster, John Thurloe. It was a dramatic fall from grace for the man who had made James's escape possible.

Charles pressured James to dismiss Sir John Berkeley in favour of his former governor, Sir George Radcliffe, whom James now considered to be 'an absolute creature' of Hyde's camp.[38] Charles ordered James to come to him, but leave Berkeley behind. The duke could not bring himself to abandon a long-time servant who had been nothing but loyal to him. James was now 23 years old, an adult, and while the king was his lodestar, he believed that, bar any serious matter, the ducal court was his own domain. James departed, taking Berkeley along. He believed he should be able to choose his own 'family', as royal households were known. It was in negotiating the tension between duty to his brother, the king, and fidelity to those who depended on him that James entered manhood.

Chapter 4

The Rover

> 'But what jewels will that cavalier present you with?
> Those of his eyes and heart?'
>
> Aphra Behn, *The Rover:*
> *Or, The Banish'd Cavaliers.* I.i.95

A tense encounter took place as James rode out of Paris, bound for the Spanish Netherlands. He ran into Cromwell's ambassador to France, Sir William Lockhart, at a roadside inn. Lockhart, a Scots Presbyterian, had originally fought for Charles II. After Scotland was absorbed into the Commonwealth in 1654, he married into Cromwell's family and soon gained the position of ambassador. Hearing that the duke was on the road, Lockhart had sought to dodge him by retreating to the inn, only to hear him arriving there, accompanied by his soldiers and trailed by a lively crowd of locals. The ambassador, to avoid giving offence, hastily directed his own men to remove their hats in a flourish of respect before James strode in. (During these years a newborn English sect that would eventually play a key role in James's life, the Quakers, were defiantly keeping their hats on as a form of egalitarian political protest.) Not only was it dangerous for the Commonwealth delegation to rub up against English Royalists, but ordinary French folk had no love for Roundheads. The handsome and gallant young Duke of York was popular among them. They stood close to him, waiting for his signal to pounce. As James was grimly aware,[1] Lockhart 'apprehend[ed] what might happen to him on the Duke's account'. Although James itched to fight it out, he decided to stand down. He knew well how tricky things could get for Cardinal Mazarin if he attacked Cromwell's delegation.

As James approached Bruges he was met first by the Marquis of Ormond, and then by Prince Henry and King Charles. The three brothers rode into the canalled medieval city. The courtiers made James welcome, and he enjoyed life at Charles's court where, as one observer noted, 'They go every day here a-hunting and every night drinking, dancing and a-wenching.'² There was no shortage of female admirers for the lively young Cavaliers. Paris was replete with pleasures, to be sure, but at his brother's court and away from his mother's gaze, James could truly let his hair down.

On the other hand, the exiles would also be entertained generously at monasteries. On one occasion, a nun asked the duke which faith he followed. He answered that he was 'too young to enter into disputes of controversy'. In response, she promised to pray that God would show him the right path.³ All in all, James reported, he was 'treated with great civility' in Bruges. However, a number of people including Charles snubbed Berkeley as a 'Louvrian' troublemaker. James remained true to his governor: 'What a miserable condition he must have been [in],' he observed, 'if he had suffered those in whom he had the greatest confidence, and in whom he had the greatest kindness, to be torn from him.'⁴ More alarming still was the fact that Charles wanted him to fight for the Spanish. This would mean taking up arms against his French comrades, men he had fought alongside for years. It would mean battling his beloved General Turenne. James was a serious man; he had nothing of the calculation and lightness that led a man like the Comte de Gramont to abandon the *frondeurs* in favour of the king when it suited his interests. But it could not be helped: Charles had committed to Spain in 1656 when it became clear that France and England would sign the Treaty of Paris, which they did the following year. Hoping to mount an invasion of England from the Spanish Netherlands (Flanders), he settled his court in Bruges. England would join France in their war against the Spanish, Cromwell having decided that they were the greater threat of the two Catholic forces fighting for dominance of the trade routes. Henrietta Maria's favourite wrote from Paris, trying to dissuade James. Jermyn reminded him of France's kindness to him, the time he had spent among the French. and failing that, his pension. But these efforts 'prevailed not with the Duke … if the King his Brother should command him, it was his duty to obey.'⁵ With great reluctance James agreed to switch sides, bringing his English, Irish and Scots regiments with him.

Princess Mary arrived in Bruges shortly before Christmas 1657 to find her brothers still at odds over Sir John Berkeley. Charles held that Berkeley had come between them and was anti-Spanish. James had just sacrificed his career in the French army to follow Charles. He was not prepared to break up his household 'family' as well. Sir George Digby, Earl of Bristol, waded into the matter. Though bold and adventurous, he failed to inspire confidence in the young duke. Bristol was inclining towards Catholicism; at the same time, he was obsessed with astrology and arcane fortune-telling. 'He talked perpetually of Crowns and Sceptres,' wrote James. Bristol insisted that Berkeley be dismissed. When argument failed, he asserted bluntly that 'it was the King's absolute pleasure that Berkeley should withdraw.' James was adamant. How would he appear if he abandoned his 'innocent Servants' ... 'to the malice of their enemies?' It disturbed Mary to see her brothers at odds, but she took James's part. 'She advised him on the whole to stick close to his trusted Servant.'[6]

Charles sent Sir John Berkeley away. Two days later, James slipped away under cover of a hunting trip and followed him. As ever, he was accompanied by Charles Berkeley and Harry Jermyn. Richard 'Fighting Dick' Talbot, a towering Irishman, had also joined the little York court after Cromwell crushed the Royalist Irish Confederacy at Drogheda. No one had expected James to depart, certainly not the king. The travellers wandered confusedly for a spell. They considered boarding 'a lusty French ship which was ready to set sayle for France',[7] but as Cromwell's navy dominated the Channel, they risked being taken prisoner. They resolved instead on visiting William of Orange's tutor at Zuylestein, near Utrecht.[8] The companions enjoyed themselves at a formal Dutch wedding. James then wrote to Charles apologising for having defied him for the first time in his life, but he felt he had no choice. He was first among his brother's faithful servants, but he had his ducal court to consider: men who depended upon and were loyal to him. James wrote of his distress at having to fight Turenne, 'one of the men in the world I am most obliged to,'[9] though he did accept it as inevitable. What he could not abide were unjustified attacks upon his servants and efforts to undermine him. The king begged him to return. James agreed on two conditions designed to discourage rumour-mongering. Number one: that any allegations against himself and his family should be investigated, and if disproven, the rumour-mongers punished. Number two: Berkeley should be allowed to clear his name. Charles agreed, but stipulated that the governor remain away from court for one month. After that, 'things past should be forgotten'.[10]

The brothers agreed they should not allow troublemakers to divide them. When James returned to Bruges, Charles ushered him in appreciatively. Now the duke could turn his attention to another, more tantalising question.

His head had been turned by a certain maid of honour in Mary's train. Her name was Anne Hyde. The daughter of the king's chancellor, Edward Hyde, she was a commoner and therefore an unsuitable mate. Nonetheless, James was drawn to her. They kept their flirtation secret – at least at first. Anne had first caught his eye when Mary visited Paris a year previously, in 1656, for carnival season.[11] She was a few years younger than the duke, no great beauty but coquettish, with shiny chestnut ringlets, large expressive eyes, a ready smile and a softly rounded face and figure. But it was her cleverness, sociability and style that really set her apart. Harry Jermyn admired her. Following in Princess Mary's footsteps, Anne had flirted with him a little. On the other hand, Henrietta Maria, who loathed Edward Hyde, wished so intensely that Mary would dismiss Anne because of it that she became infuriated when her daughter demurred. It was one thing for Mary to make Jane Lane a maid of honour – she had helped Charles escape the Roundheads. But Anne was a different matter. She was the despised Hyde's daughter. For his part, Hyde felt awkward about his daughter causing a rift between the queen and princess.

But it was time to go into battle once more, and this time they were fully invested in the outcome. Instead of being a soldier of fortune, James was fighting for the king, his brother, and against Cromwell's forces. Henry, Duke of Gloucester, was with him. Unfortunately, Henry came down with a severe fever that swept the company, and had to be sent off the field for a time. Cromwell had sent 6,000 foot-soldiers to France under the command of John Reynolds, who had served him during the invasion of Ireland and had, in fact, guarded Charles I when he was imprisoned at Hurst Castle in 1648. The English particularly wanted to gain control of Dunkirk, which was the home base for a nest of aggressive privateers. For the Spanish officers, such as Don John José of Austria, meanwhile, it was a point of pride to live on the field exactly as they did in ordinary life, taking regular siestas and dining in their tents while James strode about exploring the terrain. He could not help admiring how the English soldiers in the opposite camp were conducting themselves.

Don John was uneasy when the Duke of York was regularly invited to parley 'upon parole' with some of his old French comrades who were now ranged opposite him. Seeing what civil terms they were on, the English commander, Reynolds, developed a desire to meet with him also. He was eager to get the measure of this member of the banished royal family who had developed into such a capable officer. He approached James's companion Colonel Richard Talbot, who, as it turned out, had saved Reynolds' life in Ireland. James met Reynolds on the dunes ('sand-hills') outside Dunkirk. Reynolds ordered his soldiers to stand back and hold their fire when the duke was in the area. Each of the two brought one companion only.

General Reynolds, addressing James as 'Highness' in defiance of Roundhead pieties, begged him 'not to look on him as one sent over by Cromwell, but as one serving the King of France'.[12] The duke had the impression that Reynolds might have pledged himself if it were not for the presence of the other man: 'Keeping me very close to him, he only let fall some dark expressions, implying that he hop'd a time might come wherein he might be serviceable to me.' After half an hour, 'wee parted very well Satisfied of each other.' This meeting with a previously reliable Roundhead reinforced James's sense that his fellow Englishmen could be turned for the king. As for General Reynolds, he paid dearly for it. Some of his fellow officers complained about the encounter to Cromwell. Setting off across the Channel to account for his actions, he was lost at sea in a shipwreck.

On 14 June 1658, the Spanish faced the Anglo-French alliance on the windswept 'sand-hills' near Dunkirk. James recalled the Prince de Condé asking young Henry, Duke of Gloucester, if he had ever seen a battle. Henry replied that he had not. 'Well, within half an hour you shall behold one,' Condé assured him.[13] The English Royalists and the Prince de Condé's troops fought hard alongside the Spanish, but the Battle of the Dunes was carried by the Anglo-French alliance. Englishmen fought Englishmen, and Frenchmen likewise fought Frenchmen in this time of division and shifting alliances. James charged straight into the battalion of English horse, breaking them apart. He was proud when Henry seconded him, fighting 'as courageously as any of his Ancestors had ever done'. James noted appreciatively that the English Army 'whom I easily knew by their redcoats … came on with great eagerness and courage'.[14] They were commanded by William Lockhart of Lee, whom James had last run into at the inn. The duke narrowly avoided being taken prisoner at one point. Both Harry Jermyn and Charles Berkeley were wounded. As soon as Turenne won the battle, he resumed the Siege of Dunkirk, and shortly afterwards the city

surrendered. Meanwhile, the Stuarts were alarmed to learn that their cousin, Louis XIV, was struggling with a dangerous fever. He was nearby, at Calais. The vicissitudes of politics had put them on opposite sides temporarily, but that did not lessen the love between them.

Several months later there were unadulterated good tidings: the Lord Protector Oliver Cromwell had died on 3 September 1658. The principal signatory to Charles I's death warrant, the scourge of Ireland, the dictator described by Edward Hyde as 'a brave bad man', who had led England into a brave new world of republican military rule, had perished of malaria and kidney stone disease aged 59. Cromwell's favourite daughter had died in August; many believed that this blow had weakened him. Elizabeth Claypole had acted as Cromwell's conscience, often interceding, in the mode of a queen, on behalf of accused Royalist plotters. (The 'Sealed Knot' was one such group.) And in the mode of the Prince of Wales, Cromwell's diffident eldest son, Richard, now became Lord Protector. Oliver Cromwell had never accepted the crown, but he was accorded a royal funeral. England might have been declared a republic, but Englishmen and women still had deeply monarchist instincts. All of which presented an opportunity for the legitimate royal family ranged across the Channel. As soon as James 'received the welcome news of Cromwell's death,' he asked the Spanish for permission to leave his post and go to confer with his brother about 'this new alteration of affairs in England'.[15] As fighting was wrapping up for winter, there was no need to return until the spring thaw. He went to Breda to spend the season with Mary.

It was clear from the beginning that Richard Cromwell was no Oliver. Cromwell senior's military rule rested upon his status as a great general, his confident command of the army. Richard had little military talent and no place in the hearts of English soldiers. Writing in his diary in October 1659, John Evelyn described the state of affairs thus: 'The army now turned out Parliament ... no government in the nation; all in confusion, no magistrate either owned or pretended but the soldiers, and they not agreed. God have mercy on us!' A power vacuum opened up. Turenne, seeing the lay of the land, was quick to offer his services to Charles. The fact that they had fought at the Battle of the Dunes on opposite sides made no difference. A sincere friend to James in particular, Turenne wanted to see the Stuarts back in their rightful place. Hearing that an uprising to restore the king was to be staged from Calais, he tried to get in contact. Turenne was not the only person who had had intelligence of the plot: the town was full of Roundheads looking for 'the titular duke of Yorke', as they termed him. The city gates were locked and a search was under way. One Huguenot officer insisted he had seen James in disguise, and led the Englishmen to his quarry, only to find it was the wrong gentleman. James, having been warned, went to hide with Berkeley at his lodgings. 'Betwixt twelve and one he had a hott alarm at his lodging, and verily believed that they had come to take him, for he was wakened with a great knocking and bouncing at the door of the inn.' It was indeed soldiers, but it turned out they were bringing home the inn-master, 'dead drunk and brought home betwixt four of them'.[16]

James found Turenne at Amiens. There, the general offered the Stuarts men, money, weapons and food, enough for an invasion of England. To do this he would 'pawn his plate and make use of all his interest and credit ... what he did was freely of himself ... and out of no other motive than of kindness to the Duke and to his family.' James 'accepted of this noble offer with great joy, and lost no time in designing where to land with these forces.'[17] Turenne's own nephews were lined up to join the royal forces. The invasion was planned to coincide with an uprising in England. Charles had commissioned Sir George Booth to command his supporters in Lancashire, Cheshire and North Wales, which he did in August 1659. Unfortunately, John Thurloe had learned of the plot in advance, and deployed General Lambert to crush the uprising. When James received news of this defeat, he had been out of touch with his brother for some days and feared that Charles had already landed in England. He wanted to cross the Channel hoping to creating a distraction. However, Turenne dissuaded him: 'he was very confident his Majesty had not gone for England, and that though he were, it was not reasonable for the Duke to hazard himself, when there was no probability of Success.' (Spymaster Thurloe, it transpired, wanted nothing better than to lure James and Charles into a trap so he could kill them.) The Stuarts' time had not yet come. Knowing that James lacked money, he 'loaned him three hundred pistoles and gave him a Pass'. The duke returned to Flanders – and to Anne Hyde.

Life in exile was trying for the Cavaliers. Money was scarcer than ever, and the royal family were surrounded by people who had lost position and had lands sequestered back in the Three Kingdoms of England, Ireland and Scotland. The Stuarts were acutely aware of how much their followers had sacrificed for their cause, which had suffered one defeat after another. After the burst of hope due to Cromwell's demise, they found themselves bemoaning another failed uprising in England. James wrote that 'Their hopes concerning England' were 'now reduced to their lowest ebb'.[18] Despite these losses, or indeed because of them, the royal family had to strive ever harder to find ways to reward these courtiers with patronage, to foster reciprocal communal bonds, and to give shape to their followers' daily lives. Each time the Stuarts moved, often into modest rented accommodations, they were quick to designate a Throne Room, a Privy Chamber, a Withdrawing Room and so on; carefully observing ceremony so as to preserve the sense of court life. Yet James would one day remember these fraught years in the wilderness fondly. The wandering Cavaliers were united behind a single goal: to reimpose order upon unnatural rebellion by restoring the monarchy. There was camaraderie in struggle. Adversity called for courage and dependability, his strong suits. Moreover, adversity taught one who one's friends were. And for James, who found it difficult to read people and intuit motives, this was reassuring.[19]

James sought to anchor himself to a loyal Cavalier woman. In May 1659, just as Richard 'Tumbledown Dick' Cromwell was succumbing to pressure to renounce his role as Lord Protector, James was falling in love with Anne Hyde. Her family had been faithful to the Stuarts over the turbulent war years and the increasingly thin years in exile. Whenever possible, James would visit Princess Mary in the Hague. One of the pleasures that awaited him there was the company of her maid of honour. He loved to walk and talk with her. The vivacious and strong-willed Anne was a great favourite among Mary's courtiers, and possessed a number of admirers. One was Spencer Compton, son of the Earl of Northampton. Another was Harry Jermyn, but Anne dismissed him when Prince James began paying her close attention. There was nothing remarkable in the fact that the young blade was frequently in deep conversation with a maid of honour, that he flirted with her, or that there were snatched kisses between the pair. In fact, James's family may have assumed he was bedding her. He had an eye for women and did not try to conceal it. As one celebrated raconteur put it, Miss Hyde was 'no perfect beauty, but she had no rival at the court of Holland'.[20] For James, Anne Hyde had 'witt and other qualitys capable of surprising a heart, less inclinable to the Sex than was that of his Royall Highness in the first warmth of his youth.' But had onlookers known what was truly going on behind the scenes in the summer of 1659, they would have been concerned. For not only did Anne show 'her witt and virtue in managing the affair so dextrously', but the duke, 'overmaster'd by his passion,' secretly asked her to marry him.[21] And not only did he propose, but he put the proposal in writing and signed his name to it – in blood, according to Samuel Pepys. Reading between the lines, James believed that Anne had deftly gentled him into making the marriage contract. Her father, Edward Hyde, had no part in effecting the engagement; she had no particular advocates. She was far below James in rank. Moreover, his mother was predisposed to hate all Hydes. Yet the second in line to the throne had undertaken to wed a member of the minor gentry with no title, no alliance to offer, and precious little material wealth to bring to the threadbare Stuart dynasty. Sir John Berkeley continued to seek a grand match for his charge. Meanwhile, James had engaged himself – out of admiration, affection, lust and loyalty – to a mere commoner.

Charles, too, had his entanglements, though he avoided making rash promises of this sort. He tried to shake off the languid Lucy Walter, but she followed the court-in-exile on its peregrinations, bed-hopping as she went and causing various scandals. She gave birth to a daughter by another lover. Charles tired of Lucy, but took his relationship with their son James Scott quite seriously. The boy was growing up strong, charming and beautiful, a living embodiment of the folk belief that love-children are the bonniest. Though illegitimate, he was a king's son, and potentially a force for his namesake to reckon with. Royal bastards had to be handled carefully, for they had a way of drawing in chaotic forces. In 1656 Lucy had taken her winning little 7-year-old son to London, where the Commonwealth government, suspecting she was a spy, had imprisoned her for a time. She was released and deported along with her children to the Netherlands. At this point she tried to extort Charles for money, threatening to publicise his letters. Charles responded by having his son kidnapped, taken to Paris, and placed in the care of a Gentleman of the Bedchamber, William Crofts, ennobled that same year as 1st Baron Crofts of Saxham. Lucy followed. Before perishing of what was rumoured to be venereal disease, the ex-mistress made an allegation which would come back to haunt the monarchy – that she and Charles had wed, and that the evidence lay within a mysterious box. The boy cherished the notion that he was in fact legitimate. Blissfully unaware of Lucy's claims, and of his brother's secret engagement, Charles would soon be distracted by another tempting Cavalier camp follower. Buckingham's violet-eyed cousin, Barbara Palmer, née Villiers, crossed the Channel in 1659. Her father had died in the Royalist cause, leaving the family destitute. Newly married to Roger Palmer, the dark-haired and creamy-skinned Barbara swiftly graduated to the young king's bed. Palmer's father had rightly predicted that she would make him miserable.

What played out between James and Anne over the next year had all the makings of the sort of frisky French comedy then taking court culture by storm. According to most accounts, James signed the marriage pre-contract on 24 November 1659. Its purpose was likely to reassure his flame about their intimacy. At the same time, her hold over him grew in the hothouse conditions of seduction and secrecy. Like his brother, the king, James was driven by a powerful desire for the opposite sex, and Anne knew how to harness this passion. Moreover, she was the sort of woman who particularly appealed to him: clever, curious and strong-willed. She was very much his mistress. But Anne Hyde knew that once their secret came to light, she would face a number of challenges. Would she be able to hang onto her prince? Then something transpired in January 1660 which forced Anne's hand. She got pregnant.

Meanwhile, unbeknownst to James, Charles, and the European powers, the ground was shifting rapidly in Great Britain. The Spanish, believing that no restoration was in the offing, offered James the position of Lord High Admiral. So bleak did the Stuarts' prospects look after the failed uprisings of 1659 that early in 1660 the duke got his brother's permission to accept. But 'that Voyage was happily prevented,' James recalled, 'by the wonderfull Changes, which were almost daily produced in England.'[22] The Stuarts' political fortunes were suddenly transformed. General George Monck left Scotland, where he had helped to suppress the Royalist uprising at Glencairn, and began marching 'at the head of a great Cromwellian army'[23] bound for London. After the death of Oliver Cromwell and the failure of his son to rule, the country had once more fallen into factionalism. Monck, an old Cromwell ally, decided that the only way to rescue the realm from chaos was to offer the throne to Charles II, who alone had the power to unite it. All the fevered plotting of the Sealed Knot had failed the Royalist cause; it took an old Cromwell ally to break the eleven-year spell. Entering York, Monck was joined by General Thomas Fairfax and his troops. Together they countered republican forces raised by General Lambert. Reaching London, Monck occupied the city. Monck's contacts in the Royalist underground included his own brother Nicholas, who brought him an appeal from the exiled king. Monck replied with suggestions that informed Charles II's Declaration of Breda, designed to reassure his enemies and reconcile the nation. This included a general liberty of conscience, something that made Edward Hyde uneasy. Monck then forced the remaining members of the Rump Parliament at Westminster to readmit the Royalists. These were the men who had been driven out in Pride's Purge of 1648, the act which ultimately permitted the trial and execution of the king. Dubbed the Convention Parliament, this latest assembly differed from others because it had not been called by the monarch. Members voted to a man to restore the monarchy. The Convention then dissolved itself.

For James, everything was happening at once. In April, as the Stuart camp were negotiating the terms of their return, with prospects brightening for the first time in years, his pregnant mistress was starting to show. Anne was impatient to fulfil the terms of the pre-contract now that their lovemaking had born fruit. If the engagement predated the pregnancy, and the parents married before the birth, the child could be considered legitimate. But the duke knew that his family would be dissatisfied with such a humble match for the second in line to a throne that at long last seemed within reach. James, under pressure, confided in a friend. The two decided to purloin the document from Anne's chamber. As Samuel Pepys told it, they 'by stealth got the paper from her cabinet'.[24]

Once he retrieved the contract and burned it, James could have backed away from Anne quite easily. Everyone was against the match. Anne's own father was violently opposed to it – a sincere Anglican, he did not want to see his daughter rewarded for her loose conduct; but even more than that, Edward Hyde worried that Henrietta Maria, who loathed him, would believe that Charles's lord chancellor had pushed his daughter into the duke's arms in order to catapult himself and his family to power. And indeed, once the Queen Mother learned the truth, she was livid. Princess Mary was angry that her own maid of honour had been bold enough to capture her beloved brother. Charles opposed the match as well. He was unfazed by the prospect of another royal love child – after all, he had at least one of his own. The courts of Europe were cluttered with 'natural' children. If James was attached to Anne, surely he could keep her as an official mistress. The king was increasingly fond of the young lady in question, but he wanted his brother to reserve marriage for maximum advantage. In any case, Charles himself was still a bachelor, and he still preferred that his younger brother marry second. James had a tearful Anne in one ear, and his family and friends in the other. 'In this perplexity he opened his heart' to his friend Harry Jermyn, who admired Anne, 'and consulted him about what course he ought to pursue'.[25] Again James was faced with a dilemma, torn between loyalty to Anne and 'the duty and obedience he owed to the King.' If he was to make Anne Hyde his wife, James would have to swim against a powerful current.

Chapter 5

The Garland King

> Then early next morning I made her my bride,
> That the world might have nothing to say,
> And the bells they did ring and the bridesmaids did sing,
> And we crowned her the Queen of the May.
>
> Traditional

The next few months transformed James's world. In early 1660, despite being second in line to the English throne, the Duke of York was on the point of becoming Spanish Lord High Admiral – and at a time when republican England and Spain were at war. As Richard Talbot's Jesuit brother, Father Peter, was fluent in Spanish, he helped James to negotiate.[1] Accepting such an important post would have meant becoming a Catholic, as the Spanish would never have put their navy in Protestant hands. For reasons of expediency, therefore, James was considering conversion at that time. But by late March, thanks to General Monck, Charles II was composing his offer to the English people. Using his clergyman brother Nicholas as envoy, Monck advised Charles to offer an amnesty to former enemies in return for acknowledging him as sovereign. Charles had been at work on the declaration for some weeks when Monck suggested, for appearances' sake, that the court travel from Brussels to Breda, in the Dutch Republic. Since England and Spain were officially at war, it would look strange for the king to be proclaiming terms while ensconced in the enemy camp. The document was issued as soon as the king crossed the Dutch frontier, since Protestant Holland had friendlier associations for most Englishmen. For once, the States General, aware that political change was afoot, were completely welcoming.[2]

Back in England, a naval administrator named Samuel Pepys reported a new mood in the air. As he wrote in his diary on 11 April, 'All the news from London is that things go on further towards a King.' The rest of Pepys' April entries were full of anticipation. 'He tells me the King will come in ... the soldiers at Dunkirk do drink the King's health in the streets ... Monck did resolve to have the doing of it himself ... it was certain now that the King must of necessity come in ... we begin to talk very freely of it ... all pray for the King's coming, which I pray God send.'

Charles seized the opportunity that General Monck had given him. In close consultation with Edward Hyde; James Butler, Marquess of Ormond; and Monck's brother Nicholas, he produced a potent document. For the rest of his life, James would strive to realise the original terms of his brother's Restoration. Charles opened the Declaration of Breda with a kind of anti-masque, invoking the chaos, not just of the past years but of the present time: 'the confusion and distraction which is spread over the whole kingdom'. He offered to bind up 'these wounds which have so many years been bleeding' in taking possession of 'that which God and nature hath made our due'. In return for recognising his sovereignty, the king offered amnesty to all of his father's enemies, apart from 'only those persons as shall hereafter be excepted by Parliament'. By this he meant the regicides, those who had signed his father's death warrant in 1649. Noting that religious differences had thrown the kingdom into disorder, he concluded it was not enough to simply enforce state Anglicanism. Instead, he wanted to reach an accommodation for Nonconformists. Crucially, Charles promised 'liberty for tender consciences', provided that practitioners did not preach government overthrow. His formulation had to balance the sensibilities of Protestant minorities who had mostly opposed the Crown against the Catholic minority that had whole-heartedly supported it. The former groups had sought to root out the latter. To be charitable to them, these Protestants believed that their religious freedom *depended* upon abolishing Catholicism. But Charles envisioned a new era when a fractured people would 'unite in a freedom of conversation.' He wanted a policy to enfold the many staunch Cavaliers who had converted to Catholicism while in exile. He further guaranteed that disputes concerning property acquired during the Interregnum would be sorted out by Parliament. Finally, the New Model Army created by Oliver Cromwell would be subsumed under the king's banner – 'received into our service' – and paid arrears.[3]

Charles sent his trusty Gentleman of the Bedchamber, Sir John Greenville, to deliver the Declaration to Parliament, where it was made public on 1 May. Pepys wrote that it 'would be remembered as the happiest Mayday that hath been many a year to England.' The townsfolk of Deal had set up three maypoles: 'Today I hear they were very merry ... setting up the King's flag upon one of their maypoles and drinking the King's health upon their knees.' The old ways were pushing up with the spring.

Charles had appended a letter to MPs. Rather than stage an invasion with foreign support, he wrote, he would prefer to effect a 'reconciliation between King and People' without any further spilling of 'precious Christian blood'. Restoration was the 'best means to settle and compose the nation'. The English people could not be happy without their monarch. The Convention Parliament concurred. The time for division and experimentation was over; unity was the order of the day. On 16 May they extended a formal invitation to the king without any stipulations. They also voted him £50,000. An old opponent, Luke Robinson, set the tone by standing up in Parliament and recanting his Parliamentarian ways. The 'Fanatiques', as Pepys termed the Puritan or Nonconformist faction led by Major-General John Lambert, 'were undone.'

That evening, the Dutch fêted the long-roving exiles unreservedly. Charles, James, Henry and Mary were aglow with excitement and pleasure. Anne Hyde now knew that her baby would be born in her native land – that much seemed certain. English Navy ships sailed for Holland, and her lover was declared Lord High Admiral. Samuel Pepys and his fellow naval employees had a new official leader. Stepping into the role he had been bred for since childhood, James went down to inspect the fleet and was cheered by the sailors.[4] In England, people were replacing Parliament's arms with the royal ones left and right, and Royalist pub names – 'the Crown', 'the King's Head', 'the Crown and Sceptre' – were reappearing as well. A statue of Charles II was cast and set up in the Exchange.

Pepys records that many English 'gentlemen ... every day flock to the King at Breda', eager to submit themselves to Charles II and join his train.[5] Among them was Pepys himself; he sailed aboard the warship *Naseby* across the Channel captained by his patron, Edward Montagu, the Earl of Sandwich. They had a special mission: to carry the king of England home. Before leaving Deal they made sure to remove the figurehead, a laurel-crowned likeness of Oliver Cromwell. When the *Naseby* arrived, Charles and James swiftly redubbed her the *Royal Charles*. There would be no more sour reminders of the defeats the Royalists had suffered. (The *Worcester* was renamed the *Dunkirk*.) She sailed for Dover with the king, James and Henry aboard. The *Royal Charles* spearheaded the fleet, which would be known henceforth as the Royal Navy.

Arriving at Dover on 25 May, James touched English soil for the first time since his escape twelve years previously. He was now 27 years old, and had lived nearly half his life in exile. At long last, his fidelity had borne fruit. General Monck was on the shore to meet the royal party, while a large crowd enjoyed the spectacle of the man who had made the Restoration possible welcome the king home. All three brothers embraced him and called him Father. Another former Parliamentarian, Sir Thomas Fairfax, joined their ranks at Dover. He supplied Charles with a white steed for the ride to London. With 'Black Tom' Fairfax came his new son-in-law, the flirtatious and calculating Duke of Buckingham, who was already giving new his wife, Mary Fairfax, cause for anxiety. James distrusted Buckingham, and Charles received his overtures coldly. Buckingham, an opportunist, had been bold enough to make advances to Princess Mary in Holland; having been sent away by her furious brothers, he had returned to England and tried to marry a Cromwell. Buckingham, undaunted by cool treatment, blithely joined the Stuarts' triumphant parade anyway. Many men who had been outright enemies would be doing the same. Forgiveness was the order of the day. Only the regicides truly had anything to fear from the royal party now.

In the king's wake the Royalist exiles came flocking back to reclaim their properties, figures like royal tutor William Cavendish, Marquess (later 1st Duke) of Newcastle and his philosopher wife, Margaret. Newcastle hoped that Charles would implement his practical politics manual. A great equestrian, he envisioned the task of governance as a form of dressage. Any misgivings James had about the royal family and their true friends returning to the country where his father had met a cruel death on the scaffold abated when he saw the rapturous crowds of people who turned out to usher in the new monarch. The royal party dressed handsomely, with red plumes set off by dark clothing. James and Henry rode proudly at Charles's side. They were cheered at Dover, and well-wishers were lined thick along the route to London, strewing flowers in their path and crying out joyously. The Stuart brothers had experienced enthusiastic welcomes in their time, but never quite such an ecstatic reception as this – and from their fellow countrymen.

After stops in Canterbury and Rochester, the royal party rode into the capital city on 29 May, Charles's thirtieth birthday. It became a national holiday nicknamed 'Oak Apple Day'. As Pepys wrote, it was to be 'forever kept as a day of thanksgiving for our redemption from tyranny, and the King's return to his Government.'[6] The desperate fugitive who had been forced to hide up an oak tree had returned, in a hail of petals, as May King. As second in line to the throne, the Duke of York was lauded as a returning hero. The City officials saw that the fountains ran with wine. Londoners thronged the streets and hung out of flower-festooned windows. The Lord Mayor welcomed the returning Cavaliers (and hangers-on) at St George's Fields, and members of the army and City worthies joined their train. It took seven hours for the whole party to process through the merrymaking throng to Whitehall. Evening had fallen when the king reached the Banqueting House. There, at the very site where Charles I had been beheaded in a grim inversion of the pageantry he and his wife so loved, members of Parliament welcomed his sons back with a feast. In Charles I's own understanding, he died so that the Anglican Church might live, so that his heir would be able to reign as a traditional English king.

The green shoots which had emerged from the oak stump on 30 January 1649 now surged upwards. Whether the monarchy was reborn intact remained to be seen. Royalists stressed that Parliament did not *make* Charles II king; he was king already. But they had recognised his sovereignty, and for the present moment, that was enough to render almost everyone jubilant. The Stuart brothers celebrated beneath the Rubens ceiling glorifying their grandfather, James I and VI. Their father had been led mockingly through the hall and out to the scaffold. That had been his last walk. Now it was the scene of their triumphant Restoration. Among the guests of honour were Admiral William Penn and his meditative son, also William Penn. The admiral received a royal salute in recognition of his efforts to restore the Crown.

All the old exiles poured into London, scarcely able to believe that fortune had at long last favoured them. John Evelyn was one. He had refused to work with the Commonwealth government. He had faced arrest for attending a Christmas service, and been interrogated about offering a prayer there 'for Charles Stuart'. 'These wretched miscreants,' he recalled, 'would have shot us at the altar.'[7] Now, at last, his prayers had been answered. He beheld with joy the crowds turn out for the king as he processed through the city and into Whitehall. 'I stood in the Strand and beheld it and blessed God,' he wrote. A colossal newly built maypole stood nearby, emblem of all that had been banned under the Protectorate. Evelyn made himself known to the

Duke of York, whose hand he had last kissed at the Paris tennis-courts in the ill-starred year of 1649. James gladly led him into the king's presence.

When the feasting and dancing were over and the last toast was made, and it was finally time to turn in for the what remained of the night, James retired to a Whitehall Palace that had been speedily emptied of any lingering residents. Over the previous weeks, hasty repairs had been made. With the cultured Sir John Denham heading up the new Office of Works, the place would be properly refurbished.[8] Parliament took care to retrieve any of Charles I's possessions, in particular paintings from his marvellous collection, that were still in England. A new crown was being fashioned for the coronation, the old one having been melted down. James's now *Royal* Navy was to have new flags to fly. Royal chapels which had been used as stables were now cleared of horses, redecorated and reconsecrated to a newly re-established Church of England – and Charles I was officially added to the calendar as a Holy Martyr.

Charles II apparently spent his first night in London in the arms of his married mistress, the dazzling Barbara Palmer.[9] (He rapidly repealed the Adultery Act of 1650, which had prescribed hanging for both adulterer and adulteress.) James, for his part, had not forgotten Anne Hyde; he and his brother favoured women who had been loyal to them in exile. Anne had left Princess Mary's service under a cloud and come home to England with her father and the other triumphant exiles. Anne's swelling belly was a constant reminder of her predicament. It was a different matter for the Duke of York. He would be by no means the first lustful Prince of the Blood to make a woman pregnant. Since pleasure reigned over Charles II, Anne's condition was only mildly scandalous. The king set the tone for the court, and he had in fact just got his *own* mistress with child. That these things would bother the vanquished Puritans was actually a point in their favour. The Cavaliers' formal revenge was limited to targeting the actual regicides. Much as they might want to punish their Parliamentarian enemies, they had to content themselves with outraging Puritan sensibilities. And so they blithely dedicated themselves to scandalising the sourpusses and goading the hypocrites. They could indulge themselves with a weird sense of righteousness.

A far more serious matter than James and Anne's fornication, though, was the question of the couple's marriage in view of a pre-contract. That had implications for the succession, and now that the king had been restored, that matter took on a new immediacy and weight. The duke's paper promise to his sweetheart may have gone in the fire, but the verbal pre-contract still remained. There were two strikes against the baby, however. The first was Anne Hyde's lowly rank – not since Henry VIII had a king of England married a commoner. The second was conception out of wedlock. If the pair married soon, their child might be considered legitimate, but questions would persist. But James, considering all this, acknowledged a sense of obligation to Anne. She belonged to a family which had sacrificed all to follow his kin into the uncertainties and privations of exile. Anne had made him happy in difficult circumstances. She had given him warm affection and the fleshly pleasure he so craved. He loved her, in fact.

The prospect of a wedding between James and Anne continued to please no one. Anthony Hamilton, author of *The Memoirs of the Comte de Gramont*, held that until the Anne business marred the duke's image, he outshone his brother, the king. For his part, Edward Hyde was beyond furious with his daughter. He knew what his enemies would say – that he had manoeuvred her from maid of honour into a royal bed for personal benefit (much as the Boleyns had done over a century prior). In order to shake off such an impression, Hyde claimed he would rather 'see his daughter the duke's whore than his wife.'[10] He went so far as to suggest that King Charles send Anne to the Tower for execution. The Earl of Southampton believed the chancellor had gone 'mad, and had proposed such extravagant things, that he was no more to be consulted with'.[11] Hyde confined his daughter at home, but her servants smuggled her fiancé in for a visit.

The king continued to reject James's requests to marry, which left the duke feeling torn between loyalties. James went to reason with the chancellor, apologising for not levelling with him earlier and pleading with him to forgive Anne.[12] Henrietta Maria in France, learning of the pregnancy, was as livid as Hyde had feared. Certain onlookers were puzzled that the Duke of York, to whom every door was now open, was considering making his pregnant commoner mistress his wife. In the words of poet Andrew Marvell, James was 'thus enamour'd with a buttered bun.'[13] Samuel Pepys wrote that 'the thing is very bad for the Duke and them all,' adding that his patron, Lord Sandwich, commented on the match as follows: 'He that do get a wench with child and marry her afterward, it's as if a man should shit in his hat and then clap it on his head.' The diarist thought this attitude cynical: 'I perceive that my Lord is grown very indifferent in matters of religion.'[14] Pepys, for his part, saw some virtue in the Duke of York making an honest woman of his compromised lover. Even if no material benefit accrued to the Crown, it was the right thing to do.

In August Charles succumbed to James's pleas. The king decided to make the best of a bad situation. Having got to know Anne Hyde, he found he quite liked her. He admired her resolute character and pleasant ways. Such a woman would be good for his brother, he reasoned. As to whether a commoner was suitable to be queen – well, in any case he planned to marry a foreign princess soon enough, and there would be sons to inherit the thrones of England, Scotland and Ireland. Now that he had been restored, Charles had plenty of options. The king decided that the couple should be allowed to marry before the child was born. A bare-bones secret ceremony was held at Whitehall between 11 and 12 am on 3 September 1660. One of James's chaplains officiated, and the witnesses were James Butler, Earl of Ossory, and Anne's maid, Ellen Stroud. The new couple were delighted with one another, and Anne was of course relieved to be able to give birth as a married woman. The wedding was kept quiet, but rumours soon began to leak out.

Misfortune struck suddenly, distracting everyone from these matters. Henry, Duke of Gloucester, contracted smallpox and died on 13 September. He was buried, aged 20, in the vault of his great-grandmother, Mary Queen of Scots, at Westminster Abbey. Henry had made the best of his short time back among his family and distinguished himself fighting alongside James and Charles at the Battle of the Dunes. A dark cloud had darkened the bright day of the Restoration. Andrew Marvell's verses in 'Third Advice to a Painter' indicate bright promise snuffed out too soon: 'O more than human Gloucester! Fate did shew/Thee but to earth, then back again withdrew.' Another of the Stuart children had died young.

Princess Mary was eager to return to England, departing the Hague on 30 September. On the way she received news of her brother's death, which meant that she and her son William were closer to the throne. She arrived to find, to her dismay, that James's marriage to her former maid of honour had been recognised by the king. More than that, any heirs would take precedence. Mary had favoured Anne, given her a place and defended her against Henrietta Maria's attacks – and now she found herself deceived, and her son displaced by Anne's newborn.

James and Anne might be married, but they were not yet out of the woods. While Anne was in labour, she was subjected to hostile questioning. She affirmed that she was married to James and that he was the father of the infant boy who made his entrance on 22 October at Worcester House, London. When Henrietta Maria got wind of developments a few days later, she wrote this to her sister, Christine of Savoy: 'a girl who abandons herself to a prince will easily give herself to another man. I leave tomorrow for England to marry the king my son and try to unmarry the other.'[15] The queen's mind was full of marriage matters. She brought Henriette Anne along on the expedition. With her blue eyes, chestnut hair, lovely smile and sweet demeanour, 'Minette' enchanted everyone, especially her brother, the king. The Duke of Buckingham was even more taken with her than he had been with Princess Mary. The Queen Mother wanted to procure a good dowry for her daughter's upcoming marriage to her flamboyant cousin, Philippe of Orléans – a match Prince Rupert thought unlikely to make Minette happy.[16] Henrietta Maria also meant to find a loophole to undo the match between her treasured second son and the daughter of her enemy. By doing this, she hoped to topple Edward Hyde as chancellor. James took the fleet to Calais to meet his mother and little sister, escorting them onto the flagship.[17] The Queen Mother soon confronted him. James, unable to cope with his mother's fury, denied at first that he was married at all. Henrietta Maria eventually got the truth out of him. Her worst fears were confirmed: James had in fact married Anne by the book, and with the king's permission.

Undaunted, the Queen Mother charged that Anne was a shameless whore who had deceived her son and likely lumbered him with another man's child. Harry Jermyn and Charles Berkeley, imagining that all James needed was an excuse to escape a foolish marriage, chimed in, each solemnly claiming to have enjoyed Anne Hyde's favours. There could be no certainty about the baby's true father, they said. Anne hotly denied the accusations. James, running from pillar to post, became more and more distraught, and talked to family and friends 'with all the pain and confusion imaginable'.[18] He wondered whether, by marrying Anne, he had done a disservice to the king. Also, he had to cope with a raging mother on the one hand and a tearful Anne on the other. Seeing how miserable his friend had become, how far from feeling liberated, Charles Berkeley admitted that he had been lying in a misguided effort to serve the Duke of York's best interests. James, hugely relieved, sent his wife an affectionate note telling her to take good care of his son. Edward Hyde's tenure was safe; soon he would be ennobled as the Earl of Clarendon. Two of the most pronounced facets of James's character – lust and loyalty – had shaped this story. Lust had led him into a politically ill-advised pairing, and loyalty had made him keep his promise to the lady in question. It remained to be seen how their love would serve the duke in the long term.

In the run-up to the first Restoration Christmas, Samuel Pepys recorded new and strange experiences. His local minister gently reintroduced the Book of Common Prayer; he heard organ music in a cathedral for the first time; and he gave his wife permission to adopt the French fashion for adorning the face with 'black patches'. (These had the added benefit of covering smallpox scars.) Pepys also enjoyed several plays at the newly reopened Cockpit Theatre. With about the same regularity, he attended the executions of regicides, who were hanged, drawn and quartered at Charing Cross. The first to go was the Fifth Monarchist Major-General Harrison, 'looking as cheerful as any man could in that condition.' Harrison, a fervent millenarian who expected the Apocalypse to commence imminently, had asserted that he would soon be back at Christ's right hand to judge those who now judged him. Shown Harrison's heart and innards, the crowd responded with 'shouts of joy'. Pepys marvelled at the extraordinary political reversal he had witnessed: 'Thus it was my chance to see the King beheaded at White Hall, and to see the first blood shed in revenge for the blood of the King at Charing Cross.'[19] He had changed with the times: by his own admission 'a great Roundhead ... as a boy', Pepys was now comfortably Royalist. Anthony Hamilton recorded in *The Memoirs of the Comte de Gramont* that the English now 'delighted in the return of a natural government'.[20]

Just in time for the nation's first full-blown traditional Christmas since Parliament's 1647 edict, James made his marriage public. Anne was Duchess of York. He was proud of the way she came to inhabit this new position. 'It must be confessed that what she wanted in birth was so well made up in other endowments,' the duke recalled, 'that her carriage afterwards did not misbecome her acquired dignity.'[21] Henrietta Maria, upon receiving a stern letter from Cardinal Mazarin urging her to accept her son's new wife or face French displeasure, finally reversed her position. She received Anne and allowed the new duchess to kiss her hand. When she did, Henrietta Maria owned that her first daughter-in-law was perfectly charming. John Evelyn was among the many who went to see Anne once her marriage had been acknowledged. 'The Marriage of the Chancellor's Daughter now being newly owned, I went to see her: she being ... my father-in-law's intimate acquaintance when she waited on the Princesse of Orange, she being now at her fathers, at Worcester House in the strand, we all kissed her hand ... this was a strange change, can it succeed well!'[22] Anthony Hamilton wrote approvingly that those who once kissed the new duchess's hand out of duty came to do so out of devotion.[23]

The Stuarts prepared to observe the great festival with a new princeling in their midst. His christening was scheduled for the eighth day of Christmas; he would be baptised Charles and styled Duke of Cambridge. The English people had much to celebrate, and that openly. Under Puritan rule, Christmas had been a time of regular clashes in towns including Canterbury, London and Norwich as the people pushed back against active New Model Army suppression of church services, feasting, carolling, nativities and decking the halls with evergreenery. But now, 'roast beef and shred pie,/Pig, Goose, and Capon' reappeared on yuletide tables as the upside-down world righted itself at last.

But even as English men and women flocked to reopened churches on Christmas Eve, the royal family suffered yet another serious setback: Princess Mary died of smallpox. The disease that had just carried off her husband and brother now claimed her. Perhaps it did not help that royal physicians bled her persistently once she showed symptoms. This death was a severe blow for James, who had become so close to his sister in his vagabond days. Mary had been his confidante, friend and stalwart supporter, even when it imperilled her position in Holland. When the States General had banned her brothers from Dutch soil, she had travelled to see them and had done everything possible to support the Restoration. She had returned to her homeland, only to be cut down by disease there. It was a shame that the Anne matter had lately come between them. James was aware that his young nephew, William of Orange, was now an orphan – and third in line to the throne. Mary had named King Charles his guardian, though the Dutch would object. 'My greatest pain is to depart from him,' Mary had said of William. 'Oh my child, give him my blessing.'[24] Comprehending that death was near, the princess had asked to be buried alongside Henry. Once Mary was laid to rest, Queen Henrietta Maria took her youngest child, who had been carefully shielded from contagion, back to France. Henriette Anne's anxious bridegroom, Philippe d'Orléans aka 'Monsieur', awaited. En route she came down with a fever and red spots, which frightened everyone – Monsieur reportedly worried above all that her pretty face would be scarred – but happily it turned out she was suffering from measles. James could still claim a sister, and he was brother and right-hand man to a king whose reign had only just truly begun.

Chapter 6

The Best Revenge

It was a laughing, quaffing, and unthinking time.

John Dryden

James was awoken on the Twelfth Day of Christmas to word of an insurrection of Fifth Monarchy Men. The 'cantin' men', as he called them, were on the march. The millenarian Fifth Monarchists, after fasting when everyone else was feasting, had congregated above a Swan's Alley tavern. Two of their leaders, Thomas Harrison and John Carew, had been executed at Charing Cross as regicides. After hearing a sermon by their new figurehead, a cooper named Thomas Venner, the brethren made a wild-eyed effort to seize power. Shouting 'Live King Jesus', they charged through the streets. The rebels invoked divine kingship as a rebuke to earthly monarchy. It was their calling, they believed, to trigger the Apocalypse and usher in the reign of the literal King Jesus. Twelfth Night had once seen the Lords of Misrule invert the social hierarchy for one night; the godliest of 'godly men' sought to upend the social order for all time. Now was the time for the Fifth Monarchy Men to take charge. The manifesto Thomas Venner issued to rally the troops, *A Door of Hope: or, a Call and Declaration for the Gathering Together of the Ripe First Fruits Unto the Standard of Our Lord, King Jesus,* cast the return of the hated Cavaliers as a hideous Babylonian captivity.[1] The reinstallation of the Church of England was nothing more than another effort to bring 'popery' back to England, he proclaimed. The 'drinking the King's health' far and wide that Samuel Pepys had noted with a smile was a foul desecration enough, never mind the 'Swearing, Drunkenness, Sabbath-breaking, Whoredom, Pride, Lasciviousness, Stage-Plays, Blasphemy, Idolatry … countenanced since their coming in, as a new life given to the slain Serpent'. The stunning reversal that had seen the Stuarts restored without a shot fired had dismayed Fifth Monarchists – but this was nothing more than the ultimate test, argued Venner. He invited other factions of the 'Good Old Cause' to take part. Once they overturned the English monarchy, they would then march on the 'Antichrist' in Rome.

Few did. The outlaws were at first rumoured to number 500, though it turned out to be more like fifty. It was the last stand of the godly men. As the king was at Portsmouth, seeing off Henrietta Maria and Henriette Anne, James took control. The duke first sent forth a troop led by Sir William Howard. Then he summoned members of the nobility to arms and rode out to face the 'fanatick Crew'. The Royalists numbered about 1,500. 'Whom do you serve?' they demanded of the rebels. 'King Jesus!' came the hot reply. Over the next few days there was sporadic fighting in the streets – the Fifth Monarchists briefly took St Paul's Cathedral – until the remaining rebels holed up in a tavern in Coleman Street. When government troops broke through the roof, men on both sides died fighting. Venner, despite receiving nineteen wounds, survived to face the executioner on 19 January. 'And so ended this mad attempt of a furious zeal,' James wrote. This underscored what 'dangerous spirits', though out of power, still lay scattered about the Three Kingdoms. For James, the nation had been governed by fanatics, and it was difficult to forget that.[2] He resolved that certain regiments would not disband, but rather stay on to guard the king. On 30 January he and Charles were able to mark the anniversary of their father's martyrdom in peace – and in place.

James now dedicated himself to working hard and playing harder. 'As to affairs in the Government, and at Court, they at this time went smoothly on.'[3] He devoted himself to building up the Royal Navy fleet and seeing to trade, and proved to be a diligent and able administrator. He took careful notes on all that passed. If Charles had a particular weakness as monarch, it was that he shied away from hard work. But as James thrived on it, Charles could simply delegate tasks to his brother. Hamilton assessed James's character in contrast with the king's: 'The Duke of York was entirely different. He had a reputation for undaunted courage, meticulously keeping his word, great economy in his affairs, hauteur, application and arrogance in that order. Scrupulous in the rules of duty and the laws of justice, he was regarded as a faithful friend and an implacable enemy.'[4] As the perfect second-in-command, 'Victorious York' was immortalised by John Dryden in *Annus Mirabilis*: 'Then with the Duke your Highness rul'd the day/While all the brave did his command obey.' In a seafaring kingdom, maritime matters are, of course, paramount. Happily, Charles was well aware of this. James acknowledged that Oliver Cromwell had grown the Navy, but since his death and the intervening chaos, many ships had fallen into disrepair. He asked Parliament for money to remedy the situation, and they granted it without demur. James was the father of the modern fleet. He kept a close eye upon the Dutch, who were England's closest competitors in the maritime domain. The Dutch were expanding their trade routes and their empire; so too did England. He had plans for 'hindering the Dutch from becoming absolute masters' in this regard.[5] Moreover, Charles presented his brother with a patent for an area that had fallen into Dutch hands: 'Long Island in the West Indies' (meaning America), 'and the Tract of Land between New England and Mary Land'. There they had developed the beaver-trading port of New Amsterdam. For Englishmen like James, it had 'always belong'd to the Crown of England since it was first discover'd.' The Dutch had merely 'incroached upon it during the Rebellion,'[6] taking advantage of the turbulence in England to forge a new colony. If the Duke of York could set things to rights and win that territory back, he would have a free hand with it.

At the same time, James was a pillar of Restoration court life. Charles II presided over a sparkling milieu dedicated to pleasure, art and raillery; all light hearts and rapier wits. Court life was structured by French-style etiquette, public life by ceremony and sport. James was pleased to see Charles reintroduce ancient customs like touching for the King's Evil, which emphasised the divine nature of kingship. It was a complete inversion of the flinty years under Cromwell and the Major-Generals. Each tradition retrieved from the dust heap and polished up, and each indulgence, came with a bonus: it scandalised their enemies. For his part, the duke stepped smoothly into the role of bewigged Restoration rake. (By 1666 the fashions were codified by the king. Gentlemen were to wear a vest or waistcoat under a long coat, a periwig, a hat outdoors, a cravat and breeches gathered at the knee.) As a handsome young prince and war hero in a libertine age, James found that very little stood between him and the ladies of the court. On the one hand, he was pleased with his new wife, as everyone at court was well aware. Pepys noted squeamishly that James and Anne were given to kissing and canoodling in public in a manner he thought unbecoming to a nobleman. But Anne's power over James had limits. 'The Duke of York ... is led by the nose by his wife,' the diarist observed, 'in all things but his codpiece.'[7] The codpiece was a key exception. James's philandering caused the duchess considerable pain. The former maid of honour to Princess Mary had a train of ladies of her own to contend with now. The fact that her husband had, like Aphra Behn's Rover, 'horrible loving eyes', did not stop Anne from choosing the prettiest girls to serve her: 'The Duchess of York, to form her new court, decided to ... choose none but the handsomest,' observed Hamilton. Anne engaged a governess, but the maids of honour ran rings around her. Even prior to his marriage, James was in a dalliance with one of the first four, a Welshwoman named Goditha Price. She was the daughter of Sir Herbert Price, who had been rewarded for his faithful service in the wars and long exile with the post of Master of the King's Household. As we know, James felt most at ease with this sort of woman. Having suffered together, they could disport themselves together. A handsome young lady with wavy light-brown hair who displayed her décolletage to advantage, the witty Mistress Price was much given to intrigue. More than one young gentleman had worn a twist of her hair as a bracelet. She tried to conduct their affair discreetly, but inevitably the news leaked out. Goditha is said to have borne James a daughter, Mary.

Little effort was made to conceal the duke's attraction to a second, newly married young woman, a close companion of the king's mistress. Her name was Lady Anne Carnegie. Beautiful and giddily flirtatious, she modelled herself after her friend. Like Goditha, Anne came from a devoted old Cavalier family. Like Barbara Palmer, she had lost a father to the Stuart cause. Anne's father, William, 2nd Duke of Hamilton, had given his life for the monarchy, perishing of wounds sustained at the Battle of Worcester. While her husband, Robert Carnegie, whiled away his days bear-baiting and cockfighting, Anne threw herself into court pursuits. Her 'natural kindness did not permit her new lover to languish long.'[8] She 'seized the opportunity to add the Duke of York to her list of lovers' and proudly displayed her 'royal captive'. James would cover his visits to Anne by bringing his gentlemen along. On one farcical occasion he was in the company of his old Irish friend, Richard 'Fighting Dick' Talbot. The nickname may have derived from Talbot's warrior profession – or it may have been his habit of flinging his wig on the ground or in the fire when angered. In any case, he and James loved one another's company. The two comrades-in-arms called on James's mistress while her husband was thought to be away in Scotland for his father's funeral. Having just buried his father, Robert Carnegie was now the 3rd Earl of Southesk. Anne was entertaining James in the bedroom when her husband came home suddenly. He strode into his house to find lanky Dick Talbot loafing contentedly in his wife's antechamber. Talbot, well known for his personal loyalty and love of hijinks, was the perfect sentry for James at this time. Failing to twig the husband's identity, Talbot asked the man offhandedly 'What business brought you here? Do you too want to see Lady Southesk? If you do, my poor friend, you may go again, for I must tell you the Duke of York is in love with her ... and at this very minute in her private chamber.'[9] Poor cuckolded Southesk, not wanting a confrontation with the heir-presumptive to the crown, retreated from his own house in confusion. The absurd tale rapidly spread through London, first in whispers, then in ballad form.

It was no accident that these saucy adventures mimicked the comedies of Molière. Court life and the theatre cross-pollinated. The results exceeded William Prynne's most tortured fever-dreams in *Histriomastix*. French farce informed the sensibility of the Restoration court, and King Charles and the Duke of York were avid patrons of the London theatre, newly revived after eighteen years of Puritan clampdown. The Stuart Restoration brought glamour back to England along with merriment and ancient custom. Shortly after the royal brothers enjoyed a production of Ben Jonson's *Epicene* at the Red Lion Inn in June 1660, the monarch issued two exclusive charters – the first for the King's Company, and the second for the Duke's. The Duke's Company flourished under James's patronage. It was placed under the management of the Caroline Poet Laureate and soldier Sir William Davenant, the very sort of Stuart loyalist that James most valued. Productions took place at the Salisbury Court Theatre and the Cockpit in Drury Lane, then Lincoln's Inn Fields. Eventually the company found a new home at the Dorset Garden Theatre, decorated with miraculously delicate wood carvings by Grinling Gibbons. The 'Duke's Men' benefitted from a combination of tradition and innovation. Davenant had created a series of spectacular court masques for Charles I. He had also managed to stage, at his own home, virtually the only theatrical production permitted under Cromwell by reclassifying it as 'recitative music' in order to get a permit. Now considered the first English opera, *The Siege of Rhodes* was relaunched by the Duke's Company in 1661. It starred Thomas Betterton, the greatest actor of the day. Pepys, a habitual theatre-goer, held it was 'very fine and magnificent, and well-acted'.[10] (He bought the score to play at home and read the poetry aloud to his wife.) Davenant built on the foundation laid by Inigo Jones, using impressive sets. Because the company received the right to perform only a limited number of Renaissance classics – the King's Company under Thomas Killigrew inherited the majority from Shakespeare's troupe, the King's Men – they had an incentive to stage new works.[11] The Duke's Company was the place to enjoy 'moderns' like John Dryden, George Etheredge and, eventually, Aphra Behn.

Once the king decided that women's parts would no longer be played by pretty youths, both companies pioneered the use of actresses. The Duke's Company engaged Mary Saunderson, later Mrs Betterton, as well as Hester Davenport. The king's young protégé, beyond-bawdy John Wilmot, Earl of Rochester, proposed the introduction of actresses as courtesans. He found 'swiving' stage-players (and whores) simpler than devising complex strategies in order to seduce noblewomen. His long-term lover was the celebrated actress Elizabeth Barry, and it was Rochester who first bedded Nell Gwyn before presenting her to Charles II. The elevation of actresses led to a further intertwining of theatre and court. Unlike previous rulers, Charles II and James frequently attended both playhouses alongside the public. It brought them into contact with this new-minted breed of female, the English actress. In a sense the king had magicked her into being. Like Pygmalion, he was infatuated with his creation. Actresses like Moll Davis and, of course, Nell Gwyn would eventually join the king's seraglio. Not only did Charles and James frequently attend the theatre, they mingled and dined with the entertainers. James was enlarging the scope of his acquaintance.

A competition of sorts was unfolding: Charles II told the French ambassador that James loved women more than either of them. One tradition that *did* erode in the Restoration was courtly love. As Libertinism prevailed as an antidote to Puritanism, adultery became blatant. The fact that this handsome prince stepped from the pages of a fairy-tale was developing into 'the most unguarded ogler of his time'[12] caused his plainer wife to suffer keenly. It was a recipe for distress, and so it is not surprising to learn from Pepys that James's 'Lady was very troublesome to him by her jealousy.'[13] Moreover, their little son Charles died of smallpox at 8 months old. Despite Pepys's claim that neither seemed to mind much, this would have been a blow. It likely felt to Anne that her bond with James had slackened. He was seldom present. When her husband was not busy with government matters, he was out hunting either women or game. All this activity kept him slim; meanwhile, Anne soothed herself with delicacies and grew plump, which only made matters worse. Hamilton acknowledges Anne's sufferings in

The Memoirs of the Comte de Gramont. At the same time, he commends the duchess for her gracious conduct overall. He describes her as somewhat plain, but clever, witty, majestic and discerning.[14] In any case, she was soon pregnant again. In 1662 Anne gave her husband a healthy daughter, baptised Mary in memory of her aunt and her ancestress, Mary, Queen of Scots. The following year she gave birth to a son, James, soon after named Duke of Cambridge like his little brother who perished. Fairfax's daughter Mary, now Duchess of Buckingham, held the new baby at his christening.

Anne Hyde put her discernment to good use and rose above her jealousy when, with James's support, she developed into a royal patroness, commissioning Sir Peter Lely to paint his celebrated 'Windsor Beauties'. Just as she wanted to assemble the loveliest women to form her household, despite her husband's tendency to treat them as his personal seraglio, so she meant to commemorate the handsomest ladies in the Stuart orbit. According to Hamilton, Lely 'could hardly have had more beautiful subjects. Every picture seemed to be a masterpiece.'[15] Since the death of the master of the Caroline court, Van Dyck, Lely had cultivated his talent. Now that the Stuart monarchy was restored, and the visual arts with it, he could distinguish himself as official court portraitist. Ten noblewomen had the honour to be selected for the initial grouping, and then two more were added. The patroness appears in the series, as does Princess Henriette Anne. The languorous, heavy-lidded looks of Lely's muse, Barbara Palmer, now 1st Countess of Castlemaine, were transposed onto all the 'beauties' in their bright satin and pearls. Lady Castlemaine's influence was felt at all levels of the Restoration court. When Samuel Pepys eventually got a chance to see the portraits which the Duke of York had proudly assembled in a single chamber at his residence, the diarist pronounced them 'good, but not like'.[16] Not every belle in England had quite such sleepy bedroom eyes in reality. James himself was painted by Lely many times. In one instance he too appears in this mode, albeit in armour, looking sidelong and seductively at the beholder.

The duke's 1666 affair with one of the Windsor Beauties, Margaret Brooke, Lady Denham, is again the stuff of stage-play. *The Memoirs of the Comte de Gramont* has Mistress Brooke coming to court with the express purpose of charming Charles II. It could easily have worked. Not only was she a very pretty young lady, with long, curling light-brown hair, creamy skin, and large dark eyes, she also possessed the bold personality so much in fashion at the time. Lady Castlemaine, sensing competition, pointed James in her direction. That Margaret was married mattered very little. Charles II set the tone when he routinely kicked off festivities with a traditional country dance entitled 'Cuckolds All Awry'. It seemed that the gentlemen of the court were determined to put horns on every husband in sight – especially if he had the temerity to be aged, cranky and vigilant to boot.

Margaret's husband, Sir John Denham, had come to embody the Jealous Old Husband, a stock character in seventeenth-century comedy. Thirty years older than his wife, plagued by arthritis and looking every bit his years, he was having trouble keeping up with her. He had had a remarkable career as one of England's finest poets. Denham's greatest work, *Cooper's Hill,* had been published at Oxford in 1643. The poem offered one of the clearest perspectives on recent history. In it, the narrator surveys a landscape with a monastery left ruined by the dissolution under Henry VIII, the king who would loom increasingly large in James's own imagination. Driven by unquenched desire for Anne Boleyn, Henry had rationalised breaking with Rome. His subsequent liquidation of the abbeys and redistribution of lands had created the very class that had fought the Royalists in the 1640s. To paraphrase G.K. Chesterton – having looted the Church in the sixteenth century, this new class then pulled down the monarchy in the seventeenth.

The greatest poet of the Restoration era, John Dryden, pronounced *Cooper's Hill* to be 'the exact Standard of good Writing'. But Denham's laurels counted for little with his young wife. Over the years Sir John had transformed from a dreamy seducer, prankster and gambler into the 'naturally jealous... suspicious ... old and disagreeable' man she married.[17] Lady Margaret wanted a lover. She would happily accept the second in line to the throne, but on the condition that she become his acknowledged mistress, a second Barbara Palmer to nudge the ship of state. There would be no concealment, Lady Margaret insisted. She would be 'owned publicly', refusing to 'go up and down the back stairs like Mistress Price'. James would have no more time for Goditha. He was completely smitten with Lady Margaret. That year, Pepys' diary seems to be one long tissue of complaints about this very public affair. 'The Duke of Yorke is lately wholly given up to his new mistresse, my Lady Denham, going at noon-day with all his gentlemen to visit her at Scotland Yarde,' he writes. James's dissolute Gentleman of the Bedchamber Henry Brouncker is depicted as 'the pimp to bring it about'. Later, 'the Duke of York becoming a slave to this whore Denham, and wholly minds her.' He fears that the Lord High Admiral is neglecting naval matters: 'the Duke of York is gone over to all his pleasures again, and leaves off care of business, what with his woman, my Lady Denham, and hunting three times a week.' Pepys believed that Lady Margaret, Brouncker and Sir William Coventry made up a 'cabal'. Friend and fellow diarist John Evelyn had similar concerns, apparently. 'Denham again,' Pepys writes, accusing James of following his mistress about like a dog. 'The Duke of Yorke taking her aside and talking to her in the sight of all, all alone; which was strange, and what also I did not like. Here I met Mr. Evelyn, who cries out against it, and calls it "bitchering"'[18]

Historian David Starkey favours a certain word to describe the court of Charles II: a *pornocracy,* or 'rule of whores'. It was widely believed that both the king and his second-in-command were allowing their concubines too much political influence. Not since Anne Boleyn had a royal mistress held such sway in England. Charles II made the Portuguese princess Catherine of Braganza his queen in 1662. Producing a son and heir would have secured the Catholic queen's position, but she had trouble conceiving despite various court expeditions to take the waters at the spa resorts of Bath and Tunbridge Wells. Barbara Palmer had no such difficulty. The queen had to sit by humiliated while her husband's mistress, who had been imposed on her as a lady-in-waiting for the sake of his convenience, gave birth to one bonny baby after another. Lady Castlemaine would give the king six children in all, three sons and three daughters. (Among them was Lady Charlotte Fitzroy, a sweet and pretty ebony-haired girl who swiftly became her Uncle James's favourite niece.)

Lady Castlemaine's reign of pleasure showed no signs of abating as the 1660s unfurled, but Lady Margaret Denham's was brief, lasting less than a year. The openness of the affair with James tormented her husband. Denham went mad, claiming to be a deity. Then another disaster struck: the 20-year-old Lady Margaret became gravely ill after drinking a cup of chocolate. An expensive novelty among English courtiers, chocolate was thought to be a stomach remedy as well as an aphrodisiac. It may be that Lady Margaret took chocolate because she was feeling poorly. In any case, she then died, leading many to suppose that she had been poisoned. Her troubled husband was an obvious suspect, but the Duchess of York and even James were under suspicion as well. Another candidate was fellow Windsor Beauty Henrietta Hyde. A subsequent autopsy found no proof of poison. Instead, it found evidence that Margaret had suffered from a gynaecological malady which would account for the symptoms. Bizarrely, the examining physician opined that she was a virgin. And so, Samuel Pepys proclaims sarcastically, the report 'is an excellent invention to clear' the Duchess of York 'from poison, and the Duke of York from lying with her.'[19] Denham placated a crowd of suspicious neighbours by plying them with great flagons of mulled wine at her burial.[20] James felt chastised by his lover's strange demise, fearing that he had caused it indirectly. Pepys stated in January 1667 that 'the Duke of York is troubled for her, and hath declared he will never have another public mistress again.' The diarist was 'glad for it', and wished the king would make a similar pledge. Anthony Hamilton, that scourge of cuckolds, put the death down to 'the fatal effects of jealousy'.

James also busied himself bedding the regal yet saucy Lady Anne Hamilton. Anne came of impeccable Cavalier stock. Her father, James, 1st Duke of Hamilton, was a tenacious Stuart loyalist. He had been executed under Cromwell shortly after the death of Charles I, and the family lost their lands. Married to a member of the Douglas clan, Anne nonetheless embraced the 'make-merry-for-tomorrow-we-die' ethos of the court at that time. An erotic adventuress like her extravagant companion Barbara Palmer, she took several additional lovers.[21]

The influence of royal mistresses also manifested itself in the form of James Crofts. The presence of the king's natural son by Lucy Walter would have far-reaching consequences, not least for Uncle James (who always doubted the boy's paternity). When the boy left the care of William Crofts in Paris and came to the English court in the early 1660s, he was about 13 years old. He found the new era in full swing, the court dominated by men of gay malice like the Duke of Buckingham. He soon had to compete with the likes of his father's protégé John Wilmot, 2nd Duke of Rochester, a talented satirical poet whose father had stayed close by the king's side after the Battle of Worcester. Rochester returned from the Grand Tour in 1664 with a generous letter of introduction from Princess Henriette Anne, whom Charles adored; this gave Rochester an extra boost in the king's affections. But Crofts' beauty and charm quickly won him a place in Charles's heart. The Duke of York describes his nephew thus: 'He was tall, well-shap'd, of a good air, of a civil behaviour, and none danced better, and with all this he was very brave, which made [him] much courted by both Sexes.'[22] However, he could be 'cunning' and 'insinuating' when he wanted something. Hamilton writes of the dark-haired youth's 'astonishing beauty'. Charles made him Duke of Monmouth; inducted him into the Order of the Garter; and prompted him to renounce 'Popery' and receive the Anglican sacrament – essential steps to acquiring influence in England. When it came to religion, it transpired that Monmouth would be whatever power needed him to be. Barbara Palmer was concerned that he would upstage her children, who were 'so many little puppets compared to this new Adonis'. She decided that the best thing to do was flirt violently with the beautiful youth. Charles, desiring to protect his son's innocence and his reputation, responded by marrying Monmouth off very young indeed to a girl his age.[23] The king chose a Scottish heiress named Anne Scott, Duchess of Buccleuch, in 1663. The groom took his wife's surname. He would always resent this marriage.

Monmouth had risen swiftly from an uncertain status to being a duke twice over. He was 'in so great a splendour' at court, 'so dandled by the King', that the Duke of York was growing uneasy, according to Pepys. 'There was a French book in verse, the other day, translated and presented to the Duke of Monmouth in such a high stile, that the Duke of York, he tells me, was mightily offended at it.' One thing stood in the way of Monmouth being named his father's heir: his illegitimacy. King Charles calmly maintained that he had not married Lucy Walter. James confided further that the Welshwoman's brother had been welcomed at court and 'will talk very broad of the King's being married to his sister.' Monmouth would do the same thing out of his father's hearing. Pepys could see that a conflict between Monmouth and the Duke of York was on the cards. 'Which God prevent!' he added fervently.[24]

James had been stung, but he was still juggling women with abandon. He fitted into the court well in that respect. On the other hand, he lacked the silver tongue of a George Villiers, Duke of Buckingham, and indeed he felt somewhat uneasy in his company. Hamilton, chronicler of the Restoration court at its most glistering, describes the Duke of York as 'naturally candid and sincere, and a firm friend' – quite the opposite of Buckingham temperamentally. Hamilton writes teasingly of James's persistent tendency to regale women with endless hunting stories. On the other hand, when a fashion for guitar-playing swept through the court, James had an advantage. He had learned to play as a child. Hamilton, no fan of the 'infernal strumming' of rival instruments, allows that the duke played the Spanish guitar 'tolerably well', often treating the assembled company to a passionate and stately saraband. James was not the most sparkling conversationalist in the room, but he put his heart into making music.

One lady who responded to it favourably was Lady Chesterfield. James had been competing with his long-time friend and courtier Richard Talbot, as well as the king, for the attentions of a superlative court beauty, Anthony Hamilton's sister, Elizabeth. Sir Peter Lely's portrait of 'La Belle Hamilton' emphasises the fine features, dimples, creamy bosom and light-brown curls that captivated so many. James seems to have become infatuated with this young woman by gazing at the portrait – the series was working magic, clothing its subjects in glamour. As Elizabeth was in love with Philibert, the Comte de Gramont, she proved elusive for the Duke of York. But soon enough James was focused on another Irish beauty, her first cousin in fact. The king assured the comte that he was 'free of another rival. My brother has fallen in love with Lady Stanhope.' Elizabeth Stanhope, née Butler, Countess of Chesterfield, was the daughter of the Duke of Ormonde. Hamilton counted his cousin as 'one of the most agreeable women in the world'. The second wife of one of Barbara Palmer's lovers, Philip Stanhope, *this* Elizabeth was another Windsor Beauty. She was considered lovely, 'although not very tall, she had an exquisite figure, and was extremely fair, with all a blonde's impact, but sharp and piquant as a brunette. She had large blue eyes, highly seductive. Her manners were engaging, her wit lively and amusing; but her heart, ever open to tender feelings, was neither scrupulous in matters of constancy, nor sincere as it might be.'[25] In sum, she was alluring but unreliable.

Pepys's account of Lady Chesterfield's character is a little inconsistent. On the one hand, he deems her 'a virtuous lady'; on the other, he relates that her husband caught her *in flagrante delicto* with James. He complained that he surprised them in such a close cuddle that when the duke removed his arm, he took most of Lady Chesterfield's clothes with him. Despite Chesterfield's own extramarital romps – Pepys calls him a 'ladies' lord' – he was made miserable by her dalliance. And this, according to the logic of the bedroom-farce sensibility of the Restoration court, meant he was bound to be punished. On one occasion James visited her apartments, officially on a mission to see a most 'wonderful guitar', the best in England. As usual, he brought a gentleman lookout. Hamilton remarks that 'it is certain that they found both the lady and the guitar at home.' They were shortly surprised by Lord Chesterfield, who suspected that 'he was the instrument played upon'. Wary of the jealous husband role, he nonetheless entertained multiple suspicions, which he then confided to Hamilton. It did not simplify matters that his interlocutor was also smitten with the lady. When his wife admitted that she was 'madly infatuated' with the duke, Lord Chesterfield then sent her to the countryside in the midst of a severe winter (England was experiencing a mini Ice Age at the time). She departed in floods of bitter tears. Both men, suspecting that she wept for the Duke of York, remained implacable. Lady Stanhope became a virtual prisoner. Chesterfield averred that he would challenge the duke to a duel for making him a cuckold if 'one were allowed to show any resentment against the person who has wronged me.' Not for the first time, a wronged husband felt constrained by James's sheer rank. The court disdained Chesterfield's behaviour: 'they looked with astonishment upon a man who could be so uncivil as to be jealous of his wife.'[26] Pepys wrote that he was sorry to hear the tale, 'but it is the effect of idleness, of having nothing else to employ their great spirits upon.'[27] Rochester and his fellow wits made mincemeat of the unfortunate cuckold, and the balladeers got busy. This verse by the Comte de Gramont condemns Chesterfield for the grave error of failing to take his wife's adultery with suitable flippancy. Such a fuss, 'and all for a mere trifle'.

> Tell me, jealous-pated swain,
> What avail thy idle arts,
> To divide united hearts?
> Love, like the wind, I trow,
> Will, where it listeth, blow;
> So prithee, peace, for all thy cares are vain.

Lady Elizabeth Chesterfield never returned to London. But James was not inclined to languish and write letters. He was a here-and-now sort of lover, and there were plenty more Windsor Beauties and other women to appreciate. By the time his former mistress died in 1665 at the age of 25, his attention had been caught, a little unexpectedly, by a new maid of honour in the York household. Her name was Arabella Churchill.

Chapter 7

Apocalypse

> War, fire and plague against us all conspire,
> We the war, God the plague, who raised the fire?
> See how men all like ghosts while London burns,
> Wander and each over his ashes mourns …
>
> Andrew Marvell,
> *Third Advice to a Painter*

The year 1665 brought James a healthy new daughter, Princess Anne, to add to the royal nursery. Mary and little James were toddlers now, and the Duke of York was gaining a reputation as an extraordinarily affectionate father as well as husband. James and Anne were content. Nonetheless, his appetite for adultery remained sharp as ever. He and Charles both hankered after a distant cousin named Frances Stewart, a royal maid of honour newly returned to England after many years in France. Frances was so radiant that she managed to eclipse the king's official mistress at the Duke of Monmouth's wedding. Lely's portrait shows her radiant in yellow satin, turning to glance serenely at the viewer. 'The fair Stewart, then at the height of her glory, attracted all eyes and all respect.'[1] Frances was graceful, statuesque – and elusive. She was also playful, and a sportswoman. She has gone down in history as one of the rare ladies to refuse Charles II's advances. Predictably, this only inflamed his interest further. Hamilton indicates that the king would have married Frances if he were not already wed to Catherine of Braganza. He goes further, indicating that she was using Anne Boleyn's precise strategy to make herself queen. At one stage, the queen became deathly ill, and it looked like Frances might succeed. But then Catherine rallied. In any case, Frances eventually eloped with yet another Stewart cousin, who made her Duchess of Richmond and Lennox in 1667.

Since James had admired great beauties like Frances Stewart and bedded other lovely women like Lady Denham and Lady Chesterfield, people were astonished when he took a marked interest in Arabella

Churchill. Arabella, distant kin to Lady Castlemaine, was the daughter of a dedicated old Cavalier called Sir Winston Churchill. He had served the Royalist cause and been punished for it under Cromwell. Born in Devon, Arabella had spent time in Ireland, where Sir Winston was employed by James as a land agent. Her cousin Lady Castlemaine helped get Arabella a position as maid of honour to the Duchess of York. She made quite a contrast with her new employer. Anne was still consoling herself with delicacies, and was growing ever plumper. She had gained a reputation as having 'the biggest appetite in England'.[2] 'A tall creature, pale-faced, and nothing but skin and bone', Arabella was dismissed as an 'ugly skeleton' by sharp-tongued courtiers until James began to pay her serious attention. According to Hamilton, this first happened when the two were out riding with other members of the court. Young Miss Churchill looked anxious astride her horse, which put James off at first. A great equestrian himself, he liked women who were confident with animals – serene horsewomen such as Frances Stewart, or for that matter, his own wife, who once impressed him by handling a friend's pet snake with complete aplomb. Sensing fear, Arabella's horse bolted, shaking her off in the process. James, coming to her rescue, found her lying dishevelled on the ground with her lower limbs exposed. Onlookers marvelled that 'legs of such exquisite beauty could go with Miss Churchill's face'.[3] James was intrigued. He helped the lady up, and from then on her fortunes changed markedly.

Arabella, used to being ignored, was pleasantly surprised by the fact that the Duke of York had suddenly taken such an interest. According to Macauley, her family had the same reaction. The courtiers were puzzled. One lady, a Miss Hobart, wondered why 'the handsomest fellow in England was infatuated with an absolute fright.' Now that James was romancing a woman she thought downright ugly, the Duchess of York was more downcast than ever. Anne tried teasing him, nicknaming his mistress 'Helen of Troy'. Arabella Churchill was no Windsor Beauty. Indeed, Anne may have engaged her thinking that at least James would not be tempted – yet he had installed Arabella in a house of her own and granted her £1,000 per year once she began giving him children. There were four in all. Lady Henrietta FitzJames came first. The duke sent Arabella to the Bourbonnais region to give birth to James FitzJames, 1st Duke of Berwick. There she could 'take the waters' and recover in comfort. She followed up with Henry FitzJames, 1st Duke of Albemarle; and Arabella FitzJames. The children were educated in France. In addition to shapely legs, Arabella possessed a sharp wit. James liked her. As a special mark of favour, he gave his mistress's attractive and ambitious 16-year-old brother, John, a position as page. So now there were two Churchills dwelling in the ducal household. John would accompany the conscientious duke on frequent expeditions to review and drill the land troops. When he sank to his knees and begged 'a pair of colours in one of these fine regiments,' James granted his request.[4]

Anne was made miserable. Miss Hobart had been perched on the duchess's shoulder for some days, filling her with sweets, liquor and gossip. Everyone knew that James had only married her because he was forced to by the king, Miss Hobart whispered. 'What, Madam!' she asked, 'Must the prime of your life be spent in a sort of widowhood?'[5] Her husband galloped after every fancy that struck him. Why, if the duke was going to strive to bed every 'coquette' in London, should she not have a dalliance of her own? Miss Hobart tried to steer Anne into the arms of the presentable young Master of the Horse, Henry Sidney. When James got wind of his wife's flirtation, he gave her the silent treatment for the whole day. But his own adultery spree rolled on, and so did the king's.

Charles was all but subject to a woman whose whims knew no bounds. Evelyn dubbed Lady Castlemaine 'the Curse of the Nation', while others called her 'the Uncrowned Queen'. Whenever the king's attention wandered, the mistress would snap him back to attention with some ill-advised love affair or other. She seduced the slim and pretty John Churchill, for example, and her infatuation with a high-profile acrobat named Jacob Hall made the king look ridiculous. It seemed that when Lady Castlemaine was not in bed with a lover, or politicking, she was spending lavishly. Even now she was conspiring with her cousin Buckingham and others to bring down James's father-in-law, now the 1st Earl of Clarendon. As Evelyn put it, his 'enemies at court, the buffoons and ladies of pleasure' attacked him 'because he thwarted some of them and stood in their way.'[6] Edward Hyde had made an enemy of Lady Castlemaine when he tried to stop the king appointing her Lady of the Bedchamber to Queen Catherine. He had served Charles I, an uxorious king who strove to create an upright court, and tended to reprimand his son for these follies and vices.[7] Clarendon's presence served as a reminder – an awkward one, perhaps, for Charles and James – that a Cavalier court could promote chastity. The chancellor had a weak spot: the Portuguese match he had championed had so far produced no heirs. At the same time, his daughter's marriage to the Duke of York had catapulted his own family to fame and influence. As things stood, Clarendon's own grandchildren stood to inherit after James. These facts provoked suspicion and envy. Despite Clarendon's decades of service to the Stuarts, he would need more success in future in order to fend off his enemies and keep his position.

It seemed to many, especially the Puritans (increasingly known as Nonconformists), that the entire government had been condemned by God when England next faced a spate of calamities. The year 1665 started off well enough. James talked Charles and Clarendon into letting him personally command the fleet against the Dutch in the Battle of Lowestoft, despite the risk to him as heir to the throne. He led the English to triumph, confirming him as 'the darling of the Nation'.[8] Swashbuckling Prince Rupert was his vice-admiral. The Duke of Monmouth served under his Uncle James as well. Sir William Coventry wrote at the time that James was 'more himself, more of judgment, in the middle of a desperate service, than at other times. And although he is a man naturally martial to the hottest degree, yet a man that never in his life talks one word of himself.'[9] John Dryden addressed the celebratory verses of 'Annus Mirabilis' to the Duchess of York, who had prayed ardently for her husband's safe return. 'Victorious *York* did, with fam'd success,/To his known valour make the *Dutch* give place,' writes Dryden.

> In the English fleet each ship resounds with joy,
> And loud applause of their great Leader's fame,
> In fiery dreams the *Dutch* they still destroy,
> And slumb'ring, smile at the imagined flame.

The duke's naval prowess would also be made manifest in a vividly coloured portrait by Henri Gascar. James is depicted in Roman attire, personifying the god Mars himself, against a churning seascape. The page who attends him is clearly his cherished protégé, John Churchill.

The battle was a key episode in the struggle for commercial dominance on the high seas. Inevitably, there were fatalities. A cannonball narrowly missed James as he stood aboard the *Royal Charles*, but killed three of his close companions; his old friend Charles Berkeley, 1st Earl of Falmouth, was clean decapitated. 'Their blood covered and soaked the Admiral and a fragment of his friend's skull wounded him in the hand.'[10] Parliamentarian poet Andrew Marvell, writing under the sharply pointed pseudonym 'John Denham', memorialised Berkeley's death with a malicious couplet: 'His shattered head the fearless duke disdains,/And gave the last first proof that he had brains.'

The Great Plague hit the nation shortly afterwards. It carried off about 80,000 in London alone, about one-fifth of the city's population. Doors everywhere were painted with red crosses warning of infection within. Gentlemen who remained in town gathered in coffee houses to read the daily Bills of Mortality.[11] Evelyn was among those who sent his wife and family to the countryside, 'the Contagion now growing all about us.' Walking through the city, he beheld coffins piled high in the streets, and 'shops shut up in mournful silence, not knowing whose turn it might be next.' He noted that numbers peaked in September, 'there perishing now neere ten-thousand poore creatures weekly.'[12] Pepys wrote that losing so many close to him 'do put me into great apprehensions of melancholy, and with good reason.'[13] But he resolved to put a brave face on it for the sake of his wife and family.

London had barely recovered from pestilence when, in the ominous-sounding year of 1666, it was engulfed by fire. To Evelyn it seemed that Londoners lacked the spirit to fight the conflagration. All they could do was try to save a few goods, and soon the Thames was thick with small craft loaded with people's belongings. 'It made me weep to see it,' said Pepys of the devastation. Once he brought news to Whitehall of the 'most horrid malicious bloody' flames,[14] the king put the Duke of York in charge of fire-fighting. Both strove hard to quell the inferno. As Evelyn wrote, 'It is not indeed imaginable how extraordinary the vigilance and activity of the King and Duke was, even labouring in person, and being present, to command, order, and encourage Workemen; by which he showed his affection to his people, and gained theirs.'[15] Charles overrode the City authorities, putting James in charge. The people witnessed the duke at his courageous best. Riding the streets on horseback he worked through the night, directing the Royal Life Guards to create fire-breaks, pulling down and blowing up buildings to stop the spread of the fire. At long last it was put out, only to spring up again. The *London Gazette* reported that James stayed up all night fire-fighting, commending 'his Royal Highness's indefatigable and personal pains to apply all possible means to prevent it' blazing anew.[16]

The fire had apparently ignited in a Pudding Lane bakery, which supplied bread for the Royal Navy in the Second Anglo-Dutch War. The conflagration raged for four days. Suspicion fell on the Dutch, and, for old time's sake, the French. Rumours flew about that the two nations had joined forces and invaded England. A French watchmaker, Robert Hubert, made an unconvincing confession; it later emerged that he had arrived in London two days after the Great Fire was sparked. One of the wilder speculations had Charles II burning down his own capital city as revenge for the execution of his father. It was not long before 'papists' were blamed for the fire, the London crowd being particularly prone to nightmares of Catholics gone wild. A cartoon from the time shows Hubert accepting a fire-bomb from a Jesuit priest.

John Evelyn wandered in the razed labyrinth, seeing in it a Sodom destroyed, or a fallen Troy 'lay'd wast by an impetuous and cruel Enemy'. St Paul's Cathedral was 'a sad ruine'.[17] The embers were still glowing when Evelyn approached the king with plans to rebuild the city. Fellow members of the Royal Society, such as Christopher Wren, followed suit. The government lacked the money to implement Wren's large-scale version, but certain of his plans were realised. He famously rebuilt St Paul's Cathedral, for instance. A new, airier, more classical London would emerge from the ashes of the old. The fire could be alchemical. John Dryden, playing on the city's Roman name, 'Augusta,' captures this idea in *Annus Mirabilis*:

> More great than human now, and more *August*
> New deified she from her fires does rise:
> Her widening streets on new foundations trust,
> And, opening, into larger parts she flies.

The city was just beginning to recover from plague and fire when, in June 1667, the third calamity struck. This episode was especially humiliating for James because it concerned the Royal Navy. Taking advantage of English weakness and unpreparedness on several fronts, the Dutch sailed up the Medway and destroyed much of the fleet. They torched or captured many Royal Navy ships, towing back the flagship *Royal Charles* as a souvenir. To prevent more craft being captured, General Monck ordered that a total of thirty ships be sunk. To pull off such a daring raid, the Dutch relied on intelligence from English Protestant dissenters who had settled in

Holland – men like Colonel Joseph Bampfield, in fact. Times had changed since the colonel had aided young James to escape England. Having failed to obtain a pardon at the Restoration for joining the Protectorate side, he had joined the Nonconformist republican exiles in Holland. The Low Countries, as ever, served as a staging area for English subversives; Charles and James were consistently anxious that Holland was cultivating revolutionary forces. Now it seemed their worries were justified. Onlookers reported that English voices could be heard from within the Dutch ships, taunting and sneering at their countrymen. The Dutch blockaded the Thames.[18]

Londoners were panicked, again fearing that an invasion was imminent. English defences were severely corroded, and soldiers were demoralised. The government was forced to make peace with the Dutch. (The following year, they signed a pact with Holland and Sweden known as the Triple Alliance. It was designed to hold the French at bay in Flanders.) Evelyn was among those persuaded that these grim times were a judgement from above.[19] Most of those who could afford to leave town did so. Meanwhile, word went round that court diverted themselves with trivialities even in this extremis. As Pepys noted, 'the night the Dutch burned our ships the King did sup with my Lady Castlemaine.'[20] In his satirical 'Third Advice to a Painter,' Marvell suggests that James is too busy with his mistress to run the navy properly: 'His meagre Highness had now got astride/Does now Britannia as on Churchill ride.' The whole naval office was fair game – apart from Pepys himself, apparently ('there is not a good word said of any of us but me'). He expected the government to fall. Dryden struck a more optimistic note, arguing in the preface to his 'Annus Mirabilis', or Year of Wonders, that the catastrophes had brought Charles II and his subjects closer: 'Never had Prince or People more mutual reason to love each other, if suffering for each other can indear affection.' Still, someone would have to pay for all this misery. James noted drily that Parliament 'according to their custom, first vented their Spleen against the Papists'[21] and floated the idea of forcing all officers to take the Anglican sacrament. Having got that out of the way, MPs then changed course, awarding the role of scapegoat to Edward Hyde, 1st Earl of Clarendon.

James's father-in-law was not responsible for the war, plague and fire that had so afflicted England. However, they had occurred on his watch, so he was vulnerable. Moreover, his enemies had been circling for some time, and now drew up details of his 'mal-administration' and the failed

Portuguese match. King Charles was finally ready to hear the case against his long-time servant. In addition to the vengeful Lady Castlemaine, the chancellor had prominent foes in Parliament to contend with – the Earl of Bristol, for one. The Duke of York's own secretary, Sir William Coventry, resigned from his position so he could prosecute the chancellor. James was more favourable to Clarendon. It did not help the man that, just as his enemies swung into action, his son-in-law suddenly came down with smallpox. After recovering James returned to Parliament, his face somewhat scarred, to find the matter well advanced.

James voted against impeaching Clarendon, and laid out his reasons to the House of Lords. Certain ill-wishers were able to exploit a fissure between Clarendon and Charles. It concerned religious policy. Charles wanted to abide by the Declaration of Breda and offer his subjects liberty to practise outside of the Church of England. Clarendon, for his part, supported the Conventicles Act of 1664, which restricted and punished non-Anglicans. Both Charles and James distinguished between purely religious dissent and politically motivated nonconformism. When religious policy had constitutional implications, it was dangerous; otherwise, it could be tolerated. The political variety had already led practitioners down the path of rebellion to unrest, civil war and regicide. Both king and duke were alert to signs of republican thinking. However, they thought it wise to provide for 'tender consciences'. Dissenters should be able to practise as long as they remained loyal to the monarchy. (It was a distinction that would preserve certain friends, mostly Catholic.) They believed that complete religious repression would backfire on the government. There was evidence that banning small sects had already done so – to wit, the subversive activities of the exile colony in Holland.

It fell to James to ask Clarendon to hand over the Great Seal. The chancellor now 'succumbed to the stream which ran so violently against him.'[22] His pension was secure, and, despite certain clamourings, he would not be imprisoned, but had to go into exile in France. There, in a country whose language and way of life he had never embraced, the elderly Cavalier continued writing *The History of the Great Rebellion,* his wide-ranging account of the English Civil Wars. His fall was a defeat for the old guard, and a harbinger of the vicious politics to come. For James, it was worrying to see his brother carelessly discard such a faithful follower. It seemed to echo his father's betrayal of another faithful lieutenant, Strafford, so many years ago. James had regarded that as a colossal error. Charles II, meanwhile, believed he was coming into his own at last, stepping out of the previous generation's shadow. James was sceptical that this move would strengthen the monarchy. Parliament was always a dangerous place for 'the court party'. He perceived that, even if MPs were not outright republicans, treasuring 'their beloved Idole of a Common-wealth', they were hell-bent on transferring sovereignty from the king to themselves, leaving Personal Monarchy an empty husk.[23]

The fall of Clarendon divided the royal brothers. James held that this had been part of the purpose of engendering it. Now that Parliament had begun investigating and impeaching royal administrators once more, they would never relinquish that weapon. Several of those who had moved against the chancellor went on to replace him, forming the five-man advisory 'CABAL' (Clifford, Arlington, Buckingham, Ashley and Lauderdale). James, ever vigilant when it came to protecting the monarchy, believed that they diluted its power. Furthermore, he felt queasy seeing shimmering court wits like Lady Castlemaine and the Duke of Buckingham triumph over such a faithful gentleman.[24] Although James shared in their day-to-day pleasures, he was often made uneasy by their irreverent jests and offhand cruelty. James had a naturally serious temperament, and, at 34, the cusp of middle age, his mind was increasingly on the eternal.

He and his family had suffered two further blows in 1667. The first was the death of a new infant son, Charles, Duke of Kendal, in May. Then, in the midst of all the disarray of June, the 4-year-old James, Duke of Cambridge, had sickened, rallied and then suddenly died, probably of smallpox. The boy had lived long enough to be painted by a rising star of the English Baroque, John Michael Wright. The portrait shows a jaunty miniature knight in red, white and blue robes, and a plumed top hat. He had just been appointed to the Order of the Garter, led into the ceremonial chamber by his cousin Monmouth, and received by King Charles. Without a legitimate son of his own, Charles had focused a lot of energy on his nephew. Now that hope was extinguished. James and Anne had lost two sons; Clarendon, two grandsons. And the nation had lost the third and fourth in line to the throne.

Chapter 8

Reconciliation

> Tell me, my Muse, what monstrous dire offense
> What crime, could any Christian king incense
> To such a rage? Was't luxury or lust?
> Was he so temp'rate, so chaste, so just?
> Were these their crimes? They were his own much more...
>
> Sir John Denham, 'Cooper's Hill'

Charles I's old servant Clarendon might be banished, but the king himself was never far from James's thoughts. He kept his father close through, among other things, reading the Arminian theology he had so favoured. One particularly vivid Caroline controversialist was Peter Heylyn, who had served Charles I as chaplain. During the Commonwealth period, when the Anglican Church was dissolved, Heylyn had lost his living. As a function of the Restoration, which was as much a revival of the Anglican Church as it was of the monarchy, he wrote *Ecclesia restaurata, or, A History of the Reformation of the Church of England* (1661). In it, Heylyn lays out the events that prompted Henry VIII to sever the English Church from Rome in 1534, declaring himself its head in place of the Pope. James read the book in about 1668. In fact, he read it several times, along with the preface to Richard Hooker's *Ecclesiastical Polity*. Heylyn's work in particular would change the duke's life and the course of English history forever. Its effect, however, was not quite what the author had intended. Heylyn's detailed account of the English Reformation drove James away from the church of his youth and towards Catholicism.[1]

The figure of Henry VIII now loomed large in James's imagination. No member of the royal family of the Three Kingdoms could escape that monarch's reach, so great had been his effect upon the traditional constitution. Like James, Henry was the second son; he had been Duke of York until Prince Arthur's untimely death at 15. As a young man, Henry had been full of promise, a golden Renaissance prince, poised between More and Machiavelli. But what struck James's notice most forcefully was Henry's chief vice: lust. Like James, Henry was ridden by desire for women. They shared a frailty, and that gave James insight. Like the Tudor monarch, James had made courtesans out of maids of honour. He had also made a somewhat unsuitable one his wife. As James read Heylyn's account of Henry VIII's conduct, his detailed description of his chaotic effect on the lives of the people surrounding him, the scales fell from his eyes. He saw through Henry. Now he perceived that this man had broken with Rome and turned England upside down: he had shattered his family and alliances, ransacked the monasteries and laid waste to the Pilgrimage of Grace, disembowelled Carthusian monks and beheaded the author of *Utopia* – all because he yearned to replace Catherine of Aragon with Anne Boleyn. He did not abandon the church of his ancestors out of true conviction – James could have respected that. But any theological argument looked like post-hoc rationalisation in this case. As to begetting a male heir, Henry's method seemed to force God's hand. Henry was not a Protestant at heart, merely a bad Catholic. It seemed to him that Henry had broken with the Church of Rome first out of lust for a woman, and then greed for monastic spoils. Also, he noted, Edward VI had been governed by an uncle, Edward Seymour, made wealthy thanks to monastic lands. Finally, Elizabeth I's claim to power rested on her Protestantism; without it, she would have been illegitimate as an heir and thus as a queen. These were all unprincipled reasons to maintain separation with Rome.[2] It would have been apparent to him that Henry had stolen fire from the Catholic Church thinking to strengthen the monarchy – but that this had rebounded. Henry VIII's redistribution of church lands to people like Thomas Cromwell had fostered a new class embodied by his great-nephew Oliver Cromwell.[3] The Stuarts' greatest enemy had been forged by Henry's policy. In the long run, the attack on the Church had destroyed the monarchy – both the institution and the person of the king, Charles I. James profoundly desired to correct the damage he believed had been done by Henry VIII, damage which had culminated in the judicial murder of his father.

Reading about Henry's history with Anne Boleyn, James immediately recognised the effect that Anne's refusal to become the king's mistress would have had on him. Jane Seymour had successfully deployed precisely the same strategy to make herself queen. Because of his character flaws, Henry was easy to manipulate. James knew that he too had let desire make a fool of him, and overruled his and his family's – indeed his country's – best interests. Since his dubious marriage, James had let his passions run wild with other women. Charles II, of course, had the same proclivities. The king was less sentimental than either Henry VIII or James when it came to women, less prone to infatuation, but his addiction to pleasure was making a mockery of the monarchy, and he was too lazy to fight 'the Uncrowned Queen', Lady Castlemaine. Writing in his memoirs, James bemoans the fact that so many great men cannot control their lust.[4] His own father seemed to be the exception. Charles I had promoted married love as the court ideal. Apart from a mild flirtation or two after years of captivity, he had been faithful to his beloved Henrietta Maria.

If James became a Catholic, he would be leaving the church that his revered father had died to preserve. However, he would be joining the church that his mother was so devoted to – and his father adored his mother. Also, James came to believe that Catholicism preserved monarchy better than Anglicanism. The Protestant revolution had opened the door to political reversals, division and turmoil. And he was convinced that its premises were false. As far as James was concerned, the matter was clear. He felt he had reached the bedrock, and appreciated the sense of certainty it brought. Anglican divines Heylyn and Hooker 'had thoroughly convinced him that neither the Church of England, nor Calvin, nor any of the Reformers, had the right to do what they did, and he was confident ... that whosoever reads those two books with attention, and without prejudice, would be of the same opinion.'[5] James was an intensely patriotic Englishman. He was reminded that the English nation as such, together with the English liberties that Parliamentarians constantly invoked, had in fact emerged under the medieval church. It helped that he could describe the Reformation in English terms, and classify it as the error of a home-grown king who shared his own personal failings. Then, 'more sensibly touched in conscience, he began to think of his Salvation.'[6] There could be only one true Church, he concluded – the one that Christ instructed St Peter to found. James quoted Matthew 16:18: 'Thou art Peter, and upon this rock I shall build my Church.' The duke appreciated this sense of firm foundation. He discussed his concerns with several Anglican bishops, aware all the while that he risked drawing attention to himself and triggering a huge controversy. A high-level conversion – or *reversion,* as James termed it – would be politically dangerous for himself and for his brother. But he felt he had no choice but to proceed.

James asked his wife to read Peter Heylyn's book. Anne had been raised strongly Anglican. Her father, Clarendon, led the Church of England camp at court. But her religion was especially High Church in nature – as was her husband's. She had practised secret confession since childhood, for example. Her habits had already drawn the attention of the more Low Church Samuel Pepys, who commented disdainfully that he had seen the duke and duchess in James's 'pretty little chapel' engaged in 'silly devotion, God knows!'[7] In a sense, the Puritans were right about vestigial Catholicism in the Anglican Church insofar as it did provide bridges back to the Old Faith. High Church Anglicans saw the rupture with Rome as provisional: it could potentially be healed at some point. Still, anti-Catholicism ran deep in the Anglican Church as well. Reading Heylyn, however, Anne found that she agreed with her husband. It was apparent to her that Henry VIII had split with Rome for base reasons of lust and greed. Moreover, she concluded that doctrines of the True Presence of Christ in the Eucharist, praying for the dead and confession had Biblical support and were in fact practised in the 'Primitive Church' that Protestants wanted to recover.[8]

After much debate and consideration, the duke and duchess decided to be reconciled to the Catholic Church.[9] They were not alone among their milieu. Quite a few dramatic conversions had transpired in elite circles, particularly among Cavalier exiles who had been exposed to Catholic civilisation on the Continent. Some of these courtiers also used the term 'reversion', showing an awareness of how recently the Reformation had occurred. Many among Queen Henrietta Maria's entourage had turned to the Old Faith. An example was court dwarf Sir Jeffrey Hudson (unfortunately, he had since been kidnapped by Barbary pirates and sold into slavery in North Africa). Henrietta Maria had helped her niece Princess Louise Hollandine of the Palatinate to become a Catholic.[10] Louise was now an abbess. In the wider world, the abdicated Queen Christina of Sweden was a celebrated convert, now making her mark in Rome. In 1668, James learned that his mentor and friend General de Turenne, who had managed to achieve the rank of Marshall of France as a Protestant, had also embraced Catholicism. But it was a particularly huge step for the heir to the throne, and the couple knew it.

Anne began taking instruction with a Franciscan, Father Hunt, while James was catechised by a learned Jesuit called Father Simon. The duke eventually wrote to Rome, hoping for permission to keep taking the Anglican sacrament for reasons of state while also practising Catholicism in secret. The answer was no.[11] All this was done discreetly, but soon people noticed that although Anne still attended the Anglican services that helped shape day-to-day palace life, she was no longer taking communion there and had requested no special prayers. King Charles, who was after all the head of the national church, asked James to account for her behaviour. It was then he learned that Anne and James had left Anglicanism behind. Charles had a deeply Catholic sensibility, and it was reflected in his court. He was drawn to the faith and repelled by emphatic Protestantism. He once remarked that Presbyterianism, for example, was 'no religion for a gentleman'.[12] Charles also saw Catholicism as the religion best adapted to monarchy. However, the king was politically cautious. He made the pair promise to keep quiet for the time being. When James attended chapel with his brother but failed to take communion, people took note. John Evelyn was shocked that 'the sonn of a Martyr for the Protestant Religion, should apostasize'.[13] Rumours flew thick and fast. Now that the duke had accepted Catholicism, he wanted to be free to practise openly. He was sincere and forthright by nature. However, he agreed to hold off making a formal declaration. It was a stressful position for James, torn between his conviction and his devotion to Charles II.

The conversions dovetailed with two key developments – the fate of Henrietta Maria, and the Treaty of Dover the following year. The two royal brothers were out hunting in the New Forest in September 1669 when they received bad news from France: their mother had died. The intense, strong-willed and vivacious little Queen Mother had experienced poor health since the strains of the English Civil War. Although Henrietta Maria made an effort to be cheerful and still liked to dance, she was unwell much of the time. Her daughter organised a committee of doctors, one of whom prescribed an opiate, laudanum, as a sedative. Unfortunately, the amount was too much for the Queen Mother's tiny 60-year-old frame. Henrietta Maria died of an accidental overdose.[14]

She had endured a great deal in the 1640s and 1650s, but lived to triumph over her enemies. As James put it, 'After her great and many sufferings, God was pleased to grant her the sight of her son's restoration to his father's crown.' She excelled as 'a good Wife, a good Mother, and a good Christian. She was buryed with great magnificence at St. Denis, buriall-place of the Kings of France.'[15] Over time, James had moved from his father's to his mother's religious position. His conversion would have been another feather in her cap. Ultimately, however, James would aim to reconcile the two in himself, to do justice to father and mother. Now he inherited Henrietta Maria's mantle, albeit informally. It would be his duty to defend the Catholics of the Three Kingdoms from the synergetic forces of Parliament and the mob. A great reckoning was to come.

Charles II, meanwhile, had his own thoughts of promoting the Old Faith. He was in close contact with his cousin Louis XIV, both directly and via his 'dearest Minette' (Henriette Anne). Louis sought to extract England from the Triple Alliance with the Swedish Empire and the Dutch Republic. In the late seventeenth century, the island nation was at a crossroads. Would it align with France or Holland? As the wife of the French king's extravagant brother, Philippe d'Orléans, and a close confidante of both kings, Henriette Anne was perfectly placed to bring England and France together.[16] This ability to bridge nations was a fount of female influence in the royal courts of Europe. As for Holland, years of war with the Dutch had, of course, soured relations with that country. Charles and James had ongoing worries that Nonconformist republicans were planning another rebellion with assistance from the Dutch. Holland and France were themselves at odds over the future of the Low Countries. It was an ideal time for Charles to make a deal with Louis XIV, who wanted England's support in his dispute with the 19-year-old William of Orange and the Protestant Dutch Republic. Religion, governmental form, territory, resources, trade routes and finance – all were in play at this time.

Henriette Anne kept up with events in the country of her birth. Her life in the French court was difficult these days. Philippe (known as 'Monsieur') had proved to be a cruel husband, neglecting her in favour of his male lover, the tempestuous Chevalier de Lorraine. She cultivated her English connections, frequently corresponding with James, with Lord Arlington, and with members of her heroic governess's clan, the Villiers – the frothy Duke of Buckingham and the acerbic Lady Castlemaine. Above all Henriette Anne remained in close touch with the king. In 1668, Charles, building on his connection with his 'Minette' in order to arrange a treaty with the French, sent her a cipher so that their letters would be secure. Henriette saw a chance to harmonise the two countries and promote the cause of Catholicism.[17] Effecting a treaty would advance her own cause as well. She travelled to England, as if on a simple visit to relatives.

What became the Secret Treaty of Dover was propelled along by the fact that Charles II, like James, wanted to become a Catholic. The death of their mother seems to have crystallised a vague ambition. He was, of course, married to a devout Catholic, Catherine of Braganza. Moreover, his affectionate correspondence with Minette reveals a respect for the Old Faith. For example, he accepts the gift of a scapular from her and asks for some images for Catherine. Another factor was that Clarendon, a stalwart Church of England man who opposed Charles's plans for a toleration policy covering Nonconformists and Catholics, was out of the way. At the same time, the king knew that much of England would be disturbed by such a change. As a result, he was prepared to dissemble. Charles played fox to James's lion. He was a cunning politician, whereas James was pure warrior by nature. By initiating the Secret Treaty of Dover, Charles hoped to solve their problem. On 25 January, the Feast of the Conversion of St Paul, Charles called a meeting in 'the Duke's closet'. Present were James and three of the king's advisers – Lord Arundell of Wardour and two Cabal members, Lords Clifford and Arlington. Two of them, Arundell and Clifford, were Catholic. The third was judged trustworthy. Buckingham was bitter at being left out entirely.

James described how the king, 'with great earnestness, and even with tears in his eyes', spoke openly of his desire to promote the Catholic religion in his Three Kingdoms and liberate himself and his brother from the constraint they were under.[18] There were a trio of considerations: one's own soul, the souls of the Catholic minority, and those of the people at large. The king of England, Scotland and Ireland had to keep all three in mind. But he also had to be aware that Parliament and public opinion could work against him. That is why, Charles argued, he and James had to act while they still had the youth and vigour to face the challenge.

The result of this long and intense meeting was an agreement that 'there was no better way to do this great work than in conjunction with France and with the assistance of his Most Christian Majesty'. 'Madame' was chosen as chief negotiator for this tricky business because she could visit England without causing suspicion. Though she kept her true purpose from the malicious 'Monsieur', she did confide in James's trusted mentor, General Turenne, 'one of the privileged few ... admitted into the Royal secrets'.[19] James had certain reservations about the secret plan, fearing that it would backfire and ruin the cause of Catholicism. In any case, Minette crossed the Channel in May 1670, and was greeted by the royal barge off Dover. Aboard were King Charles, Queen Catherine, the Duchess of York, Prince Rupert and the Duke of Monmouth, who was highly attentive to Minette.[20] The still-infatuated Buckingham was never far from her side; she 'got him restor'd again to his Majesty's favour and trust.'[21] For his part, James was detained in London for a few days before he could join. People noticed that Minette seemed thin and pale, and suspected she was being made miserable by her spoiled and capricious spouse. But she succeeded at her task. Arriving at Dover Castle, she sat down with Charles to work out the details of the agreement. James was a bit wary of his little sister's immense sway with their brother, as well as, perhaps, of her closeness to the unreliable Duke of Buckingham. He wrote that she 'had at that time so much credit with the King that ... she should have perswaded him to have done almost any thing she had a mind to.' At one level, the visit was a public spectacle – Evelyn records his 'son John having ben at Dover to see the intervieu of Madame & His Majestie and having accompanied that Court at her return into France.'[22] In a secret addendum to the treaty, however, Charles undertook to become a Catholic at an unspecified point in future. Louis XIV agreed to make Charles financially independent of Parliament, giving him £200,000 a year. He would also supply troops in case of a revolt.

For Louis, the Anglo-French alliance was key. He particularly wanted Charles's support in his struggle against William of Orange. As James put it, 'when the Catholick religion was settled here, the King was to joyn with France in making war upon Holland.'[23] If they won, they would divide Flanders up between them. James worried that the costs of 'this new Dutch war' would far outstrip the funds the French had promised. Moreover, the need to raise money for war would inevitably increase the king's reliance upon Parliament, which in James's view had to be avoided. Nonetheless, the treaty went ahead. Henriette Anne then returned to the Continent laden with a gift of 2,000 gold crowns to build a chapel at the Chaillot convent in honour of the queen who had founded it. Henrietta Maria would have been endlessly gratified to learn that her treasured faith had won her sons over at last. That was certainly true of James. When it came to Charles, the results were less straightforward.

Another blow was in store for the Stuarts. A few scant weeks after her diplomatic accomplishment, on returning to her house at St Cloud, Henriette Anne fell fatally ill. On 29 June 1670, she called for refreshment and was given a glass of chicory water, which had been prescribed as a tonic. Upon drinking it down, she immediately cried out that she was dead. She sent for a confessor, and spent the next few hours writhing in pain. It was a piteous spectacle. When Monsieur came to her bedside, she reproached him, saying 'For a long time past, you have not loved me, but that was unjust, for I have never failed you.'[24] Henriette died in agony the next day. She left behind two young daughters, Marie Louise and Anne Marie.

Courtiers immediately surmised that the princess had been poisoned. Such things were not unknown at the court of Versailles. News reached England in the form of a letter from the ambassador. 'God send the King, our master, patience and constancy to bear so great an affliction,' he wrote. 'She asked for me,' he added, 'and it was to charge me to say all the kind things to her brothers, the King and Duke.'[25] Charles, sobbing frantically, pointed the finger at Philippe of Orléans. Others suspected the Chevalier de Lorraine. The London crowd blamed France generally, and additional guards had to be put on the French ambassador's residence. The grief-stricken Louis XIV called for a post-mortem, which found no proof of poison. 'The lamented Princess' had likely died of colic. Buckingham was sent to France to represent Charles and James at the funeral.

Shortly afterwards James himself became ill with a 'violent cold' and had to spend all summer recovering at Richmond Palace 'for change of air'.[26] This was the residence of his royal daughters, Mary and Anne. There, in those spacious gardens and hunting grounds, he could disport himself with his family as he so enjoyed. Samuel Pepys remarked with surprise upon the affectionate way the duke behaved with his children. He was more doting than was thought strictly dignified for a man of his rank. The diarist recorded that he 'saw him with great pleasure play with his little girle, like an ordinary private father of a child.'[27] James was especially close to his eldest daughter, Princess Mary, who turned 8 years old in

1670. Princess Anne had been with her grandmother in Paris receiving treatment for an eye condition, but she had returned when Henrietta Maria died. James ensured that his daughters received a good education and cultivated their artistic abilities, employing long-time courtier and now portrait miniaturist, Richard 'Dwarf' Gibson, as drawing-master. The girls learned to dance gracefully and to amuse themselves staging court entertainments.

James and Anne Hyde were quietly practising Catholics now, but for reasons of state King Charles took care to ensure that the 'daughters of York' were raised Protestant. He had to reassure Parliament, especially in view of the treaty with France against Holland, that England remained on a Protestant course. Mary and Anne shared a Protestant governess, Lady Frances Villiers, née Howard, and studied theology with Anglican divines. Meanwhile, their mother was writing about her newfound Catholic faith. Rumours of her transformation had spread through the court, and she had been fielding queries for some time. Now that the king knew the truth, the duchess felt free to lay out her reasoning, but discreetly; her account would circulate in manuscript form. In it she asserts that she was once 'one of the greatest enemies the [Roman] Church ever had'. No one, she says, had ever approached her about converting. She describes being exposed to the Catholic way of life while in exile on the Continent, but says that she had no thought of changing her religion until she read Peter Heylyn's account of the English Reformation. 'It is a blessing that I wholly owe the Almighty,' she avers, that she came back to Rome. She prays that the 'poor Catholics' of the realm are not harmed by the reaction to her conversion.[28] Anne understood how likely it was that recusants would experience further suppression if Protestant elites detected a larger Catholic movement.

It is not clear whether Anne understood how dearly her popular husband would pay for turning to Catholicism. His conversion was still officially secret when, later that year, the duchess developed breast cancer. It advanced quickly. Obese and suffering great pain, she told James that 'death is very terrible'.[29] One of her ladies-in-waiting, Margaret Blagge, wrote to her mentor John Evelyn as follows: 'the Duchess dead. She was a princess honoured in power. She had much wit, much money and much esteem.'[30] Blagge, a Protestant, claimed rather sourly that Anne's newfound faith had failed her at the end. She was unaware that her mistress did, in fact, receive

Last Rites and the Catholic Holy Sacrament before dying. What occurred was this: Anne's brothers, Laurence and Henry Hyde, tried to ensure that she took the Anglican sacrament, but she refused it. She then asked for the viaticum of the Catholic Church. Palace visits from Catholic priests had to be effected discreetly, and this one certainly was. James records that 'she dyed with great devotion and resignation, and the morning before her death, finding herself very ill that she could not long hold out, she desir'd the Duke not to stir from her till she was dead.'[31]

James had lost the woman who had joined him in the drama of conversion, and would now have to face the backlash without her. He characterised their marriage as 'extraordinary', and observed that it had had both good and bad effects. On the one hand, their affair was a product of his chief vice, lust. On the other, their eventual marriage reflected one of his main virtues, loyalty. Although James could have easily slipped his collar and avoided responsibility for his pregnant commoner mistress, he instead persistently begged the king to let him marry. As a result, the Hydes were grafted onto the Stuart dynasty. Most likely, James fully expected Charles to produce legitimate children. As it transpired, however, Anne had given the Stuart family children for the line of succession. It remained to be seen how that would play out.

Chapter 9

Numerous Charms

> Bless't were the hours when thro' attendance due,
> Her numerous charms were present to my view,
> When lowly to her radiant eyes I bowed,
> Suns to my sight, but suns without a cloud.
>
> Anne Finch on Mary of Modena

James was scarcely out of mourning for Anne when his household began pressing him to remarry and beget a male heir. (Evelyn was dismayed at how quickly the court seemed to forget the poor dead Duchess of York.) There was no shortage of candidates, and no lack of immediate distractions. Initially James's gaze was fixed upon a dark-haired widow temptingly close at hand, another of Sir Peter Lely's subjects. Her name was Susan, Lady Belasyse, née Armine, and she was about 25. Lady Susan was the lively Protestant daughter-in-law of an unflinching Cavalier and devout Catholic, Lord Belasyse. She and James each tried persuading the other to convert, but without success. He seemed prepared to overlook this gap, so charming did he find her. At first, history seemed to be repeating itself. In the throes of passion, James sent his mistress a letter offering marriage. When he approached his brother on the matter, asking for permission to marry Lady Susan, Charles was withering. The passionate lover was briskly told off. He had played the fool once by marrying a commoner, the king told James. This time he would wed a foreign princess so that the realm would benefit from the alliance. Charles retrieved the letter from Lady Susan, although she is said to have kept a copy.[1]

As 'First Subject' to the king, James submitted dutifully. He insisted on one thing, however: the lady in question had to be beautiful. The duke knew himself. If this match was to have a fighting chance, given his philandering tendencies, he should at least be drawn to his wife. Charles directed his counsellors to begin hunting for someone suitably appealing and well connected. Courtship portraits began to stream in. The king would have preferred a French princess to secure that alliance, but as none were available, he turned to the Habsburg possibilities. James was enchanted by the regal image of Claudia Felicitas, Archduchess of Austria. A fine-figured lady, she was a skilled huntress, a gifted singer and a devout Catholic. He was eager to wed her. The English were negotiating for the archduchess's hand when the Holy Roman Empress died. Soon afterwards, the Emperor let it be known that he wanted Claudia Felicitas for himself. Leopold then offered James his sister as a replacement. The duke's response was graceful: he would not marry the sister of his rival.[2] A disappointed James withdrew from the fray.

Over the next few months he was showered with possibilities. The negotiations were conducted by Henry Mordaunt, 2nd Lord Peterborough, the duke's trusted Groom of the Stole. Eventually he steered James towards a young lady of the d'Este family of Modena, a north-western Italian duchy allied to France – the 14-year-old Mary Beatrice. Mary's mother, Laura Martinozzi, was one of the seven fashionable nieces of Cardinal Mazarin known at Versailles as the 'Mazarinettes'. Mary of Modena was initially misrepresented to James as a redhead (she was raven-haired) and homely (she was pretty and graceful). He also gathered that she was too frail to bear children, and he learned something more accurate: the young *principessa* had little interest in marriage. Instead, she felt called to join a convent.

Mary Beatrice was initially dismissed from the running, but then reconsidered. The widowed Duchess of Modena persuaded her daughter to marry well for the good of the d'Este family. Laura Martinozzi had, in fact, been hoping to wed Mary Beatrice to the 11-year-old Charles II of Spain. When that match fell through, they made a greater effort as regards the English monarch's soldierly brother, who might well become king of England since Catherine of Braganza appeared to be infertile. In this case, the duke's newfound religion was an advantage. Once they had assured themselves of his conversion, they were pleased with him. Laura resorted to asking Clement X to write to her daughter on the matter. He did, urging her to accept James. There was a chance that Mary Beatrice could one day help shepherd a Protestant kingdom back to Rome.

Mary of Modena was lovely, willowy, young and pure-hearted. She had been well educated at a nearby Carmelite convent, and would bring a generous dowry. Like James, she spoke fluent French in addition to her native Italian, and had good Latin. Far from speaking English, he recalled, she was so 'innocently bred' that until the negotiations began 'she had never heard of such a place as England, nor heard of such a person as the Duke of York.' James dispatched Peterborough to meet the Italian princess and, all being well, secure her hand in marriage. After meeting the young woman and finding her to be beautiful, Peterborough wrote to his master saying that she 'was tall and admirably shaped. Her complexion was of the last fairness, her hair as black as jet, so were her eyebrows and her eyes, but the latter so full of light and sweetness as they did dazzle and charm too.'[3] For James, 'a better choice could not be made than of her person'.[4]

The English agreed that the *principessa* would have freedom to practise her religion, although they could not guarantee her a chapel for public worship. As James was in a hurry to secure the match before Parliament met again, he did not bother to clear it with Pope Clement X. The difficulty was that the Vatican still considered the duke a Protestant because he continued to appear at Anglican services for the king's sake. James was under pressure from both camps. The Protestants wanted him to take Anglican communion at high holidays like Christmas, but he declined. He could not be swayed 'in so tender a point of Conscience ... receiving in one Church and being of another ... would make him dispised by all good men'.[5] As the duke's status was not crystal clear, the couple would need a dispensation to marry. A proxy wedding was nonetheless held on 30 September 1673, with Peterborough standing in for his master.[6] His wife Penelope, née O'Brien, became one of Mary Beatrice's ladies-in-waiting. The *principessa* was able to bring along an Italian companion, 18-year-old Contessa Vittoria Davia Montecuccoli. Vittoria would prove a true friend over the turbulent years to come.

Peterborough and Mary Beatrice left Modena on her fifteenth birthday, travelling to the French court en route to England. The Duchess of Modena came along to ensure that her daughter settled in properly. Mary Beatrice's reception at Versailles seemed to augur well. Louis XIV presented his first cousin's young bride with a costly brooch. After all, he had approved the match in advance. Meanwhile, across the Channel, in the mysterious Isle of Great Britain, there were mixed signals – a peal of church bells here, a pontiff burned in effigy there. Parliament was back in session and 'the noise of the match coming to the ears of the House of Commons,' as James put it, was 'mightily heated'. They 'entered into a hot debate.'[7] The background to all this was Charles II's effort to introduce official toleration of Catholics (and Protestant dissenters) in the form of a Royal Declaration of Indulgence in 1672. Dissent could either be suppressed or accommodated, and the royal brothers preferred the latter. It meant that anti-recusancy fines would be suspended. Catholics had no churches, but they would be able to practise in their own homes unmolested. The purpose of the declaration, according to James, was to 'foster a Union amongst ourselves before we fell upon our enemies', the Dutch.[8] There were 'due limitations to preserve the Church of England', which remained after all the backbone of the state. However, the perceived menace to the Protestant status quo resulted in widespread alarm and intensified rhetoric. In March 1673, Parliament struck back against the king and his brother with the Test Act, subtitled 'An Act for Preventing Dangers Which May Happen from Popish Recusants'. It required anyone in, or aspiring to, public office to take an oath rejecting the Doctrine of Transubstantiation. He would also have to take Anglican communion. As no Catholic could in good conscience deny that the body and blood of Jesus Christ was truly present in the Eucharist, James resigned as Lord High Admiral. Many courtiers lost their places – even Barbara Palmer had to resign as lady-in-waiting to the queen – but James was the single greatest casualty of the Test Act. No longer would he lead the Royal Navy that he had personally built up and cultivated. It was momentous, as his whole life had been oriented towards the post. Instead, it would be Prince Rupert who led the fleet against the Dutch. A number of other key noblemen resigned their posts as well. By so doing, moreover, James was making his conversion public for the first time. His enemies had achieved their goal of forcing him to declare himself. England's champion would now become the national scapegoat.

A 'papist' spouse for the heir to the throne in combination with the French alliance added up to 'Popery and Arbitrary Government' and was denounced as such. This political formula, designed to oppose the Stuart monarchy, would be repeated more and more often. Another frequent theme concerning property played on fears that long-ago redistributed church lands might be under threat. The new order that had emerged as a result of Henry VIII's dissolution policy defended itself vigorously. Lord Arlington advised Charles II to stop Mary Beatrice, who was on her way from Paris to Calais, from coming at all. Lord Shaftesbury stood up to demand that the marriage remain unconsummated; the king responded by proroguing

Parliament until after Christmas. The London mob, meanwhile, devised a nickname for this latest Catholic royal consort. Mary of Modena would be dubbed 'the Pope's Daughter', based on wild imaginings that she was the love child of Alexander VII. Anti-Catholic feeling was bubbling up in part due to talk of high-level conversions and the pro-French policy. So intimidating was the political atmosphere that Mary Beatrice's reception party on the beach at Dover was sparsely attended.

James was delighted with his new spouse, but Mary Beatrice burst into tears when they first met. It was a trying situation for a sensitive young girl who had longed to join a convent. James was now 40, twenty-five years older than she. His good looks had suffered somewhat. Time, tide and a run-in with smallpox had hardened his features. His fashionably full light-brown wig was becoming, but something else was in store for Mary Beatrice. Her new husband had taken, like other gentlemen, to cropping his natural greying hair close to the skull. Attending the duke as he dressed, Samuel Pepys had seen him without his wig and was dismayed at the shorn-lion effect. Mary Beatrice, young and far from home, had a lot to contend with all at once. She had arrived in a mysterious northern land just as winter was setting in, and now faced sharing a bed and life with a middle-aged foreigner. But once she got to know her bridegroom a little, chatting in French, she found him kind and reassuring. James scrubbed up well for the in-person marriage ceremony at Dover Castle, wearing a becoming suit of grey broadcloth embroidered in gold and silver thread and lined in orange silk, together with a lace cravat. The confirmation of vows was performed by a spiritual confidant of the duke's, Bishop Nathaniel Crewe of Oxford.

The new couple had a few days to get to know one another before they sailed up the Thames to Whitehall Palace. Unfortunately, the reception there was nearly ruined by the behaviour of a group of peeresses who were resentful ('humped')[9] because Laura Martinozzi, Duchess of Modena, outranked them seating-wise. Upset by their snub and by the fact that her daughter was denied a chapel, Laura cut short her stay in England, leaving Mary Beatrice to fend for herself. Lord Conway wrote that 'the Dutchesse of Modena hath gone away in wrath and displeasure at most of the Ladies in our court.' Meanwhile, James's enemies in Parliament were denying that Mary Beatrice was as beautiful as advertised. Peterborough's nephew remarked cattily that Parliament should reward his uncle for his matchmaking efforts with a pair of spectacles. Trying to make his new wife at home in a somewhat inhospitable land, James soon presented her to his two daughters, saying hopefully 'I have brought you a new playfellow.'[10] At 11 years old, Princess Mary was only four years younger than her new stepmother. She immediately warmed to Mary Beatrice, and the two became friends. Anne was on good terms with her as well.

After this shaky start, James's marriage became a great success. The progress of their union echoed that of his parents. The two found that they truly enjoyed one another's company. Mary Beatrice was a cheerful and sociable new force at the ducal court. She picked up English quite rapidly. Like her husband, she loved the arts. She was a skilled and confident horsewoman, something James particularly appreciated in the opposite sex. The new Duchess of York looked especially elegant in the masculine-inspired riding attire that stylish women like Frances Stewart also wore. Like James, Mary Beatrice revelled in outdoor pursuits. Husband and wife played afield in the remarkably cold weather that England was experiencing at that time, taking toboggan rides and throwing snowballs at each other.

Mary Beatrice grew to love her husband deeply. He was attentive, spending plenty of time in the splendid bed made to mark their marriage. Gold and silver, it was decorated with cupids, arrows and flaming hearts. She soon became pregnant. Everyone was aware that the duchess could be carrying an heir to the thrones of the Three Kingdoms. As Lord Conway also noted, the Duke of York still visited his mistress at the house he had provided for her in St James's Square, and continued to ply her with expensive French gifts – gowns, muffs, looking-glasses and furniture.[11] The existence of this liaison was painful and humiliating for his young wife. A blatant reminder was that Arabella Churchill had borne her fourth FitzJames, also Arabella, in August 1673. (Arabella senior was an Anglican, but she complied with her lover's wish to have their four children educated at Catholic schools in France.) But between James's new marriage and his transformed Christian faith, he felt more ashamed of his adultery than previously and would try to be more discreet about it.[12] Charles, for his part, continued to flaunt his seraglio. 'God would not damn a man for a little irregular pleasure,' he once asserted to Bishop Gilbert Burnet. The incorrigible Earl of Rochester had introduced the king to orange-seller turned actress Nell Gwyn – 'pretty, witty Nell', as Pepys had it. There was something piquant in this unlikely union, which had produced a son, James Beauclerc, in 1671. (The boy was christened in honour of the Duke of York, who was friendly with Nell and often joined her and Charles for dinner after the theatre.)[13] Light-hearted Nell made a pleasant contrast with the ever-turbulent Barbara Palmer. On the whole, people expected great men to have mistresses, but it was, of course, a trial for their wives nonetheless. Anne Hyde had known of James's chief vice only too well in advance of their marriage, and yet suffered when he strayed. Mary Beatrice was an innocent, little prepared for the distress she would experience when the husband she had come to love was unfaithful to her. Overall, however, the union flourished, especially as the two grew ever closer spiritually speaking.

The solid marriage was a blessing, because the Duke of York continued to face sustained political resistance in the face of his Catholicism. A strong oppositional faction organised by the Earl of Shaftesbury and the duplicitous Duke of Buckingham was emerging in Parliament. These men now inherited the political mantle of the Puritans, striving to weaken the sovereign monarch in favour of a sovereign Parliament. James himself equated the plan to corrode kingly power with outright republicanism. But instead of clinging to 'their beloved Idole of a common-wealth',[14] the Shaftesbury faction would instead strive for a republic with a royal figurehead, along Dutch lines. (In the following century, Montesquieu would characterise Great Britain as 'a republic disguised as a monarchy'.) James's detractors, who came to be known as Whigs; and his supporters, who would be dubbed Tories, would eventually form the basis of the party system in England's Parliament. In a sense, therefore, our modern political history turns around James.

Having forced the duke to resign his offices, these enemies now began worrying away at his right to succeed Charles. Although England was broadly Protestant, there was as yet no formal barrier to a Catholic becoming monarch. It was the goal of the quickening Whig faction to introduce one. One of their strategies against the Duke of York was to adopt the Duke of Monmouth as their figurehead.[15] If James could be pushed aside, Monmouth could perhaps succeed. On the one hand, they attacked James's right; on the other, they worked to legitimise Monmouth. As a result, an informal court began to assemble around the appealing but dissolute royal bastard. When Monmouth was out of his father's hearing, he was quite happy to be toasted as the Prince of Wales, a king-in-waiting. The young man had been educated Catholic on the Continent by Father Stephen Goffe,[16] though he had never converted. In order to stand a chance of becoming king, he would have to seem unimpeachably Protestant. The problem of his legal status remained, however, so Monmouth's promoters continued to insist on the unlikely tale that Charles II had secretly wed Lucy Walter at his court-in-exile. They alleged the existence of a 'Black Box' containing marriage documents. An approach was made to the Bishop of Durham. If he could sign a fake marriage certificate, he would defeat 'popery' in the realm. The bishop refused to sign and reported the incident to the king. Undeterred, the 'factious party', playing on Monmouth's ambition, 'desisted not to put such fancies into the Duke of Monmouth's head, who greedily swallowed the poison, as shall hereafter appear,' James recalled.[17] Seeing how fondly the king loved Monmouth, the Shaftesbury crowd calculated that Charles might connive with them for the sake of convenience. They tried to make it easy for him to 'acknowledge' his son as legitimate. Perhaps if they made it temptingly easy for the king to lie, he would do so.

They were mistaken. Sowing division between the royal brothers turned out to be more difficult than expected. Although the fall of Clarendon had caused disagreement, they had moved on and now their relationship was stronger than ever. It was true that Charles II could be practical to the point of cynicism. He caroused with blatant libertines like John Wilmot, Earl of Rochester, who thanked him by penning filthy yet accurate poems like 'In the Isle of Great Britain'. (It runs in part 'Poor prince, thy prick, like thy buffoons at court/Will govern thee because it makes thee sport'.) The king was often flippant. Anglicans were dismayed to see the head of their Church snoozing pointedly during sermons. Charles laughed many things off. But when it came to his brother's right to succeed to the throne, he was utterly serious. The 1670s would show that the king was not seeking an excuse to put James, the rightful heir who had produced two legitimate daughters, aside. It is true that Charles found James's tendency to see things in black and white frustrating, as he himself perceived most matters in shades of grey. He worried that his brother lacked the Machiavellian skills which are arguably necessary to rule. On the matter of religion, he regarded James as a blunt instrument. However, the king recognised that James possessed talents that he himself lacked. While Charles tended to be lazy, the duke was hard-working and an able administrator. Yes, he was stubborn, a quality James ascribed to his nationality. 'The English are stubborn whether they are right or wrong, so your arguments can make no impression on me,' he once told the French ambassador.[18] However, one man's *stubborn* is another's *resolute*. The duke's human flaws were in any case beside the point – the principle of traditional monarchy was at stake. Charles II would have been in agreement with Sir Robert Filmer's case in *Patriarcha* that subjects no more choose their sovereign than they do their parents. That is why monarchy was characterised by its proponents as 'natural government'. Moreover, Charles recognised that the axe that lopped off an oak branch would soon come for the trunk. So James was his heir, and that was that. 'The crown was his by right and he knew none more worthy of it.'[19] As for the Duke of Monmouth, the king declared that as much as he loved him, he would 'rather see him hanged at Tyburn than own him as his legitimate son.'

Charles also demonstrated reliability when it came to Catherine of Braganza. Anti-Catholic forces in Parliament targeted her, along with James. Certain other advisors were not so much bigoted against her religion as they were anxious about her infertility. Charles was advised to put his queen aside, to send her to a nunnery as Henry VIII had tried to do to Catherine of Aragon. Or, since that monarch had wiped out England's convents, she might be exiled to one of the New World colonies. There she could be filed away and forgotten. Although Charles was wildly unfaithful to Catherine, he rejected any plans to replace her as queen. No matter how easy certain people tried to make it for him to dispose of his wife or brother, the king demurred. He loved them both and honoured the principle of legitimist monarchy.

The all-charming young Duke of Monmouth would soon have competition as Protestant front-runner. His father set about strengthening the existing line of succession, seeking a husband for Princess Mary. Meanwhile, Monmouth went from strength to strength as a soldier. He fought at the head of a group of 6,000 English and Scottish troops sent to aid the French against the Dutch in 1672. In 1673 he distinguished himself at the Siege of Maastricht. Under him was a contemporary, James's feisty protégé John Churchill, who saved Monmouth's life in one skirmish and got wounded. They were backed up by the storied D'Artagnan and his musketeers; the Frenchman died on that day. Returning to England triumphant, Monmouth found a more open field, since his long-time superior, James, had been compelled to resign his offices. The king, his father, made him Master of the Horse. All military commands had to pass by him, including those related to uprisings. This put the Duke of Monmouth in an ideal position should he ever decide to command a rebellion of his own.

Chapter 10

The Duke's Company

> Willmore! Welcome ashore, my dear rover! What happy
> wind blew us this good fortune?
>
> Aphra Behn, *The Rover;*
> *or The Banish'd Cavaliers* I.ii.67

Dashing young John Churchill rapidly became James's favourite. He was 'by all accounts of singular beauty and address, with qualities of force and fire which were already noticeable'.[1] Churchill's sister Arabella kept her place through the mid-1670s. Meanwhile, his FitzJames nephews and nieces were raised in some splendour in France, with little James and Henry attending the Duke of Monmouth's former college at Juilly. All of this was a step up for the struggling family of Sir Winston Churchill. Described as 'a decayed Cavalier and sharp-set place-hunter,'[2] Sir Winston was widely thought to have pimped his daughter out 'for preferment'. If that was the case, it seems to have worked. Arabella made her family's fortune. Her brother rose speedily through the ranks, duelling frequently as he went. The Duke of York promised his page the coveted position of Gentleman of the Bedchamber once the young man returned from serving in Tangiers and the Low Countries.

The king overrode the order. The difficulty was young John's dalliance with the sybaritic Lady Castlemaine, who had managed in 1670 to make it to Duchess of Cleveland. According to gossip spread by the French ambassador, Barillon, Charles II began to find the bedroom farce he found himself living in a bit trying. He once visited his official mistress's bedchamber, only to find John Churchill hiding his slender form in a cupboard. Both lovers sank to their knees, and Churchill begged his pardon. 'Go; you are a rascal,' was the king's rejoinder, 'I forgive you because you do it to get your bread.'[3] The biting jab, so prized in the Francophile courts of Europe, is characteristic of Charles. James felt it from time to time. Once he encountered his brother out in nearby Hyde Park with what he declared to be an inadequate guard. He worried that the king might be at risk. Charles parried, 'No kind of danger, James, for I am sure no man in England will take away my life to make you king.'[4] (Charles believed that his subjects 'would not kill a lamb to have a lion rule over them.') At any rate, despite being a persistent annoyance to the monarch, Churchill did eventually get his promotion. James made him Gentleman of the Bedchamber, and gave him increasingly important assignments in the tense years that followed.

The king remained loyal to James when it came to the succession, but he opposed his brother over Princess Mary's marriage prospects. Charles ensured that Mary (and Anne) continued to be educated Protestant at Richmond Palace. The girls' tutor was Bishop George Compton. He also fostered a love of gardening in Mary. She was developing into a lovely young woman, with chestnut hair and regular features in a pink and white oval face. Mary was slender and graceful, while Anne took more after their mother and had a tendency to chubbiness. The sisters mastered French, played the lute and harpsichord, and studied painting with the talented Richard Gibson. Bathsua Makin, the Stuart family tutoress who had accompanied Princess Elizabeth into captivity, went on to champion female education in *An Essay to Revive the Ancient Education of Gentlewomen* (1673). She dedicated the work to 'Her Highness the Lady Mary, Eldest Daughter to His Royal Highness the Duke of York', describing Mary as 'the first among ingenious and vertuous ladies' on a list which included the Royalist philosopher Margaret Cavendish, Duchess of Newcastle.

In about 1673, James commissioned Sir Peter Lely to paint his 11-year-old daughter dressed as the goddess Diana. There was a fashion for painting young noblewomen in this specific guise, which sounded themes of chastity, mystery and elevated femininity. Lely depicts the grave eyes of the virgin huntress in motion, bow in hand. The portrait perfectly conveys just how rare and precious a being the Duke of York's eldest daughter was. Appropriately enough, Mary's coming-out was marked by an elaborate court masque written by John Crowne and dedicated to the princess. Set in Arcadia, *Calisto, the Chaste Nymph*, tells of a follower of Diana. Mary, who danced 'most finely so as almost to ravish' Samuel Pepys,[5] was cast as Calisto, and Anne appeared as her sister, Nyphe. Both girls had studied elocution with the wife of the actor Thomas Betterton, which enhanced their performances. In the words of the Epilogue, the sisters are 'Two glorious Nymphs of your one God-like line'. The moon goddess was played by John Evelyn's protégée, Margaret Blagge. Mary and Anne's cousin the Duke of Monmouth displayed his fine form in the ballet. Lady Henrietta Maria Wentworth, who played Jupiter, would soon become his mistress. She uttered these words celebrating the debut of England's princess before the king: 'Beauty and Youth more than a God command/No *Jove* could e'er the force of these withstand./'Tis here that Sovereign Power admits dispute,/Beauty sometimes is justly absolute.' Perhaps it was then that she captured Monmouth's heart.

How would the accomplished Mary serve her country? As a princess, it was her role to bridge nations by marrying. After the performance she had a higher profile, and now accompanied her father and stepmother more frequently in public.[6] James would have liked to match his treasured girl with a great Catholic prince, preferably the Dauphin, who was also nearing marriageable age. But as the Third Anglo-Dutch War wound down, King Charles saw an opportunity to balance his French treaty with a Dutch marriage. It would offer an olive branch to Holland and placate the Shaftesbury faction, those who castigated the French model as 'Popery and arbitrary rule'. A union between William of Orange and his first cousin Princess Mary rhymed insistently with the marriage of William's parents, also William and Mary, in 1641. In both cases, the Stuart princess was arguably marrying down, but the king determined that the political situation demanded the match. William had expressed an interest in 'the Lady Mary' when he visited in 1671, but war had intervened. Now the idea was being floated once more. Royal advisers Temple and the Earl Danby approached James with the idea of a peace agreement with Holland. To this end, they said, they would suggest marriage to the Prince of Orange. (Danby in particular sought to provide a Protestant alternative to James's rule.) Once James realised that his daughter's future was already bound up with this peace plan, he resisted: 'it startled the Duke to see his daughter dispos'd of without his privity.'[7] Charles, however, was persuaded it was best to 'soothe Protestant disquiet.'[8] The Duke of York had stopped attending Anglican services in order to get papal dispensation for his second marriage, so his hand was weakened as regards his brother. Charles wished that his brother would conform outwardly, as he himself was doing after a fashion, but that went against James's nature. The dispensation which finally came through in 1676 was most welcome to both James and Mary Beatrice. The disadvantage was that Charles was now less inclined to mind his brother's objections. At one point he assured James he would not marry his daughter off without his agreement. Soon, however, Charles shrugged off his promise, saying: 'But, odds fish! He *must* consent.' The duke felt powerless: 'The King seem'd so resolved in the matter, that the Duke had nothing to do but acquiesce.'

Bishop George Compton, a man 'very eminent in his zeal against Popery', now approached James asking for permission to confirm Mary and Anne as Anglicans. The duke demurred as a matter of conscience, obliging the king take command. James wanted to have his children raised Catholic, but he knew this was impossible. He told Bishop Compton that if he had tried to do so, 'they would have immediately been quite taken from him.' James's memoirs are scattered with references to accepting his brother's commands. By leaving it to Charles to give the order, James was letting the world know two essential facts in one fell swoop. One, he was a true Catholic (like his mother). Two, he was an obedient monarchist (like his father). This was one of the most difficult, and most consequential, instances of obeying the king. Also, he hoped that by accepting a Protestant bridegroom, he had demonstrated that he had no plans to alter the country's religion, that 'all he desir'd was that men might not be molested merely for conscience sake.'[9]

Mary had, of course, been raised to expect a marriage with a foreign prince. Because of Queen Catherine's misfortune in conceiving a child and the question marks over her father's status, Mary's plans were regarded as crucial. In the meantime, she had developed a passionate friendship with an older girl which was echoed in Princess Anne's growing attachment to the vivacious Sarah Jennings, who had been appointed maid of honour to Mary Beatrice in 1673, at the age of 15. Frances Apsley, the young lady in question, was nine years older than Mary. She was the daughter of James's trusted household cofferer. Mary and Frances carried on a fanciful correspondence, addressing each other using names drawn from the romantic-pastoral genre they were so steeped in. As 'Chlorine', Mary addressed Frances's 'Aurelia' as an imaginary husband, 'a dear crual loved blest husban' in fact. 'You are loved more than can be exprest by your ever obedient wife vere affectionate friand humble sarvent to kis the ground where on you go to be your dog in a string your fish in a cage your humbel trout,' she poured forth.[10]

The prince that ardent Mary found herself engaged to in 1677 was rather remote from the romantic ideal. That her cousin was ten years older, 26 to her 16, was unremarkable. But William of Orange was much shorter than his prospective wife, who at 5' 11" took after her ancestress, Mary, Queen of Scots. At 5' 6", he just passed Mary's shoulder. He was also asthmatic, thin, had a large hooked nose, blackened teeth and a hunched appearance. All of this prompted the sharp-tongued Sarah to nickname him 'Caliban', and Anne mimicked her. On the other hand, William had large dark eyes and thick, dark, and eminently visible hair; in defiance of French fashion, he refused to wear a periwig. The Prince of Orange's dislike of all things French robbed him of the high heels that Louis XIV, also a small man, had also made modish in European courts. A wig and heels combined might have made up the height difference between William and Mary, but William had no regard for such artifices. The Stadtholder was imbued with a stern republican spirit, which dovetailed inextricably with strict Calvinism. He was allergic to all forms of enchantment.

William was invited to return to England on a mission to see his potential bride and discuss a treaty. Concerned about whether a match with a Stuart princess might alienate the English Dissenter faction he had so long cultivated – they had had one foot in Holland for most of the seventeenth century – he consulted the Shaftesbury camp. They reassured him. They were happy to see the royal family diluted, as William might push the Stuart monarchy in a 'constitutional' direction. His chief concern, however, was to limit the power and influence of Louis XIV. By wedding the second in line to the throne, he would be able, at a bare minimum, to draw England some distance away from France.

Now it was time for William to make court to his uncles, James and Charles. The prince visited the Duke of York, attending his *lever* and *coucher*, despite being impatient with etiquette. James was already uneasy about one of his nephews, Monmouth; he hoped that this legitimate one would serve him better. He had expressed to William's envoy, De Benting, that 'he should always have that kindness for his Nephew, which his own merit, and the interest of the Royal Family, which consists in being united, should require of him.' James was beginning to warm to the idea of William as a son-in-law, and looked forward to talking about business and military matters with him, since his nephew was intelligent and a capable soldier. The duke also perceived that the marriage might reassure the Protestant majority and improve his public image.[11] Learning that Charles had accepted William's offer, James simply said 'the King shall be obeyed.' He wrote a letter of apology to Pope Innocent XI and communicated this unwelcome news to Barillon. Louis XIV responded unhappily that James 'had given his daughter to his [the French king's] greatest enemy.'

Mary cried for over a day when she was told that the marriage to William had been settled. Both father and daughter were unhappy. It would, of course, mean leaving her household, her family and friends, to be marooned in a foreign land with an unpromising suitor that Anne and Sarah tittered at from behind their fans. Mary had only ever left the South of England to visit York with her father. On her wedding day, 4 November 1677, Queen Catherine tried to offer comfort by reminding the bride how similar her own case had been. Mary answered, 'But Madam you came into England; but I am going out of England.'[12] It was her Uncle Charles, rather than James, who gave her away – appropriately enough, since he was the matchmaker in this case. Anne could not attend, as she was in bed with smallpox. Neither could Mary Beatrice, as she was about to give birth. But there were plenty of celebratory church bells and bonfires. The king was in good spirits and full of ribald encouragement at the bedding ceremony that evening, drawing the bed-curtains and calling out 'Now nephew. Hey St. George for England!' William seems to have consummated his marriage handily enough, but gossip held that he treated his new wife coolly. He seemed to pay her little mind in public. Onlookers noted 'the prince's sullennesse, or clownishness' at a birthday ball for Catherine of Braganza, and that apart from dancing with her once as custom required, 'he took no notice of the princess at the playe and balle.'[13]

The departure of James's beloved daughter was delayed by the fact that Anne now came down with smallpox, the dreaded disease that had carried off so many, including both of William's parents. The now-Princess of Orange wanted to remain until her sister pulled through. In addition to the new bride Mary and the bedridden Anne, James had a third daughter to think of, an infant. Mary Beatrice had given birth to little Isabella in 1676. Now, two days after the wedding, she delighted James by giving him a son. Unfortunately, the child did not live long, but Mary Beatrice was clearly able to provide heirs to compete with Anne Hyde's Protestant offspring. Soon she was pregnant once more. Once Anne had recovered, meanwhile, Mary tearfully said goodbye to her family and friends and put away girlish things, among them 'Aurelia'. The princess now had a real-life 'husban' to attend to.[14] She found some comfort in affectionate letters from her stepmother, Mary Beatrice, who addressed the new Princess of Orange by a new pet name – 'my dear lemon'. Young Mary had sought to reassure herself by peopling her new household with familiar faces. Before long, William had made one of them, the none-too-gorgeous but remarkably clever Betty Villiers, into a mistress.

It was a time for mid-life reflection. The same year that James saw his first child married off, 1677, he enjoyed a production of *The Rover, or The Banish'd Cavaliers* put on by the Duke's Company at the Dorset Garden Theatre. The playwright was Aphra Behn, a member of the Earl of Rochester's circle. She was an adventurous Stuart loyalist who had engaged in Royalist espionage in the Low Countries. She liked to use her assigned code-name, 'Astraea', as a pen-name. Her comedy was designed as a compliment to James, and, in fact, it stole his heart. Set in Naples during the uproar of Carnival-time, the play is a layered expression of Restoration court culture. Thanks to Rochester's influence, it was now a world in which actresses held nearly as much sway as noblewomen did. In the original production the lead female role of Hellena was played by Rochester's mistress, Elizabeth Barry. He had managed to introduce another of his favourites, Nell Gwyn, into the king's bed; she was now jostling for influence with the king's more aristocratic courtesans. (Her high spirits served her well. One night when she was at the theatre with the king and the Duke of York, Nell learned that neither had money on them to tip the performers, as was customary. 'Odds fish!' Nell said, mimicking her lover with his characteristic turn of phrase. 'What company am I got into?')[15]

James was particularly taken with the subject matter of Behn's play. The male protagonist, Willmore, is 'the rover' in question; a rakish naval captain. 'Thous know'st I'm no tame sigher,' he states, but a 'rampant lion of the forest'.[16] Behn evokes a specific milieu, that of the courtiers who followed Charles II into exile – young, poverty-stricken, uprooted, pleasure-seeking English gentlemen fighting their way through the maze of 1650s Europe. It was a sketch of the duke's own wanderings, and it filled him with nostalgia. Yes, the 'banish'd' Cavaliers had suffered defeat, ruin and the unthinkably awful execution of Charles I, something they were still coming to terms with even now. They had been cast out into the wilderness.

Meanwhile, the enduring Lent that was Commonwealth England took hold. But there had been light-heartedness and camaraderie out in the desert. The triumph of 1660 had still been in store for the Royalists then, with all its promise for the future. In the present time, some of the sheen had gone off the Restoration. James attended *The Rover* again and again, and ensured that it was twice performed at court. Charles II, for his part, was less sentimental. He hoped that their wanderings were over, but the way James's conversion was playing out had the king worried. 'I am weary of travelling,' he remarked. 'I am resolved to go abroad no more. But when I am dead and gone, I know not what my brother will do. I am much afraid that when he comes to the Crown, he will be obliged to travel again.'[17]

James wanted to fulfil the promise of 1660. In particular, he desired to see the toleration policy that Charles had promised at Breda implemented. For the royal brothers, the edict was a tool that might solve the greatest political problem of the day – the religious division that had contributed so much to the Wars of the Three Kingdoms and the Thirty Years' War. Of course, this thirst for toleration was sharpened by the fact that he himself was now a dissident. James had always found the slivered Protestant sects alien and menacing, but now he began to perceive a glimmer of potential for a dissident coalition. Catholics might ally with any number of Nonconformist groups – with one proviso. James drew a distinction between revolutionary sects and what he called 'mere religion'. By *mere*, he meant *pure*, unadulterated by political ambition. Subjects of the realm who refrained from attending Anglican services simply for reasons of conscience could be tolerated. What he could not endure were those whose religious convictions led them to directly oppose the monarchy itself – as Oliver Cromwell and his ilk had done in the 1640s. They had warred against monarchy and smashed the episcopate that buttressed it. Finally, they had murdered the king.

Probably the single greatest Nonconformist influence on the duke in this period was William Penn. James had lived his life distrusting the adherents of small sects. Becoming close to an earnest Quaker, however, made him see that a coalition of Catholics and Protestant dissidents might be possible. This extraordinary friendship holds the key to James's ambitious toleration policy, something which has been minimised by his critics. William Penn was the thoughtful son of the admiral who had served the Stuarts in multiple ways – helping to bring about the Restoration, battling against the Dutch, and lending the king a large sum of money. Considering his elite background, it was remarkable that William selected that novel sect in the first place. Quakerism emerged in the wild atmosphere of the English Revolution, a time when anything seemed possible. It spread chiefly amongst the lower-middle orders[18]. 'The Society of Friends', as the Quakers are known formally, promoted a deeply unorthodox egalitarian doctrine, stripped of the sacraments and formal prayer. (The nickname derived from George Foxe's habit of shouting 'Tremble! Tremble before the Lord!' to one and all.) Followers simply worked to discern the 'Inner Light', assembling to 'testify' as the spirit moved them. Quakers refused to doff their hats before men of higher social rank, and addressed all individuals using the familiar pronoun 'thou/thee/thy/thine' in a fashion that declared equal status. This Quaker mode of address was often interpreted as needling by social superiors – though Charles II handled odd dissident deportment with his characteristic good grace. Pepys records the king's serenely hearing out 'a pretty Quaker woman ... who 'thou'd' him all along.'[19] In another instance, William Penn the Younger insisted upon wearing his hat before the king. Charles doffed his own, remarking that he believed it was customary for *someone* to do so on these occasions.

It was exceedingly rare to encounter a gentleman Quaker like Penn the Younger, whose dramatic conversion got him thrown out of Oxford University. After this incident, Penn Senior sent the young man on the Grand Tour of France and Italy, hoping to distract him from Nonconformist ideas. All this did was make William a more well-dressed and polished radical. In no time at all, Samuel Pepys was noting with much eye-rolling that 'Mr. William Penn is a Quaker again, or some very melancholy thing. He cares for no company, nor comes into any, which is a pleasant thing.'[20] The admiral was dismayed and even more worried when William began bombarding the government with pamphlets and convening illegal meetings ('conventicles'), and getting imprisoned for it. As the older man lay dying, however, he grew reconciled to his son's beliefs and exhorted him: 'Let nothing in this world tempt you to wrong your conscience.' Admiral Penn then wrote to James and Charles, beseeching them to protect his son.

Quakerism was not calculated to appeal to a man like James, Duke of York. Yet his loyalty to the admiral outweighed these considerations. Penn Senior had been a pillar of the Royal Navy. His work had formed the basis for a key document, 'The Duke of York's Sailing and Fighting Instructions'. The duke was prepared to help Penn's boy. Obviously, James was no egalitarian; he firmly believed that a harmonious hierarchy best served God and man. And yet Quaker sincerity appealed to him, being an earnest soul himself. This worked both ways, as certain Protestants respected the duke's seriousness when it came to religion, especially since the king often came across as irreverent. And there was something else that impressed James about young William Penn's position: Quakers were pacifists. Although the 'Friends' opposed monarchy in principle, they also rejected force of arms. Penn argued that, for this reason, Quakers should be exempt from 'anti-conventicle' laws which outlawed non-Anglican gatherings. Pacifism distinguished them from the Puritan groups which had gone to war with the Stuarts, groups whose heirs were now launching a new campaign in Parliament. Quakers refused moreover to swear oaths, rejecting those had been designed to weed James and other Catholics out of public life, so fellow feeling obtained there as well. The two converts understood one another. James agreed to protect William Penn following the death of the admiral in 1670 and engaged him as a royal counsellor. He told Penn in 1673 that he looked upon Quakers 'as a quiet industrious people, and though he was not of our judgement, yet he liked our good lives'.[21] For William Penn, the Duke of York was now 'Friend James'.

Both James and William Penn were founding members of the nascent Royal Society, founded by Charles II in an effort to fulfil Sir Francis Bacon's prophetic vision of scientific collegiality, the House of Solomon, in his *New Atlantis*. James only ever made one formal presentation to the Royal Society, but the project he now embarked on with Penn took experimentation to a new level. Several of England's American colonies had, from the outset, functioned as political laboratories.[22] Massachusetts was home to two explicitly Puritan settlements. The sovereign permitted these because they solved one political problem by siphoning off irritating dissidents. Colonies also allowed the government to try out various political formulas at a safe distance; in other words, they hoped to solve the persistent problem – again, the single most important issue in governance – of religious division at home. Occasionally one such experiment backfired on the king, as, for example, during the 1640s, when Puritan New England contributed to the Roundhead war effort in Old England, sending soldiers and incendiary pamphlets back across the Atlantic. But this danger was offset by the presence of Cavalier colonies such as Virginia and Maryland, which served the monarchy. Overall, the colonies benefitted England greatly.

William Penn proposed creating a refuge for Quakers in particular and religious dissidents in general. Quakers in England faced persecution. On the other side of the Atlantic, Puritans had driven them out of Massachusetts as heretics.[23] The great moral energy of 'the godly men' could be generative or destructive of community. As James would have been aware, Maryland had been founded in the 1630s with his parents' patronage as a refuge for English and Irish Catholics, a place where they could co-exist with Anglicans. Neighbouring Puritans' fierce opposition made the Catholic colony impossible to sustain. This new place would be a 'Holy Experiment' where the Friends could assemble to usher in and become worthy of the End Times, said Penn, weaving the scientific language of the Royal Society into an apocalyptic tapestry. In 1681, James would award his fellow dissident a portion of the vast territory that the king had bequeathed him after the Second Anglo-Dutch War. It added up to over 40,000 square miles of land. 'I eyed the Lord in obtaining it,' wrote Penn, '... and desire to keep it that I may not be unworthy of His love and do that which may answer His kind providence and serve His truth and people, that an example may be set to the nations.'[24] Charter in hand, Penn travelled to America and met with local tribes and previous settlers in the region which the king called, overruling the modest proprietor, Pennsylvania, or 'Penn's Woods'. More 'planters' began arriving, and a 'Frame of Government' stressing religious liberty was drawn up with the freeholders. The friendship of James and William Penn had borne fruit. And their collaboration was not over yet.[25]

Chapter 11

Fountain of Impudence

> Plots, true or false, are necessary things/
> To raise up commonwealths and ruin kings.
>
> John Dryden,
> *Absalom and Achitophel*

In 1678, the year the 'Popish Plot' hoax kicked off, James needed reliable friends around him more than ever. It was not the best moment to make an enemy of his long-time mistress Arabella Churchill, but that is what happened.[1] A new maid of honour arrived to serve Mary Beatrice, and she caught James's notorious eye. Her name was Catherine Sedley. Catherine was the daughter of the politician and dramatist Sir Charles Sedley, a member of Rochester's 'Merry Gang' of strenuous libertines. She had impeccable Cavalier credentials, and had inherited her father's facility with words. In short, she was just the sort of young lady James especially favoured. Evelyn described her as 'none of the virtuous, but a wit'.[2] Catherine was considered a bit plain, but she was observant and employed the spiky drollery so celebrated at the Restoration court. Her portrait miniature by Peter Cross shows an unfashionably skinny, pale girl with dark hair and an inky, penetrating gaze. Her insulting yet self-deprecating humour was perfectly in tune with the mode of the day. Surprised at having won the duke's favour, she remarked: 'It cannot be my beauty for he can see I have none. And it cannot be my wit for he has not enough to know that I have any.'[3] Charles Sackville's lines on Catherine Sedley paint a picture of a lady whose acute jibes could indeed wound: 'Dorinda's sparkling eyes, and wit, united/Cast too fierce a light.'

Like Arabella Churchill, Catherine was a Protestant; in fact, she frequently teased James about his priests. For his own part, Charles II liked to jest that these Catholic clergymen had assigned the duke homely mistresses as a penance. It is unlikely that any of these ladies was truly unappealing, since attractive looks had always been a prerequisite for the highly sought-after position of maid of honour. These days, James limited himself to one such liaison at a time. He discarded Arabella Churchill in favour of Catherine Sedley. Stung and humiliated, Arabella retreated to France for a time. She was, however, able to sell the London house that her royal lover had given her for the tidy sum of £8,000, and this made it possible for her to marry, in 1680, a distant cousin named Charles Godfrey.[4]

James may have broken with Arabella, but he remained highly attentive to the four promising children she had given him – Henrietta, 11 in 1678; James, 10; Henry, 7; and Arabella, 6. Also, Arabella's brother continued to advance in his service and esteem. John Churchill was as lively and daring as ever. That year he was wounded in yet another duel, this time with the poet Thomas Otway, over the beating of an orange-wench at the Duke of York's theatre. The Duchess of Cleveland had moved to Paris in 1676, clearing the way for Charles to promote another courtesan, Louise de Kéroualle, and for John Churchill to court a young lady.[5] Churchill's father had a wealthy heiress in mind for him – oddly enough, that heiress was Catherine Sedley, the woman who would shortly become James's mistress. It is not clear whether Churchill resented the fact his master had replaced his sister with the woman he was slated to marry, but he certainly took note. In any case, Churchill preferred Sarah Jennings of 'Mrs Freeman' fame, employed by Mary Beatrice as a maid of honour to Princess Anne aka 'Mrs Morley'. For Sarah, this young gentleman was 'as beautiful as an angel'.[6] Clever, bold and ambitious, Sarah was a female version of her suitor. She was a lovely blonde, though not quite as stunning as her sister, the fresh-faced and dimpled Frances. The historian Macaulay calls her 'beautiful Fanny Jennings, the loveliest coquette in the brilliant Whitehall of the Restoration'[7]. The yellow-haired young widow was pursued fruitlessly by the king and his brother, but Frances had no desire to become a mistress when she could make a good marriage. Hamilton writes that she 'had both virtue and pride, and the duke's proposals were consistent with neither'.[8] 'La Belle Jennings' would marry, become a Catholic, be widowed and eventually go on to marry James's towering Irish friend, Dick Talbot, in 1681. Sarah, meanwhile, was wed to John Churchill in a low-key ceremony facilitated by the Duchess of York, who was also their sole witness. Once the Churchills were able to reveal their marriage publicly, it became clear that they were becoming a political

'James II when Duke of York', John Michael Wright, circa 1662. (Wikimedia Commons)

James's parents, Charles I and Queen Henrietta Maria, grew into a devoted couple. Anthony Van Dyck, 1632. Kromeriz Archdiocesan Museum. (Wikimedia Commons)

Charles I, a great art collector, particularly treasured the family paintings he commissioned. From left to right: Mary, James, Charles, Elizabeth and Anne. Anthony Van Dyck, 1637. Royal Collection. (Wikimedia Commons)

The three young children of Charles I – Henry, Elizabeth and James – who were kept captive together once Parliament's forces triumphed. Sir Peter Lely, 1647. National Trust Collections. (Wikimedia Commons)

James was permitted to visit his father in captivity at Hampton Court Palace. Both dreamed of escape. Sir Peter Lely, 1647. (Wikimedia Commons)

Above left: An anonymous portrait miniature of James's first love, Anne Hyde, when she was serving as maid of honour to his sister Mary, Princess of Orange. Circa 1658. Rijksmuseum. (Wikimedia Commons)

Above right: Portrait miniature of the handsome young James, Duke of York, in armour. Samuel Cooper, circa 1660. Royal Collection. (Wikimedia Commons)

Mary, Princess of Orange, gave a celebratory ball at the Hague just before her brother, Charles II, departed for England to accept the throne from Parliament. Charles dances with Mary. James, seated, is just to his right. Hieronymus Janssens, 1660. Royal Collection. (Wikimedia Commons)

Above: The Duke and Duchess of York with their daughters, Mary and Anne. Painted by Sir Peter Lely, 1668–70, and completed by Benedetto Gennari. Royal Collection. (Wikimedia Commons)

Right: Margaret Brooke, Lady Denham, was married to Cavalier poet Sir John Denham. Her blatant affair with James nearly drove her husband mad. Circa 1665. Sheffield Galleries and Museums Trust. (Wikimedia Commons)

Left: James commissioned Sir Peter Lely to paint the seductive 'Windsor Beauties' series. Here he is presented in a similar mode. Circa 1665. Royal Collection. (Wikimedia Commons)

Below: This sculpture by Caius Gabriel Cibber is part of the monument to the Fire of London. A helmeted James, who led the fire-fighting efforts of 1666, is shown beside his brother, the king. The City of London is personified sitting at left. Envy is underfoot at right. 1671–77. (Wikimedia Commons)

This swagger portrait of James as Lord High Admiral commemorates his win against the Dutch. The page at right is recognisable as John Churchill. Henri Gascars, 1672–3. Royal Maritime Museum, Greenwich. (Wikimedia Commons)

Believed to depict James's mistress Arabella Churchill. Mary Beale, circa 1675. (Photo © Philip Mould Ltd, London/ Bridgeman Images)

The charming James Scott, Duke of Monmouth, was Charles II's most prominent illegitimate son. He would become James's rival. After Willem Wissing, circa 1680. National Portrait Gallery. (Wikimedia Commons)

James's eldest daughter, Mary, as the goddess Diana. Sir Peter Lely, circa 1672. Royal Collection. (Wikimedia Commons)

James's second wife, the lovely Mary of Modena. Sir Peter Lely and studio, 1679. National Trust Collections. (Wikimedia Commons)

Above left: Much to his wife's chagrin, James awarded his mistress Catherine Sedley the title Countess of Dorchester. Portrait miniature by Peter Cross, 1685. National Portrait Gallery. (Wikimedia Commons)

Above right: Lady Charlotte Fitzroy, Countess of Lichfield, was James's cherished niece. Portrait miniature by Richard Gibson, circa 1682. Welbeck Abbey Collection. (Wikimedia Commons)

Queen Mary Beatrice dazzled in her coronation robes. Sir Godfrey Kneller, 1685. (Wikimedia Commons)

King James II and VII by Sir Godfrey Kneller, 1685. (Wikimedia Commons)

The birth of a son and heir, James Francis Edward, sent the Whigs into a panic. Nicholas Largillière, 1691. National Galleries Scotland. (Wikimedia Commons)

James's daughter and nephew plotted and succeeded to replace him. 'William III and Mary II', detail of the Painted Hall of the Old Royal Naval College at Greenwich. Circa 1710. (Wikimedia Commons)

Right: The valiant James FitzJames, 1st Duke of Berwick, remained utterly loyal to his father. Attributed to Pierre Mignard, about 1689. Beurret & Bailly. (Wikimedia Commons)

Below: King James and family in exile at St. Germain-en-Laye. From left to right: James Francis Edward, Mary Beatrice, Louisa Maria Theresa and James. Pierre Mignard, 1694. Royal Collection. (Wikimedia Commons)

Prince James Francis Edward Stuart depicted as an angel guide to his sister, Princess Louisa Maria Theresa, whose birth in exile was a great solace to her parents. Alexis Simon-Belle, 1699. Royal Collection. (Wikimedia Commons)

force to be reckoned with. It seemed to James that he had a strong asset in John Churchill. The younger man was promoted to Master of the Robes, and became the duke's key envoy.

If Shaftesbury's faction was going to block the Duke of York from succeeding, it would need to corrode, somehow, the sense of legitimacy indivisible from the ancient institution of monarchy. James's birth was unimpeachable. It is true, however, that Catholicism was decidedly unpopular in 1670s England. The land that Richard II had once dedicated as 'the Dowry of the Virgin Mary' now defined itself in opposition to Rome. Still, no formal legal barrier existed at that time to prevent a Catholic prince from becoming king. It was Lord Shaftesbury's goal to create such a barrier. Once a scion of the court, he now opposed it, prompting Charles and James to nickname him 'Little Sincerity'. Shaftesbury now spearheaded 'the country party'. James decried it as 'the Republican Party', adding 'he became an outrageous enemy to the Crown itself.'[9] John Locke, having joined Shaftesbury's retinue, was shaping his famous arguments against Filmer, Hobbes and 'absolute monarchy'. Shaftesbury's goal was to drive a wedge between the royal brothers, to somehow depict the steadfast James as a traitor. This was a tall order. But the perfect weapon soon presented itself in the form of a disreputable cleric named Titus Oates.

The son of a Baptist minister, Oates often switched religious affiliation. He turned Anglican and served as a chaplain at Tangiers, but was dismissed for showing a prurient interest in the young sailors.[10] Converting to Catholicism, he tried and failed to join the Jesuits at Valladolid. It turned out he had faked a doctorate in divinity. Full of resentment against the Society of Jesus for rejecting him, he returned to England and soon fell in with a morbidly anti-Catholic fantasist named Israel Tongue. The latter blamed 'papists' for every misfortune that had befallen England from the Civil War onwards. After working each other up into a frenzy, they began making public accusations of a Jesuit plot to murder the king. As James noted, it was the 1640s all over again. Oates's fervid imaginings 'had so perfect an air of the fabulous reports which preceded the late Revolution', the designs Pym alleged to 'kill the King, subvert the government to bring in Popery, and arbitrary power.'[11] The second generation of rebels had been activated.

Charles II prided himself on possessing the common touch. Despite the concerns of his brother and other advisers, he liked to stroll in London parks unguarded. There, in principle, anyone could approach him. He was quite confident that no one wished him ill. Oddly enough, it was on one of these walks that he first learned of the so-called 'Popish Plot' to murder him. It would turn the country upside down for the next three years. A chemist acquaintance, someone who shared the king's interest in scientific experiments, sought him out there and told him of Titus Oates's feverish allegations. James was alerted to the claims of a conspiracy by his confessor, Father Thomas Bedingfeld, who came of an old recusant family. He had been sent letters purporting to be written by fellow Jesuits; in reality, Oates and Bedloe had hastily forged them to lend credence to their dramatic claims. At first, Oates claimed that the Duke of York was also a target of the conspiracy. Eventually, however, James was accused of being complicit, as was Queen Catherine, her personal physician and many others. As James's loyalty to the king was among his defining traits, he was outraged by the accusations. In fact, no Catholic was safe from this 'unexhaustible fountain of impudence'.[12] Also, the king permitted every recusancy law on the book to be energetically enforced. Ordinary Catholics lost positions, property, the right to live within 10 miles of the capital, and more.

Charles was unruffled by the initial report of a plot to take his life. He went off to enjoy the horse races at Newmarket, leaving Lord Danby to investigate the claims. James soon joined him at the new palace there.[13] Unfortunately, the situation in London soon span out of control. Attention fell on James's secretary, the pale and black-wigged Edward Coleman, who had embraced the Old Faith at about the same time as his master did. Coleman was a skilled controversialist. His public debate with two Anglican divines, Gilbert Burnet and Edward Stillingfleet, had netted at least one important convert. Coleman was tipped off by Sir Edmund Berry Godfrey, the magistrate who had been appointed to adjudicate the matter, and James ordered him to prepare for a raid. Despite these warnings, Coleman neglected to get rid of papers in which he discussed plans to root out Protestantism in England – an approach that James himself may have considered, but never endorsed[14] – with Cardinal Philip Howard in Rome. (The cardinal had served Queen Catherine at Somerset House until, in the wake of James's conversion, the tense political climate drove him out of England. Rome had since appointed him Protector of England and

Scotland.) The papers also revealed that Coleman had received money from Louis XIV's confessor to be distributed as bribes to MPs. Its purpose: to discourage a war against France and lessen Charles's reliance upon Parliament. Seeing Edward Coleman as a born intriguer, the king urged his brother to dismiss him. Coleman soon went to the block. 'Having now dipp'd their hands in blood,' the accusers ran on.[15]

Titus Oates testified before Sir Edmund Berry Godfrey. Unfortunately, Godfrey was found murdered two weeks later, and this fleshed out the 'Popish Plot' phantom somewhat. Evelyn's diary entry reflects the public perception: 'The barbarous murder of Sir Edmund Bery-Godfrey, found strangled about this time, as was manifest by the Papists (he being a Justice of the Peace, and one who knew much of their practises, as conversant with Coleman, a Servant of the ... now accus'd), put the whole nation into a fermentation against them.'[16] The real culprit was never discovered.

Oates found a rapt audience in Shaftesbury and his rebellious 'Grandees', men who wanted to see James excluded. They opposed legitimist Personal Monarchy and supported watering down the king's power in favour of Parliament. The modern party system as we know it emerged out of this question of James's right, and modern newspapers developed in tandem with it. His detractors came to be known 'Whigs', a pejorative reference to outlaw Scottish Covenanters. The Duke of Buckingham participated in the 'popish' prosecutions, but he was less enthusiastic about the efforts to deny James the throne. The duke's supporters, the 'Tory Party', were named for Irish papist outlaws; the majority-Anglican Tories supported James's hereditary right in spite of his newfound religion. Tories understood the monarchy as sacred, a vision that Charles II emphasised through ceremony and customs like the use of the royal touch for scrofula ('touching for the King's Evil'). The Whigs sought to disenchant the monarchy. They knew how to whip up the London crowd and deploy them to achieve political ends, making skilful use of newspapers, gossip and demonstrations. James viewed the Whigs as 'the party whose study it was to inflame the people'. The crowd, meanwhile, were all too ready to 'take fire at the least rumour of a Popish Conspiracy.'[17] The Whigs understood how to create a demand for their policies. Soon enough, hair-raising stories sped through the city: the cut-throat papists were planning to murder the entire populace in their beds. The Whigs pointed to the Catholic population, who were extremely thin on the ground in the London area. Nonetheless, they were perceived to be a colossal threat. To stave off this apparent menace, 'Solemn Mock Processions' were organised in order to burn the Bishop of Rome and others in effigy. The 5 November bonfires, commemorating Guy Fawkes's failed scheme to blow up Parliament with the entire government inside, raged hotter than they had ever done. It would not be long before the Whigs got bored with effigies and turned their attentions to flesh-and-blood priests, especially Jesuits. Many would be hanged, drawn and quartered over the next three years.[18]

The problem from the Protestant perspective was not so much ordinary recusants – though they did hate and fear such people. Rather, they were particularly disturbed by the numbers of Catholics at court, the sense that the numbers of elite conversions were growing. Charles had a Catholic queen, and that queen was permitted a chapel at Somerset House and priests to go with it. Like Henrietta Maria's chapel there, it was open to the public and might draw converts. Catherine of Braganza was also patroness to Catholic projects, such as a school for young ladies. She showed no sign of producing an heir, but she did have considerable influence. Furthermore, the king's prominent mistresses tended to be Catholic. A prominent exception, Nell Gwyn, nearly fell victim to the unrest. Famously, she was out in her carriage one day when a fired-up mob laid siege to it, believing that the seductive Louise de Kéroualle, now Duchess of Portsmouth, was inside. ''Tis the Catholic whore!' they shouted, starting to rock the carriage. Nell thrust her head out the side and yelled, 'Pray good people, be civil! I am the *Protestant* whore!'[19]

But it was the example of the Duke of York, the former 'darling and idol of the people' that caused the most concern. To summarise, James, the second in line to the throne, was now an open Catholic. His first wife had been another high-profile convert. His second wife shared his faith. Any child James and Mary Beatrice might produce would be raised in their religion. They favoured the French alliance, and Louis XIV suppressed his Huguenot subjects. It was feared that James – and indeed Charles, though the details of the Treaty of Dover remained secret – meant to replicate the French model of governance in England. Another factor was the haunting fear that long-ago redistributed church properties would be reclaimed. The main political questions of the day turned on the figure of the Duke of York, and the modern party system of liberal-revolutionary Whigs versus legitimist Tories emerged in response. It foreshadowed the left/right structure of the eighteenth-century French *Parlement*. Furthermore, modern newspapers emerged in connection with these political parties, aided by the fact the

Licensing Act, that regulated the printing press, expired in 1679, allowing for a storm of activity closely tracking events in Parliament.[20] Day after day, the Whiggish set filled up London's coffee houses to read and discuss the broadsheets. The Tories, meanwhile, grew to favour chocolate houses, where they could sip cocoa and absorb the news of the day. It would be several years before the government once more clamped down on political speech with a new act, although they did make use of libel suits.

Titus Oates fulminated tirelessly, targeting one 'popeling' after another for arrest and interrogation, which could mean prosecution and death. Indeed, it did mean a brutal execution for over thirty people. James's trusted confessor, the 61-year-old Father Bedingfeld, did not survive the stresses of interrogation and imprisonment; he died in the Tower awaiting trial.[21] Frequently contradicting himself, Oates lurched from insisting that he had nothing to say against 'any person of quality' to accusing the Queen of England of 'intending to Poyson the King' one week later, something that Evelyn for one dismissed out of hand.[22] Nonetheless, there were renewed calls for a royal divorce. The Duke of Monmouth made a show of snubbing the Duke of York, while whispering far and wide that he was ready to prove his own legitimacy. His 'cunning managers' among the Whigs 'had dazled his eyes with the glimering of a Crowne'.[23] Meanwhile, several of James's close friends, such as Lords Belasyse, Petre, Powis and Arundell of Wardour, were sent to the Tower of London. Propagandists took advantage of the febrile political climate to try and pass a law blocking James from the succession. Shaftesbury sent Monmouth on an ersatz royal progress through the West Country to whip up popular support, presenting himself as the Prince of Wales and even touching for the King's Evil.[24] Charles reproached him for his part in stirring up trouble. In 1679, the king ordered the wayward Monmouth into exile in Holland, where he worked his magic on his cousin Mary. He then returned to London without permission, only to be fêted by adoring Whiggish crowds with bonfires and church bells.

Each effort to pass an Exclusion Bill in Parliament was accompanied by a storm of inflammatory speeches, parades, ballads and pamphlets designed to sway the vote, to lend a sense of inevitability to the Whig project. Aphra Behn of the Duke's Company did return fire with plays satirising Monmouth and the City Dissenters, but the tide of Whig propaganda was overwhelming. One common rhetorical strategy was to invoke another Tudor monarch, Mary I. Her image had been tarnished beyond recognition by John Foxe's

Acts and Martyrs, a work which could be found alongside the Bible in every Anglican Church. Mary I had made it her mission to course-correct England and restore England's traditional relationship with Rome. In so doing, she persecuted Protestants. The burnings now defined her reign, whereas, for example, Elizabeth I's torture and subsequent hanging, drawing and quartering of English Catholic priests was shrugged off. Such Englishmen had been redefined as 'foreign' for clinging to the faith of their ancestors.

The fact remains that Mary I did indeed have a fearsome reputation in England. Now, 120 years after her death, the prospect of a Romish successor made the figure of the last English Catholic monarch truly politically useful. It was in the late 1670s that Mary Tudor was truly branded 'Bloody Mary' in the English mind. Obligatory Roman Catholicism and mass burnings at the stake for heretics: this, according to the Whigs, is what the English faced if the Duke of York ascended the throne. The Tories asserted that the Whigs were whipping up an anti-Catholic miasma to screen their attack on the English Church and monarchy.[25] Inevitably, James had to mull over Mary's example in addition to that of her father, Henry VIII. She haunted the scene as much as he did. The duke would go on to formulate a far different religious policy to hers, one which reflected how much the landscape had changed since her day.

The king feared for his brother, for himself, and for the very institution of monarchy in the midst of this frenzy, which cast a pall over court life and culture – right down to the theatres. There were more florid imaginings, such as that the duke intended to boil Parliament men to death, make an ampoule of their remains and use it to anoint himself at his coronation. It felt like the run-up to the civil wars all over again – with all that that implied. James wished that, since the ideal of harmony between king and Parliament was so elusive, Charles might be persuaded to live within his means and thereby break his dependence upon that assembly. The king intuited that the 'Popish Plot' was nothing but a fever dream, but for the time being was resolved to let the law take its course.[26] Charles ordered James to leave the country for a while. As it turned out, James had been 'obliged to travel again' sooner than expected. He also received a visit from Lady Powis, who begged him on behalf of her husband and the other lords in the Tower to retreat abroad. Anti-recusant law was being more strictly enforced, and in this atmosphere there was no telling who else might face arrest. One such unfortunate was the former court dwarf and fighting Cavalier Sir Jeffrey

Hudson. Queen Henrietta Maria's long-time companion had joined the Old Faith while in her service. He was kidnapped by Barbary pirates in the English Channel and sold into slavery in North Africa, where he laboured for over twenty years. After being ransomed by King Charles, 'Lord Minimus' finally made it back to London in 1676, only to be scooped up in the anti-Catholic hysteria and thrown into prison shortly afterwards.[27] Irish Archbishop St Oliver Plunkett was one of those martyred at Tyburn. Long-time Stuart devotee Archbishop Peter Talbot was arrested and locked up despite ill health. Shortly afterwards, his brother Richard – James's old friend – joined him there, though the king permitted him to go into exile in France. The archbishop was accused of conspiring to assassinate Ormonde, the Lieutenant Governor of Ireland, a claim that Ormonde himself laughed off in private. Peter Talbot died in prison in 1680. It was a bloodbath.

James was losing old friends left and right to the fantasies of Titus Oates. The injustice of it disturbed him. 'Scarce went to his heart more than the cruel treatment his friends met with in England, on account of this pretended conspiracy.'[28] Shortly before he was due in Parliament at a particularly tense juncture, he received a visit from the Archbishop of Canterbury and the Bishop of Winchester. Their purpose was to entice him back to the Anglican Church, which they represented as 'a lily among thorns'. How could he leave the church that his beloved father was martyred to preserve, they asked? It was an excellent strategy to invoke Charles I and the tribulations of the 'late Rebellion'. But it failed, as previous efforts by James's friends to reclaim him had done. He had informed himself thoroughly before leaving the church of his youth, he explained, in the full knowledge that he would likely go from being 'one of the happyest Princes in Europe, to that of the most unfortunate and abandon'd man upon earth'.[29]

Obeying his brother out of duty and 'sincere affection', James once again prepared to leave the country of his birth. 'For whatever his Majesty commanded, had always the force of a most sacred law with him,' he remarked. He was gratified to find that Mary Beatrice was eager to come along and help him shoulder misfortune.[30] Little Isabella eventually came along as well. He had succeeded at one thing at least – convincing Charles to send a declaration of Monmouth's illegitimacy to the Privy Council. James understood how torn the king was between his love for his brother on the one hand and his son on the other. At first Charles would not permit James to take 'the Lady Anne' out of the country too. The couple's first destination was Holland, where they paid a visit to William and Mary. The duke was miserably anxious that in his absence Charles would be persuaded to sacrifice him, to set him 'aside like an infant or lunatick'. The king insisted that such a thing would never happen. James, however, was aware of his brother's 'ductile spirit', and grasped that 'his enemies were willing to move heaven, earth, and even hell to prevent him coming to the crown.'[31] His friends on both sides of the religious divide worried that he would not be able to weather the storm. James made the point that the Scots would object to English tampering with the Stuart royal line, 'one of the antientest in Monarchys in the world,' and would likely seek to break off as a result. James had a sense of right on his side and was determined, with his wife's help, to cultivate the virtue of patience. He followed events carefully, and was relieved by his brother's steadfastness in the face of repeated efforts to pass bills excluding him from the succession. The couple soon moved on to Brussels, where they stayed with the Duke of Villahermosa, former Governor of the Spanish Netherlands.

James was concerned about Mary's wellbeing. She had suffered a miscarriage, which led her father to write William various pieces of advice. She had been rather melancholy since realising that William had taken up with one of her ladies. Mary's solution – apart from pastimes like needlework, music and card-playing – was to begin corresponding with her 'dear Aurelia' once more. As for 16-year-old Anne, James was pleased when, after several pleas, the king allowed her to join them in Brussels. There she attended a grand ball and feasted on 'sweet-meats'.[32] The auburn-haired Anne had grown into a presentable young woman. It was time to select a husband for her. Most likely, James knew, Charles would oblige him to choose from among the Protestant princes of Northern Europe. Great care was taken by her household to shelter Anne from additional 'Romish' influence, which meant she could not visit many landmarks in Flanders. 'All the fine churches and monasterys you know I must not see, so can give you no good account of them,' she wrote to a friend. She was unfavourably impressed by the religious images she glimpsed in shops and on streetcorners. 'The more I see of those foolerys & the more I heare of that Religeon the more I dislike it,' she wrote. The English princess was encouraged to be vigilant about her Protestant faith. Anne continually braced herself for James to try to persuade her away from Anglicanism, but he made little effort apart from recommending reading. He believed that his best strategy was to set an attractive example to the daughters he loved so deeply, and occasionally bring up the example of their mother. Meanwhile, he had little to do apart from disport himself. Although, in England, he had been forced to resigned his offices, he had continued to work behind the scenes. Now he had little to do, which did not suit his restless temperament. Bored and anxious, James hunted relentlessly, soon sending to England for his personal foxhounds. Often he was joined outdoors by Mary Beatrice and Anne.

In addition to concerning himself with his three daughters, James also continued to cultivate his relationship with his most charming niece, Lady Charlotte Fitzroy. A dedicated uncle, he kept in close contact with her on his travels with little sketches of daily activity. The daughter of the notorious Duchess of Cleveland had inherited her mother's ebony-haired beauty but not her difficult character. Sweet and agreeable, Charlotte had married Edward Lee, 1st Earl of Lichfield in 1677. The bride and groom were 13 and 14 respectively, and became a devoted couple. They would go on to have eighteen children.

James worried incessantly about the five Catholic lords detained in the Tower of London thanks to the wild imaginings of Titus Oates. He frequently pleaded with Charles to let him return, but his brother turned him down. The duke's *ennui* was interrupted by a burst of panic when news reached him in August 1679 that the king had taken seriously ill at Windsor Castle. He was worried for his brother. He was also concerned that the Duke of Monmouth, 'whose ambition gave life to all these commotions,' would try to seize the throne with Shaftesbury behind him. A committee consisting of Charles's ministers and mistress, now Duchess of Portsmouth, sent for him, and he hastened back to England.[33] At his brother's request, James came virtually incognito, leaving Mary Beatrice in Brussels. He brought only a tiny entourage consisting of Lord Peterborough, the trusted John Churchill, and a barber to groom the gentlemen, dress their wigs and attend to certain medical matters. James was told to pretend that he had come of his own accord. Arriving at Windsor to find Charles much improved, he went through a little charade of apology at his sudden appearance. Charles appeared surprised to see him. 'This Scene being over, all the Courtiers flock'd about him to make their compliments, his Enemys as well as his friends.'[34] The Duke of Monmouth was the exception to this. He had trouble masking his dismay. Monmouth had taken pains to keep his uncle and rival away, and yet here he was. James could sense the younger man's discomfiture. It was apparent, moreover, that the Tories, the 'Abhorrers' of popular tumults, were growing in number and in confidence. The 'Popish Plot' frenzy had at last begun to abate.[35] James assured the English bishops that he would never force Catholicism on the nation, which shored up his Tory support.

John Evelyn's diary entries are a microcosm of the public's gradual disenchantment with the whole affair. What had seemed like a frightening plot was gradually revealed as a hoax. When a jury acquitted Catholic lords in the Tower, he wrote this of Titus Oates: 'I do look on Oates as a vaine, insolent man, puff'd up with the favour of the Commons.' Evelyn believed that while Edward Coleman had been conspiring with Jesuits, the subsequent claims were the product of delirium. Even his old friend and fellow diarist Samuel Pepys had been arrested by this point, accused of popery and leaking secrets to the French. Having worked closely with the Duke of York at the Admiralty, Pepys had come under exaggerated scrutiny and spent time in the Tower.[36]

Charles judged that the time was not yet ripe for his brother to return to his side, but he had a mission for him, one for which James was immensely grateful. In November 1679 he was appointed as Lieutenant Governor of Scotland. Effectively, he would serve as viceroy – stand in for the king and rule in his stead. Since James I had departed Scotland to become James VI of England, Scotland had been ruled from afar. The nation had been instrumental in the Wars of the Three Kingdoms, both in opposing and supporting the Stuart monarchy. Recently another Covenanter rebellion had broken out. It had begun with the cruel murder of the Archbishop of St Andrew's. To James's profound annoyance, Charles had sent the errant Monmouth rather than himself to put the revolt down. 'He had the mortification of seeing the honour conferr'd upon his greatest enemy.'[37] Now, however, James would rule Scotland. Hearing that he had to go a-rovin' once more, Aphra Behn wrote a sequel to her famous play and dedicated it to the Duke of York. For the first time since the chaotic civil war years, a senior member of the Stuart clan was coming to Holyrood Palace. Scotland, the land of his ancestors, was a home that James had never known. The Scots had longed for 'a king to live amongst them' once again.[38] Now, in a sense, they would have one. And James would have a chance to showcase his abilities once more.

Chapter 12

The High Road

> His brother, though oppressed with vulgar spite,
> Yet dauntless, and secure of native right,
> Of ev'ry natural virtue stands possessed,
> Still dear to all the bravest and the best,
> His Courage foes, his Truth his friends proclaim,
> His Loyalty the King, the world his fame,
> His Mercy, even the offending crowd will find,
> For surely he comes of a forgiving kind.
>
> John Dryden,
> *Absalom and Achitophel* l. 353–363

The Duke of York and Albany's experience in Scotland contrasted greatly with that of his brother. Charles had been under a great deal of strain following their father's death. In 1650 the wandering young king had been forced into an agreement with the Scottish Covenanters. If he was to have the ghost of a chance at winning against Cromwell, he had to co-operate with them. He was ill at ease with what he saw as their grim approach to religion, with its emphasis on long charged sermons in chilly outdoor settings. The Covenanters' general abstemiousness did not suit his temper. He disliked their stripped-down coronation ceremony, with its pointed lack of bishops. He was their king, but at that moment the Covenanters had seemed sovereign. Later on, once Charles II was properly restored, it did not escape their notice that he had not kept his earlier promise to make England Presbyterian.

Twenty-eight years later, James was in a wholly different situation. The duke came to Scotland to assert royal authority as a guarantor of property rights and to gain knowledge of that nation which would help his brother rule well.[1] He also wanted to show that he could judge fairly among Scottish lords despite his conversion. James had to tangle with the same 'fanatick' faction, but from a position of strength. In dealing with the Scottish dissidents, such as the hard-line Cameronians, he was careful to treat theirs as a political rebellion rather than a 'merely' (purely) religious one,[2] as dissent for the sake of conscience was something he respected and identified with. The Scottish Privy Council made efforts to persuade the duke to take the 'Test' oath, but he declined, arguing that it was designed for Protestant dissidents. In Scotland, he could run his court as he chose. He may have intended to bring Whitehall to Edinburgh, but the final result was a distinct fusion. Travelling through England with a considerable train of courtiers, the duke and duchess stopped at York en route. At the border, the Scottish nobility turned out to greet James and Mary Beatrice formally.[3] The couple progressed to Lauderdale's house in the Borders. When they reached Edinburgh 'he was received with expressions of all imaginable joy and gratitude, for the honour, they say, that his Majesty the King and his Royal Highness did, in his comeing to reside amongst them.' There were bonfires, wine gushed, and James received the keys to the city. The Duke of York and Albany would eventually be welcomed at Stirling, Linlithgow, Glasgow and Dumbarton. A 'cult of tartan' developed at court. 'I live here as cautiously as I can,' wrote James, 'and am careful to give offence to none and to have no partialities and preach to them laying aside all private animosities and serving the King his own way.'[4]

The renovation of Holyrood Palace had begun in 1673, when Sir William Bruce was appointed King's Architect. Sir William was a Stuart loyalist who had served their cause while living in Rotterdam, carrying messages between General Monck and the exiled king. He had been rewarded with a baronetcy and a number of commissions to develop country houses and gardens. He also became the subject of a handsome portrait by the best home-grown royal painter of the day, John Michael Wright. Sir William, a Palladian in the vein of Inigo Jones, had refreshed and updated Holyrood to suit contemporary tastes. He had been tasked with erasing any traces of the Cromwellian troops who had been housed there in the 1650s. Their additions were pulled down. Now, in late 1679, James wanted to go further, ensuring that the Stuart Restoration truly came to Edinburgh. He also wanted a palace that would be comfortable for his household – for Mary Beatrice, her ladies and maids of honour, and, of course, the gentlemen courtiers as well. Charles had insisted upon keeping little Isabella in England, which distressed the duchess. Anne had to remain as well, though she would join the Holyrood court in 1681, where she was delighted to reunite with Sarah Churchill once more.

Now that Great Britain's second greatest patron of the arts was in Edinburgh, culture flourished there. James invited natural philosophers to present their experimental findings in the mode of the Royal Society. He directed Sir William Bruce to commission portraits of the entire Scottish royal line. In a painted echo of the coronation recital, it ran from the storied Fergus to Charles II, and was exhibited in Holyrood's Great Gallery. The architect brought a Dutch Catholic painter, Jacob de Wet the Younger, to Edinburgh. He would go on to produce the 110 portraits over the next several years at the rate of one per week. De Wet also decorated the state apartments with classical allegorical scenes.

The duke beautified the palace and made it comfortable for the household and guests. As pleasant as it became indoors, he was as eager as ever to enjoy outdoor sports, and chafed when poor weather 'imprisoned' him. Horse races were held, and James went 'a-buck hunting' for the palace table. 'The Dutchesse and my Daughter … and all the ladies that care to … ride abroad almost every day, the weather being very good,' he wrote to Charlotte on one occasion. 'The Dutchesse likes that sport now very well, and had a very fine chase the other day.'[5] At one point Mary Beatrice damaged her leg in a fall and was consigned to the sofa. He himself had learned the eminently Scottish sport of 'Goffe', a pastime his ancestors James IV and Mary, Queen of Scots had enjoyed. The duke also availed himself of the tennis court, and everyone enjoyed country dancing.

The court were as eager as ever to stage and enjoy plays. 'I am sure that we do not pass our time so ill as you in England think we do,' James told his niece. 'For we have plays, ride abroad, play at Basset, and have plenty of company, but for all that,' he added affectionately, 'one wishes oneself in London with one's friends.' The Puritan tide was still high north of the border, and many local people found the stage shocking. For the Scots, the theatre became an index of their willingness to embrace royal mores.[6] A number of actors and actresses from the Duke's Company came to Holyrood and performed John Dryden's *The Indian Emperor*. (Back in London, due to their struggles during the Popish Plot crisis, they would soon merge with the King's Players to form the United Company.) The tennis court was converted into a theatre. There were frequent amateur theatricals as well. When Lady Anne was not playing cards or hunting with her father, she was rehearsing for masques and plays. She and her maids of honour appeared in Nathaniel Lee's drama *Mithridates, King of Pontus* to mark Queen Catherine's birthday, with Anne in the role of Semandra.

Anne's accomplishments were winning praise. She drew the appreciative gaze of the 35-year-old John Sheffield, Lord Mulgrave, who put himself forward as a suitor for the 17-year-old princess. Mulgrave, 'a known philanderer', was judged to be an inadequate match for the third in line to the throne; the following year he was deprived of his offices and banished from court for overstepping the mark.[7] Anne's family now began searching in earnest for a more suitable husband. Two candidates were mooted, both distant cousins of the princess. One was George, the son of Sophia of Hanover, whom Anne met and admired when he made a three-month visit to England in 1680. James preferred the second option. Also named George, he was the mild-mannered younger brother of Christian V of Denmark. Evelyn would describe him as having 'the Danish countenance, blound', he was 'a young gent of few words, spake French but ill, seemed somewhat heavy, but reported Valiant'.[8] Charles and James were eager to create an Anglo-Danish pact in order to counterbalance Dutch power – a plan that naturally enough annoyed William of Orange and gratified Louis XIV. The duke also accepted George as a potential son-in-law to demonstrate that he was not biased against Protestants. He sent John Churchill to Denmark to meet with Prince George at a time when Anne's friendship with the canny Sarah Churchill was deepening. Anne, five years Sarah's junior, seems to have become more interesting for Sarah now that a royal marriage was on the cards. It meant that the princess had entered the political fray, and that was Mistress Churchill's natural habitat. On the matter of marriage, Anne was bracketed by Churchills. She was forming a close association that would turn out to be hugely consequential for her father.

James was immensely satisfied with his sojourn among the Scots. He gave 'his whole attention to the affairs of Scotland, where, by his industry and together with his affability, and kind reception of the gentry and nobility, whereby he gained such credit as did not only better the King's affairs in that Kingdom, but acquired to himself universal love and esteem, and his enemys were hugely dejected at it'.[9] However, he still experienced his time there as a banishment. The sense of exile became all the more painful when

4-year-old Princess Isabella, who had been held back in England much to her parents' dismay, took ill with smallpox and died at St James's Palace in March 1681. Mary Beatrice had long been pining to see her daughter and was, of course, shocked to learn that Isabella was dead. James recalled that 'it was the more afflicting because they had not the pleasure of seeing and assisting her in her sickness.'[10] The distraught Mary Beatrice sought consolation in unceasing prayer to the point that her physicians began to worry. There was concern that she might not recover well in the harsh northern climate so unfamiliar to her. It was painful for James to see his devoted wife's sufferings made worse because she had chosen to remain by his side in his 'misfortunes and hardships, rather than to enjoy her ease in any part of the world without him'.[11] Her torments continued when the bizarre allegation came off an English printing press that her mother, Laura Martinozzi, had put a price on the king's head. Charles, having lost patience with these kinds of claims, swiftly had the pamphleteer put to death. After some months, the duchess was well enough to fall pregnant once more.

The king also lost patience with Parliament. The Popish Plot had turned out to be such an utter hoax that James was eventually able to sue the loquacious Titus Oates successfully, winning a huge settlement. Shaftesbury faced a grand jury. They failed to indict him, but much of his political power was spent. Nonetheless, what James called 'the Phantom of Popery' seemed to haunt the scene as much as ever. The Whigs, having noted how much power could be generated from whipping up sectarian strife, were loath to let this ghost flit away. Shaftesbury and his fellow Whigs continued their frantic efforts to cut the duke out of the succession. The second Exclusion Bill passed the Commons but stalled in the Lords.[12] James was dismayed to learn that his cousin and comrade-in-arms Prince Rupert had voted in favour. He imagined himself as a stag at bay. The Whigs prepared the third Exclusion Bill. Various arrangements were considered, including a regency that would see the Duke of York exiled upon pain of death. All such proposals were offensive to James; ultimately, the king could no longer put up with this threat to his brother's right in particular and the principle of hereditary succession in general, which also structured society at large. He decided that Parliament would convene at Oxford, choosing that historically Royalist city because, unlike in London, there would be no rebellious crowd for 'the factious party' to whip up and pass off as the English people at large. Financially secure thanks to additional funds from Louis XIV, Charles was setting the stage for a big announcement. He also had the support of James's brother-in-law Laurence Hyde, Earl of Rochester (he had received the title not long after the notorious poet John Wilmot burned himself out and died in 1680). The new Rochester stood strong against exclusion.

Parliament met on 21 March. The king used the Whigs' favourite themes to reproach them for their behaviour: 'I, who will never use Arbitrary Government myself, am resolved not to suffer it in others.' He proclaimed, in an echo of his father's last speech, that 'neither your Liberties nor your properties could subsist long when the just Rights and Prerogatives of the Crown are invaded.' Charles I haunted the proceedings of this chaotic Parliament. Touching upon 'the just care you ought to have of religion,' he asserted that it could not justify fanning 'unnecessary fears, as may be made as a Pretence for changing the foundation of Government.' The recent storm of excesses had divided the nation and made it look foolish: 'Let us remain united at home, that we may recover the Esteem and Consideration we us'd to have abroad.'[13] After hearing the many strident speeches that followed, Charles understood that the Whigs would never back off. 'In their fury against the Duke, no bitter or intemperate thing was left unsaid ... they could think or talk of nothing but Popery'.[14] The least thing was blamed upon James's 'hellish practices'. There could be no reasonable discourse in such an atmosphere, the king concluded. One week later, enthroned and wearing his robes of state, he dissolved Parliament for what would be the last time. For the remainder of his reign, Charles ruled alone. Both calling MPs and dismissing them entailed risks, but the king judged that allowing them to proceed was the greater peril.

James was delighted with his brother for taking this firm stand. He felt that perhaps his troubles were ending. In 1682, with encouragement from Louise de Kéroualle and Laurence Hyde, Charles invited James back to his side in 1682. The duke first promised that he would not 'meddle' in English affairs, but instead remain focused on Scotland. Though satisfied that he now had a better understanding of the land of his ancestors, he was delighted to return to Whitehall. It seemed that the Whigs were in retreat at last. This time, town after town celebrated his arrival with bonfires, bells and songs. James marvelled that the London mob 'who had been ready to hound him to death' were now chorusing 'The glory of the British line/Old Jimmy's come home again!' He felt 'unspeakable joy' at being welcomed home at Whitehall. 'Old Jimmy' then set sail on the HMS *Gloucester*, John Churchill at his side, to 'fetch the Dutchess bigg with child out of Scotland.'[15] (His mistress Catherine Sedley was also pregnant around this time.) Unfortunately, the *Gloucester* ran aground off the Norfolk coast. Conscious that they were carrying the heir to the throne, the crew urged James to abandon ship. He lingered as long as possible, then departed, carrying a strongbox filled with papers, on a smaller craft. Churchill and other nobles came with him. Swords were drawn to stop mariners piling into the little boat and capsizing it. Disastrously, some 150 passengers drowned in the shipwreck, among them a member of the Hyde family. Charles had a silver medal cast to mark his brother's providential escape.

No Parliament meant no money for foreign wars. William of Orange, wanting England to take his side against France, made a visit to plead with the king to mend fences with Parliament. James worried that such a measure would 'now lead him back into the Laberinth' he had only just escaped.[16] William, ever aware that his wife Mary was second in line to the throne, allowed himself to be fêted by Whiggish supporters in the City. This annoyed the king greatly. Another sore point was that the Dutch Republic continued to harbour the dissident English Protestant community, people who also tended to be unhappy about Charles's Personal Rule as well as James's reappearance on the scene. Shaftesbury and the 'discontented faction' had spent much political capital trumpeting that a plot was afoot to murder the king. As Evelyn remarked, 'The Popish Plot also (which had hitherto made such a noise) began now sensibly to dwindle, through the folly, knavery, impudence and giddynesse of Oates.'[17] Now, with their star witness dimmed, certain Whigs hatched a real scheme of their own to kill the monarch and his 'papist' brother to boot. It would be dubbed the Rye House Plot.

Once again, the king who had prided himself on the love of his people was hearing of a threat to his life. As usual he was loath to accept it – but the evidence was mounting. It emerged that radical Whigs led by the Council of Six had mooted a variety of different plans for ridding themselves of Charles and James. Evelyn notes that some were for seizing the king and 'perswading him to new councils', while others were for killing him. James held that 'sometimes they were for executing in St. James's Park, or when they should be going down to the river, or to Hampton Court, or to Windsor, or in the play-house, but at last pitched upon Rye-House.'[18] These 'fiery spirits' disagreed on how to bring down the government and on whether to bring back the republic or install another, more conformable, monarch, such as their standard-bearer, the Duke of Monmouth.

The assassination plan they settled on was quite detailed: they would ambush the royal party en route from enjoying the Newmarket races. Armed men would be stationed near the road at Rye House, a moated Hertfordshire mansion which had been leased by one of the conspirators. In the event, the plan was foiled when a huge fire swept through Newmarket. The races being cancelled, the king and duke set off for London early. They had passed Rye House before the assassins could ready themselves. On 1 April 1683, Charles and James unwittingly made fools of their would-be murderers. Meanwhile, however, in London, the Whigs had imprisoned Tory aldermen in Skinners Hall as part of a co-ordinated effort to seize the Tower and effect a rising.[19] This made it clear that the 'Monmouth cabal' plotters were in earnest about seizing the royal brothers. Harsh punishment was in store for them. Many were imprisoned and executed as traitors. Political theorist Algernon Sidney was among those beheaded. A number of men were hanged, drawn and quartered. A woman named Elizabeth Gaunt, who had sheltered the plotters, was burned at the stake. William Penn, witnessing her death, marvelled at her cheerful demeanour. The Earl of Shaftesbury and his secretary John Locke were among those who fled to Holland. The republican writings of Locke and fellow conspirator Algernon Sidney would later inform the American Revolution.

Monmouth, the prodigal whose 'ambition gave life to all these commotions', first 'absconded' and then wrote to Charles begging for mercy for his part in the planned attack on his own father, not to mention uncle.[20] Panicked, Monmouth insisted that he did not know the armed men meant to *kill* them. As soon as he received his pardon, he recanted and fell right back in with 'the party of rebellion', was banished from court once more, and withdrew again to Holland. This time Charles directed William and Mary not to welcome Monmouth, but they paid no heed. Instead, they blithely fêted him at the Hague. James wrote, pleading with William 'not to countenance one who had lately done his best to destroy them all and involve the kingdom in blood and confusion'.[21] Apparently William of Orange had dismissed the rift as just another squabble that would soon blow over. But Charles II was serious this time. He refused ever to see Monmouth again. He and James considered recalling certain British regiments backing

William in the Low Countries.[22] The whole business had rendered the king melancholy.

James believed that Charles, generous to a fault, had helped to make a rebel angel of a royal bastard by indulging him. Now Monmouth had repaid his father's love with betrayal. It was a story that captured the nation's imagination. Of all the king's natural sons, the bewitching James Scott, Duke of Monmouth, made the biggest splash. His betrayal of his father at Shaftesbury's behest had already been allegorised by the Poet Laureate Dryden in *Absalom and Achitophel*, even before the Rye House Plot played out. Now both were in Holland, welcomed as heroes by the dissident English Protestant settlement there, people united by their opposition to the Duke of York. Shaftesbury, a 'crafty & ambitious fox', according to Evelyn, did not last long. He died in Holland a few months later, but his protégé Monmouth lived on to fight another day. Monmouth brought along Henrietta Wentworth, the young noblewoman he had danced alongside in the masque *Calisto*. Falling passionately in love, he had proposed marriage to her despite being already wed to the Duchess of Buccleuch. Henrietta was received as his official mistress at the court of William of Orange. Monmouth tried to bring revelry to that slightly austere place and encouraged Mary to ice-skate.[23]

With the Whigs in retreat, James's supporters consolidated their power. The Tories aka 'church party' pressed forward in defence of James's right and traditional monarchy, making their arguments in sermons, books and pamphlets. However, they also enforced laws against religious dissenters of all stripes. James and his friend William Penn looked forward to a day when a general toleration would be possible – although that posed a threat to the very party who affirmed his place in the succession most emphatically. For now, the duke would have to satisfy himself with the Tories' support of the royal line. Both James and the Tory Party were gratified when Princess Anne married Prince George of Denmark in July 1683 at Whitehall. The Tories were partial to Anne, and she returned their affection. Charles gave Anne and George the Cockpit as a wedding present. The building that had been dedicated to pleasures of all sorts – cockfighting, tennis, bowling, tilting and, finally, theatre – was now refitted as a home for newlyweds, 'her court and house-hold to be moduled just as the Duke her Father's,' noted Evelyn.[24] The king found George dull, saying 'I have tried him drunk, and I have tried him sober, but odds fish! There is nothing in him.'[25] But Anne found George immensely agreeable. James had successfully married off his second daughter. Meanwhile, Mary Beatrice had given birth to a 'lusty' baby girl, christened Charlotte as a compliment to James's beloved niece. The child would not survive long. When she died, her grief-stricken parents buried her in the vault of Mary, Queen of Scots. Before long, Mary Beatrice would make another therapeutic visit to Tunbridge Wells, an increasingly popular resort amongst royal ladies, to take the waters.

With a husband and a court of her own, Princess Anne was of more interest than ever to the social-climbing Sarah Churchill. Sarah understood that 'Mrs Morley' craved her attention and desperately wanted to please her 'Mrs Freeman'. 'A friend was what she most coveted,' wrote Sarah.[26] She and John moved into the Cockpit. Anne asked her father to appoint Sarah Groom of the Stole, but her aunt by marriage, the bookish Flower Hyde, née Backhouse, was in the way. Sarah launched a malicious campaign of mockery against Flower, sniping at 'the scholar' to the accompaniment of Anne's giggles. Meanwhile, Prince George visited his wife's bedchamber nightly. Soon Anne became pregnant, but she lost the baby and made a trip of her own to Tunbridge Wells. In Protestant England, it seemed that spa towns had overtaken holy wells in the quest for fertility.

Charles settled into cosy domesticity with the Duchess of Portsmouth. Now that he was older, his appetite for new mistresses was waning. Portsmouth was so influential with the king that people would approach her with requests. James was still seeing the acerbic Catherine Sedley, much to the chagrin of his wife, but conscious of his Achilles heel, he tried not to permit Catherine political power. She had given him a daughter, also named Catherine, in the early 1680s. A small question mark hovered over the little girl's paternity, however, as Catherine Sedley was rumoured to have taken the duke's Keeper of the Privy Purse as a lover. Nonetheless, James acknowledged the child. She was christened Lady Catherine Darnley after her paternal ancestor, Lord Darnley, husband of Mary, Queen of Scots. She was also awarded a coat of arms suitable for a duke's natural daughter.

James's fine sons by Arabella Churchill visited from France in 1684. James was 14, and Henry was 11. There they met their uncles, Charles II and John Churchill. Charles welcomed them to court warmly and offered to ennoble young James. Their father declined on this occasion, probably because the passionate Mary Beatrice objected even to the name FitzJames.[27] The duke was extremely proud of the boys who were pious children. A serious and conscientious child, James particularly took after his father.

He showed great aptitude as a soldier. On the advice of one of their father's preferred priests, the Jesuit Father Edward Petre, they returned to France to complete their education at La Flèche.

Charles and James did not have long to enjoy their leisure together after so many difficult years. One day in 1685, aged 54, Charles II suffered a stroke while shaving. The royal physicians subjected him to the usual rounds of bleedings, enemas and emetics intended to draw out evil humours. He did not recover, but took to his bed, certain that his time had come. James knelt continually at his bedside with Queen Catherine. The Duchess of Portsmouth was as eager as they were to see that Charles died a Catholic. He had already refused the Anglican sacrament. When James asked him whether he should fetch a Catholic priest, the king replied urgently, 'For God's sake do, brother, and please lose no time.' He then worried that this might get James in serious trouble. The duke replied that he would complete the mission even if it cost him his life. He sent for Father John Huddleston, the modest Benedictine priest who had long ago tended to Charles during his flight after the Battle of Worcester. The priest was slipped into the palace. James then led Father Huddleston into the royal bedchamber. 'This good man once saved your life, Sire,' he said. Now he comes to save your soul.' 'He is welcome,' whispered the dying king.[28]

It had been a long time coming. Before the Treaty of Dover, Charles II had desired to become a Catholic. He had always enjoyed discussing theological matters, opining that it was a shame that the Bible had been so widely spread and interpreted, for it had led to fragmentation of the body politic. When Anglicans complained of the smaller sects, he reminded them that they had set the precedent by splitting with the Roman Church. For reasons of expediency, for reasons of state, he had waited until now to make his position clear. Now Charles made his first and last confession. Among other things he apologised to his wife and to James, begging forgiveness for any harm he had done them. Many tears were shed. Finally, the king received the Eucharist and the Last Rites. He spoke of the Duchess of Portsmouth. He remembered Nell Gwyn. 'Let not poor Nelly starve,' he told James.[29] The king spoke of 'my poor children', who numbered eleven in all. He did not mention the Duke of Monmouth, who had broken his heart, by name. Charles passed out of this world on 6 February and was buried on St Valentine's Day, mourned by huge weeping crowds. Charles II was dead. And James was proclaimed king of England, Scotland and Ireland.

Chapter 13

A King of England Too

> To that soft charm, that spell, that magic bough,
> That high enchantment I betake me now:
> And to that hand, the branch of Heaven's fair tree,
> I kneel for help; O! lay that hand on me,
> Adored Caesar! And my faith is such,
> I shall be heal'd, if that my King but touch.
> That evil is not yours: my sorrow sings,
> Mine is the evil, but the cure, the King's.
>
> Robert Herrick, 'To the King, to Cure the Evil', *Hesperides*, 1648

Poor Nelly did not starve. After fifteen minutes of solitary prayer and meditation, James met with his council. As Evelyn tells us, the new king promised clemency and the protection of property, and the maintenance of church and state 'as by law established'. He asked that they be 'good and loyal subjects'.[1] James rapidly honoured his brother's last wish as regards their old companion Nell Gwyn, settling her debts and seeing that she lived comfortably. Louise de Kéroualle also got a generous pension. James was quick to release a number of Quakers from prison, a gesture which solidified his friendship with William Penn.[2] The Quaker leader now became a close advisor to the king. James envisioned his own main agenda for the Three Kingdoms as a fulfilment of Charles's true desires: he would now fully implement the Restoration by bringing in a broad religious toleration. Charles had alluded to such a policy (provisions for 'tender consciences') in the 1660 Declaration of Breda. He had followed up by issuing a Declaration of Indulgence in 1672, only to see his plans trampled by Parliament. James meant to use the royal prerogative to ensure that toleration took hold at last.

He called for the Lords and Commons to convene in three months' time. It would be the first Parliament in four years. In the meantime, James had a coronation to stage. It was to be a double ceremony, the first since his grandparents, James I and VI and Anne of Denmark, were crowned at Windsor Castle in 1603. Anne, a recent Catholic convert, had caused upset by refusing communion that day. One result was that neither Henrietta Maria nor Catherine of Braganza had been crowned at all. James and Mary Beatrice would both abstain from Anglican communion at the ceremony. Apart from that one item, the event was to be traditional in every respect.

James was to be crowned on St George's Day, honouring England's patron saint and dragon-slayer exactly as Charles II had done.[3] On the evening before 23 April 1685, he and Mary Beatrice attended mass as part of a private coronation ceremony officiated by James's Capuchin confessor, Father Mansuete, at Whitehall. The next day the pair rose early. In keeping with tradition, the new queen had the settled the debts of those imprisoned for less than £5, and they were set free. As a tribute to the loving wife who had willingly shared in his tribulations, James had paid a great deal of attention to her queenly regalia. He had new jewel-encrusted consort's crowns and sceptres made to replace those liquidated under Cromwell – one for the moment of consecration at Westminster Abbey, and a second for the procession out to Westminster Hall. Upon glimpsing the newly fashioned crowns, Lady Warwick commented: 'Shee will be all over jewls besides, never was any quene so richly decked.' A Modenese guest observed that in her gold-embroidered robes sewn with jewels and plenty of pearls, the new Queen of England shone like an angel. Some members of the crowd had tears pouring down their faces, he said. Mary Beatrice and James processed separately, each under a silken canopy borne by numerous attendants, to Westminster. Lords and ladies crowded around. 'My dress and royal mantle were covered with precious stones,' Mary Beatrice recalled, 'and it took all the jewels of all the goldsmiths of London could procure to decorate my crown.' She wore a long ermine train. The whole area between abbey and hall was covered in blue carpet, and costumed maidens strew fresh-smelling flowers and herbs there.[4]

Westminster Abbey's chorister Henry Purcell had composed the joyful coronation music. Two songs in particular stand out – 'My Heart Is Inditing' and 'I Was Glad' – both performed by eight voices, accompanied by strings and organ. In Modena, the court heard music written by Giovanni Battista Vitali to honour the occasion. King and queen were liberally anointed on the head and chest; the Archbishop of Canterbury placed a large ruby coronation ring on James's hand. He swore to serve and protect the nation. A Catholic was now head of the episcopal Churches of England, Scotland and Ireland. Aphra Behn's coronation ode emphasised James's long road to the throne: 'Great prince of wonders, and welcome to that throne,/Both your virtues and your sufferings due,/By Heaven and birth-right all your own,/You shared the danger, now share the glory too.' That last line might have been addressed by James to his queen.

King James possessed the traditional understanding of sovereignty – single, visible, personal and accountable.[5] As king, he had a role in shepherding his people to Heaven. In one aspect, however, his was a post-Reformation vision. He intended to course-correct Henry VIII, but not as Henry's daughter Mary I had done. England had changed too much since the sixteenth century to simply return it to Rome overnight. Whatever the Whigs might claim, 'Bloody Mary' still slept soundly in her grave. There were no heretic burnings scheduled at Smithfield post-1685. As a convert himself, King James prized the human conscience and respected its workings. After all, he had arrived at his present position freely. Yes, he was an ardent and convinced Roman Catholic, but he had learned some of the lessons of the turbulent previous century and a half. 'Though he wished all men to be like himself in religion, yet thought it unlawful to force any man much less a whole kingdom to embrace it.'[6] James wished to grant his subjects religious liberty so that they might arrive at the truth in freedom. It was a paradox, but it might just have worked. To that end, he proposed to set his subjects free to practise as they pleased, provided that they did not use religion as a stalking-horse for politics. Admittedly, the previous era had also shown the difficulty of disentangling the two. But he wanted to use his position as monarch to advance this new formula. (Meanwhile, in Holland, John Locke was composing his *Letter on Toleration*. His version of toleration would exclude Catholics entirely.)

King James planned to set a visible example in order to attract the people to his faith. He sought to be a good king, a magnetic one. His efforts echoed those of his father to create a virtuous and beautiful court. Evelyn noted that James wanted to reform 'the former vices & prophaneness of both Court & Country'.[7] Whitehall was now a place where two faiths existed in parallel. Princess Anne had the Chapel Royal, and the king and queen would have a new one. Now the couple would practise more openly. James commissioned Christopher Wren to build him a new chapel at Whitehall, with two life-size kneeling angels, cherubs and saints. The master carver Grinling Gibbons partnered with the Flemish sculptor Arnold Quellin to realise Wren's designs for an altarpiece and intricate reredos. Antonio Verrio painted the chapel ceiling and walls there, at Hampton Court Palace and at Windsor Castle. The king also commissioned the architect James Smith to restore Holyrood Abbey, which was to be re-established as the Chapel Royal.[8] It would provide the setting for an Order of the Thistle revived, the king wrote in 1687, 'to its former lustre, glory and magnificency'. Dedicated to St Andrew, the order had lapsed with the Reformation and aftermath. Now it would flourish once more, giving James a way to reward loyal Scots subjects.

The times were changing, and certain people found it distressing. John Evelyn, for example, seemed incredulous that 'papists' were now out in the open, bold as brass: 'To my grief I saw the new pulpet set up in the popish oratory at Whitehall ... Masse being publiqly saied & the Romanists swarming at court with greater confidence than had ever ben seene in England since the Reformation.'[9] He was anxious that the country would face divine punishment for it. Evelyn was alarmed by evidence that Charles II had embraced the Old Faith on his deathbed. More worrying still, King James's example was making converts in high places. The Poet Laureate was one such: John Dryden soon laid out his position in the remarkable allegorical poem *The Hind and the Panther.* James hoped that Buckingham might follow suit. Hearing in 1687 that this one-time companion was dying, the king sent a priest to his bedside. Buckingham merely mocked the man's arguments.

James and Mary Beatrice fostered a new, rather Italianate musical culture centred on their new chapel. One effect was that Westminster Abbey composer Henry Purcell was somewhat sidelined when it came to sacred music, but he did contribute a 'harpsicall' to James's newly reorganised 'private musick', or chamber orchestra. Among the many performers was the celebrated castrato Francesco Grossi aka Siface. Sent by the Duke of Modena to join James and Mary Beatrice's chapel choir in 1687, Siface was passionately admired in London. On account of the English climate, however, he did not stay long. The singer's departure inspired Purcell to write the plaintive instrumental 'Sefauchi's Farewell'. In the same year, an English delegation to Rome visited the academy of Queen Christina of Sweden to enjoy a concert. Arcangelo Corelli conducted an orchestra, 200-strong, in celebrating the first accession of a Catholic to the English throne since Mary I. The Paquini cantata was set to a poem by Alberto

Guidi in honour of James II and VII. Many Italians felt a deep connection to this king and his Modenese queen consort.[10]

Mary Beatrice took easily to the role. She had always been graceful; now she was stately. She adored her husband and continued to suffer torments because of his attentions to the clever Catherine Sedley. The queen wanted him to choose between the two of them. James, keenly aware of his frailty when it came to other women, was receptive when his priests urged him to set an example and put Catherine away – at least initially. He heard out one of his trusted chaplains, Father Bonaventure Giffard, a man from an old Catholic family whom James particularly trusted because he came of Cavalier stock. His father had been killed early in the English Civil War. Father Giffard wrote that the king had taken his advice 'in a very kindly way' out of deference for his station. Some of the lords chimed in, pressing him to break with his mistress, at which point James remarked ironically that he had not realised they too had joined the priesthood.[11] He then decided that Catherine should go to Ireland for a time. Meanwhile, he continued to keep an apartment in Whitehall for assignations. The conflict between lust and self-discipline raged on.

An election was held in May 1685, with excellent results for the Tories (468 seats, including four in the enemy territory of London). The Whigs got 57. The Tory Party now dominated the Lords and Commons. King James spoke reassuringly to what became known as the Loyalist Parliament.[12] He reiterated his earlier statement: he had no wish to interfere with either his subjects' liberty or their property. Knowing that the opposition were animated by fears dating back to Henry VIII's Dissolution policy, James was careful never to give formerly monastic lands back to Catholics. Mary I herself had been careful to offer protection to those who had bought church properties post-1536, and yet worries persisted. Parliament, reassured, voted James the money he needed in order to govern. Whereas Charles II had shied away from hard work, his brother was as industrious and conscientious as king as he had been in previous roles.

In June, the Duke of Monmouth played his hand. Word reached the king that his nephew had sailed from Rotterdam and landed in Lyme Regis in the West Country with about 100 men. Another nephew, William of Orange, had allowed the rebel to rally his forces in Holland, but had afforded him no aid.[13] For that, they had had to rely upon such strategies as pawning the jewellery of Monmouth's wife and mother-in-law. His mistress, Lady Henrietta

Wentworth, also pawned hers. The Duke of Monmouth, proclaiming himself king and accusing James of having poisoned his brother, raised an army largely composed of untrained peasants wielding scythes, pick-axes and pitchforks. The gentry mostly stayed home. Monmouth's chaplain, Robert Ferguson, whipped up the West Country fighters by appealing to their strongly Roundhead sensibilities. Flowers were scattered at Monmouth's feet at Taunton, and 'twenty Puritan maids' presented him with a Bible and a sword. 'I come to defend the truths defended in this book,' he declared, 'or seal them with my blood!'[14] As there already was a King James, the rebels dubbed their leader 'King Monmouth'. Meanwhile, Archibald Campbell, 9th Earl of Argyll, had landed in Scotland in an effort to trigger a second rebellion, which was swiftly put down. Monmouth emphatically failed to raise Bath: his messenger was slain. With the financial backing of Parliament, King James dispatched John Churchill, Lord Feversham, and an army of redcoats to the West Country. He recalled the Scottish regiment from Holland to join the fight. The Battle of Sedgemoor went badly for Monmouth. Soon he was on the run, disguised as a shepherd and with a price on his head. In the meantime, his supporters faced harsh punishment under five judges who toured the south-west. This came to be known as 'The Bloody Assizes'. Many were executed, and some 850 were transported to the West Indies as slave labour.

The Duke of Monmouth was discovered hiding in a ditch and brought back to London. He wrote frantic apologies to the king. He appealed to James's queen, hoping she would intercede on his behalf. He appealed to Catherine of Braganza, who convinced James to see him. Monmouth then threw himself at the king's feet, begging for his life. He vowed to become a Catholic. He blamed Robert Ferguson, alleging that the chaplain had duped him into revolt and into accusing the king of murder. James wrote to William of Orange that such evasions were unworthy of one who wanted to wear the crown. In any case, Monmouth's time had finally run out. He was condemned to beheading on Tower Hill. The king behaved affectionately to Monmouth's children, however, and saw that his wife, Anne Scott, Duchess of Buccleuch, received his forfeited property. For his part, Monmouth treated his wife frostily when she visited him in prison, reserving his heart for Henrietta Wentworth. He sent her a final memento before setting out for the scaffold. Unfortunately for the beautiful royal bastard, Jack Ketch, the executioner, so botched the job that the onlookers were infuriated. But few were surprised by Monmouth's fate under the circumstances. Samuel Pepys had once opined that this 'skittish leaping gallant' would not be fit for anything.[15] Monmouth had seen some military glory in the past, but had stirred up unrest once too often. After the execution Evelyn wrote that the 36-year-old Monmouth, 'a favourite of the people, of an easy nature, debauched by lust, seduced by crafty knaves ... took this opportunitie of his Majesty being of another Religion, failed of it, and perished.'[16] Rebellion is a harsh territory.

The wayward Duke of Monmouth was dead. King James would inspire much more loyalty in his natural sons by Arabella Churchill, James and Henry FitzJames. The two youths were growing tall, strong and confident. They returned to London shortly after the Monmouth uproar. It was their first visit since James's accession. Paying close attention to their education as always, the king decided they should study with a French master in the art of fortification and other military essentials, such as fencing and riding. Before leaving for Paris, the two paid a visit to their older sister Henrietta, who was cultivating a household of her own since marrying Sir Henry Waldegrave. Their plans were delayed when Henry ('Harry') suffered a riding accident. James sent a messenger with a worried letter ('They say his face will not be marked with it. Pray let me know the truth out, and how soon they think he may be well enough to go. Remember me to your brother James ... and tell Harry I hope he will be carefuller for the time to come.'). After a stint at M. Vaudeuil's academy, young James was sent to Hungary, where he distinguished himself tangling with elite Janissaries at the Siege of Budapest in 1686. (The Pasha summarised the action in this way: 'They came at us like lions, but were received by devils.') An observer reported that 'Mr. FitzJames' behaved 'with remarkable gallantry'.[17]

When the young man returned to England, bringing M. de Vaudeuil along, his proud father made him Duke of Berwick and gave his companion a knighthood. James also appointed his son colonel of Princess Anne's regiment. These honours distressed Mary Beatrice, who had recently had to contend with the ennoblement of Catherine Sedley. The king's acerbic favourite had returned from Ireland, ostensibly to take the waters at Tunbridge Wells. Before long the two had renewed their affair. Evelyn attended 'the creation of Mrs. Sedley, concubine ... to Countess of Dorchester, which 'tis certaine the Queene took grievously ... she hardly ate one morsel, nor spake one word to the King, nor any about her, who at all other times used to be extremely pleasant, full of discourse, & good humour'.[18] Not only that, but James had set Catherine up in Arabella Churchill's former house on St James's Square. It was painful and humiliating for Mary Beatrice to cope with mistresses and to see their offspring being flaunted, especially since she had lost little Isabella and several others. As for Anne and Mary, it was different. They had been there since before her time and she had always embraced them. But the queen longed for children of her own and to give her husband a legitimate son.

To that end, King James and Queen Mary Beatrice made a pilgrimage to the ancient well shrine at Holywell, Wales, in autumn 1687.[19] There they prayed for a son. The site is dedicated to St Winifrede, virgin martyr. The tale goes that a certain Prince Caradoc tried to seduce her. When she spurned him, he had her decapitated. When her head fell to the ground, the sacred spring gushed forth from the earth. Many miraculous healings were associated with the site, and a long line of James's predecessors had visited it over the centuries. He and Mary Beatrice made the pilgrimage as part of the broader re-enchantment intrinsic to the Stuart vision of Restoration. All they had had to do was lift the prohibitions, and the beloved old pagan-tinged customs once listed affectionately by Newcastle – 'May games, Morris dances, the Lords and Ladies of the May, the fool and the hobby-horse' – sprang back up. Simultaneously, from on high, Charles and James re-emphasised abandoned court ceremonials and made generous use of the healing royal touch, distributing gold touch-piece coins embossed with St Michael the Archangel. Now the king was going one step further. He and Mary Beatrice paid for Holywell to be repaired, and James donated a relic to the guardians there – a piece of a dress belonging to his great ancestress, Mary, Queen of Scots. And their prayers were answered. At Christmastime the king announced that Mary Beatrice was pregnant.

Tradition co-existed with innovation under James, as it had done under Charles. Science, 'natural philosophy', was in no way seen as antithetical to religion. Instead, it was believed to deepen the human appreciation of God's creation. For instance, Sir Isaac Newton's *Principia* was published in 1687, laying the basis for classical mechanics. Yet Newton was equally at home analysing *Revelation*. The work of another particularly active member of the Royal Society, Sir William Petty, was of special interest to James. A naval architect as well as an inventor and musician, Petty is one of the originators of laissez-faire economics. The king was keen to adopt his ideas on land registry, a credit bank and coinage reform. Previously a republican, Petty decided that the royal prerogative could be put to good use, saying 'I am starting the world again, and endeavour instead of quarrelling with the King's power shall make use of all he hath for the [use] of his subjects.'[20]

This combination of tradition and innovation also characterised James's defining policy – the Declaration for the Liberty of Conscience of 4 April 1687, which was intended to be read out in churches across the land. A second such document was issued the following year. The king used his prerogative in an effort to solve a persistent problem and establish something new: a broad religious toleration which would overwrite the legacies of Henry VIII *and* Mary I. James's cherished plans aimed at suspending recusancy laws, permitting worship outside the Church of England, and getting rid of the 'test' oaths for holding public office, serving in the military, graduating from university, or indeed living within 10 miles of London. It would go some way to repairing the damage done to Catholics, but would include other minority faiths as well, especially Nonconformist Protestants, but also Jews and, in principle, Muslims and others. Now he sought to prepare the ground for his 'new Magna Carta', as he called the declaration. It was 'another great Charter, to bury all our prejudices, and establish a lasting Civil Union in this great and Ancient Kingdom.' This peace, he argued, would increase the nation's prosperity. James believed that he had a vocation to solve the religious question for his peoples. Leviathan would forge a new kind of unity. Rather than determine the faith of his subjects, as Henry VIII had, the monarch would instead have the role of guaranteeing their liberty of conscience.[21]

Louis XIV had damaged James's position when, in October 1685, he revoked the Edict of Nantes. The French king had used *his* power to outlaw Protestantism in his country, leading to a new influx of zealous French Huguenot refugees into England and the Dutch Republic. There were fears that James would one day copy his cousin and ally. But the reality was that while James might admire Louis' bold exercise of kingly authority, he had too much respect for individual conscience to simply impose Catholicism on everyone. Taking the fatherly tone traditional for monarchs, he stated that he could not 'but heartily wish … that all the people of our dominions were members of the Catholic Church. Yet … conscience ought not to be constrained nor people forced in matters of mere religion.'[22] Again, by 'mere', James meant not 'incidental' but 'pure', *unadulterated* by political content. And yet this was a tall order in a time when sound worship and good government were seen as indivisible. In practice, a broad toleration would have meant that local populations were governed in the main as a 'congregation of congregations'. As for the monarch, he would *propose* Catholicism as the ideal. The new order would leave his subjects at liberty to choose it. It was an innovative vision. The difficulty was, however, that so many Protestants of the British Isles perceived the very existence of Catholicism as a threat to religious liberty by definition.

To promote the policy so dear to his heart, the king sought to solidify his proposed alliance with Protestant dissenters, who came to be known as 'Repealers'. Quakers were especially unhappy with the Test Act because oath-taking was anathema to them. William Penn consulted closely with 'Friend James'. In 1686 James sent William Penn on a Dutch mission to ask William and Mary to assent to the repeal of the recusancy laws and the Test Acts. They agreed to the first item, but not the second.[23] Penn also accompanied James on a tour through the western counties, speaking to local electors. The two were closely aligned intellectually. James trusted Penn enough to leave his comrade's experimental Pennsylvania project out of his plan to consolidate various New England colonies into one dominion under a single governor. The king was satisfied that Pennsylvania religious policy would accommodate Catholics.

As they travelled, they found that certain local people expressed surprise when their 'papist' monarch turned out to be a normal man instead of the hideous monster that fevered pamphleteers had led them to expect. In Chester, the king engaged in a public discussion with a Whig MP, Sir William Williams. In defence of toleration, James appealed to the kind of justice and liberality upon which Englishmen prided themselves. As a member of the audience noted, the king remarked that 'we had as little reason to quarrel with other men for being of different opinions as for being of different complexions.' It is a striking analogy – not perfect, since opinions change more readily than complexions. James meant to emphasise that conscience is intrinsic to the human person, and 'he was sure no Englishman could desire to see others persecuted for differences of opinion.' Furthermore, 'the King said he hoped we would join with him in making a Magna Carta for conscience as well as properties and other liberties,' and 'he was sure no man should be debarred of either while he lived.'[24] Essentially, he was arguing that religious intolerance was un-English. In his appeal to English liberality of spirit, James was building upon the home-grown political tradition in order to advance his core vision. It was a strategy calculated to appeal across the board.

The rub was this: in appealing to the Protestant dissenters, James risked alienating his Tory base, a group that had originally formed to support him. The 'church party' had affirmed the Duke of York's right to succeed to the throne despite his conversion. Once James became king, Tory MPs had voted him the money he needed. Now, it seemed, he was asking them to saw off the branch they were sitting upon. This new toleration would effectively disestablish the Church of England – not abolish it, but deprive it, the majority denomination, of special status. It would become just one church amongst many. Directed to read out the declaration from their pulpits, a great many Anglican clerics refused, saying that it would let in any manner of sect. Seven key bishops defied the king, refusing to have the document read out in their churches. They distributed a printed petition to the king, essentially accusing him of acting outside the law. For the first time, a cleavage appeared between James and the Tory Party that had formed around him. Those who stood with him would eventually be known as 'Jacobites' after *Jacobus*, the Latin word for James.

Events were dovetailing rapidly. James, infuriated, had the seven bishops arrested for libel and sent to the Tower of London to await trial. Meanwhile, Mary Beatrice's pregnancy was advancing. Its significance was apparent. As long as James had only Protestant heirs, his reign might be nothing more than a temporary exception; his religion was a private matter. The Princess of Orange would succeed, and if she remained childless, Anne would come next. With the support of figures like the enterprising Sarah Churchill, now her Groom of the Stool, Princess Anne was very deliberately presenting her court as a rival alternative. Sarah wrote that Anne, having heard anti-'popery' sermons in her chapel and other churches she visited, was aware of rising tensions. 'God be thanked,' Anne wrote to Mary in 1686, 'we were not bred up in that communion, but are of a church that is pious and sincere, and conformable in all its principles to the Scriptures.'[25] She remained vigilant against any effort to convert her, writing, 'I expect it any minute, and am resolved to undergo anything rather than change my religion.' However, she freely admitted that her father had 'used no harshness with her' in his efforts to win her over. He had sent only a reading list featuring Peter Heylin and her own mother 'had she any inclination that way'.

Both daughters were married and considered likely to produce children. But if Mary Beatrice gave birth to a son, that prince's claim would trump those of 'the daughters of York'. Anne's hopes of becoming queen would be dashed. It was apparent, moreover, that any such child would be raised in the Old Faith. England would have a Catholic dynasty once more. It was another reason to worry for the fate of Anglicanism – and another reason for Anne to present herself as the saviour of that tradition. Unlike her Whiggish friend Sarah, Princess Anne was a Tory. 'It is a melancholy prospect that all we of the Church of England have,' she wrote. 'Everyone has the free exercise of their religion, on purpose no doubt to ruin us.'[26]

Added to that, James was using his prerogative to appoint various Catholics to high positions, including at Magdalen College, Oxford. He did this, in part, because he wanted loyal people in key spots. More than that, though, he believed it was a matter of justice. Recusants had lost much over the years in terms of position, property, and liberty – in part due to the Whigs' focus on him. James believed that he was obliged to right the scales. But some grumbled that one had to turn papist to gain favour in this court. 'As things were carried on by King James,' Sarah Churchill opined, 'everybody sooner or later must be ruined, who would not become a Roman Catholick.'[27] There were quite a few high-level conversions, such as the Drummond brothers in Scotland. In a move that made many nervous, the king appointed the Jesuit Father Edward Petre to his Privy Council.

Little did James know that his daughters were gossiping behind his back about Mary Beatrice's pregnancy. It was in their interest to cast aspersions, and indeed to believe the worst of their father and stepmother – and that is what they did. Unfortunately, much of the public were prone to whispering of dark Jesuitical schemes, so these rumours were rapidly amplified. Now that her cousin Monmouth was dead and gone, the Princess of Orange was keeping company with Gilbert Burnet, the Whig Bishop of Rochester, who had gone into exile after the discovery of the Rye House Plot. She went so far as to employ her father's enemy as a personal chaplain. Burnet, always willing to believe the worst of 'papists', turned her against James. So when Anne wrote to Mary, hinting that their loving stepmother might be faking her condition in order to bring in 'popery', she nodded along gravely. Both ladies claimed to be sceptical that Mary Beatrice was truly expecting a child. Either their stepmother lacked the proper confidence that she was pregnant, or she was too confident: everything raised suspicion in their willing minds. Anne had developed a disdain for Mary Beatrice. She accused the queen of haughtiness and secret bigotry: 'She pretends to have a great deal of kindness for me, but I doubt it is not real, for I never see proof of it.' Writing ominously of court Catholics, she claimed that 'they will stick at nothing, be it ever so wicked, if it will promote their interest … there may be foul play intended.' Anne assured Mary that she would investigate further.[28] On 20 March, the princess wrote that she suspected 'a false belly', essentially because Mary Beatrice retreated to her chamber instead of offering her torso to be felt. Thanks in large part to Anne, the Whig rumour machine, built up with the Popish Plot hoax, swung back into action. The story grew and then billowed thoroughly out of control.

Chapter 14

Another Exile

Goneril. As much as child e'er loved, or father found;
A love that makes breath poor and speech unable;
Beyond all manner of so much I love you.

Shakespeare, *King Lear,* 1.i.

Just as Mary Beatrice was going into labour, the seven defiant bishops were acquitted by a London jury, and there were jubilant public demonstrations. Evelyn describes 'infinite crowds of people on their knees, beging their blessing & praying for them as they passed'.[1] And shortly afterwards, on 10 June 1688, Prince James Francis Edward of Wales was born at Whitehall Palace. For the first time in English history, the birth of a princeling, instead of securing a dynasty, toppled it. The queen's bedchamber was even more crowded than was usual at royal births. When King James had learned of the rumours concerning his wife's condition, he was incredulous. The story ran that the pregnancy was fake, that a suppositious child would be magicked into its place. A sincere, honourable and straightforward man, James struggled to grasp the import of these tales. But once the king understood what he was being accused of – plotting to pass off a mystery infant as the Prince of Wales – he invited a range of Whigs and Tories to witness the lying-in. Poor Mary Beatrice was humiliated at having to give birth under a microscope. The back of the bed was curtained, but the sides were open. She asked the king to conceal her face with his periwig, 'for she said she could not be brought to bed and have so many men look on her'.[2]

A certain number insisted on turning their backs to the bed so they could not be called on to testify. Sidney Godolphin, fence-sitting, later claimed he was too far away to see anything. As for Princess Anne, she happened to be taking the waters at Bath when her half-brother was born, recuperating from one of her many miscarriages. 'I shall never now be satisfied,' she wrote to

Mary, 'whether the child be true or false. It may be it is our brother, but God only knows.'[3] Both daughters of York preferred to leave the matter obscure. Before, during, and after the prince's birth, interested propagandists clouded his whole existence with mystery. Either, they claimed, the pregnancy had been faked; alternatively, the child had died and an impostor was supplied by shadowy entities. Because the boy's very being was deeply inconvenient for the king's enemies, they redefined him as a changeling, a weird fairy child. He was not murdered like poor Cesarion or the little Princes in the Tower – his father made sure of that. Instead, however, the brand new Prince of Wales was rendered uncanny in the public mind.

King James stayed up all night in tearful thanksgiving.[4] Outside, the birth celebrations, bonfires and fireworks mingled with chorusing cheers at the bishops' acquittal. The effect was unsettling. Nonetheless, it had been a few years since Mary Beatrice had last given James a child, and the king was thrilled. At 55, he had a new son to continue the Stuart line. Prince James Francis Edward of Wales was an appealing baby, with the brown eyes and very dark hair that would win him the nickname 'Blackbird'. He resembled his mother and his Uncle Charles. The anxious court doctors tried the tiny prince on a complicated diet which made him unwell. 'I believe it will not be long before he is an Angel in Heaven,' wrote Anne.[5] Once his father insisted he be given a wet nurse, he rallied. All was well.[6] Catherine, the Queen Dowager, was named godmother. Meanwhile, William's camp hailed down hostile pamphlets, pictures and even floor plans alleging an intricate Jesuitical scheme. Faced with claims that the baby had been spirited into the queen's bed in a copper warming pan, the palace fought back with material celebrating the birth with odes and fireworks. Aphra Behn composed two celebratory poems to welcome the child. One read in part 'O happy King! To whom a son is born/What more can Fortune, Heaven, and you perform?/Behold, with joy three prostrate Nations come/Albion, Hibernia, and old Calendon/Now join their in'trests, and no more dispute/With saucy murmurs, who is absolute.' Various portraits of Prince James Edward were produced, including one by Sir Godfrey Kneller showing the infant in velvet robes. Kneller later asserted to one gossipy gentleman that the baby was no changeling. 'His father and his mother have sat for me about thirty-six times apiece, and I know every line and bit in their faces,' the painter averred. 'I say the child is so like them both that there is not a feature in his face but what belongs to father or mother.'[7] In addition to paintings, there were black and white depictions of Mary Beatrice and her little son which could be printed and circulated widely. Some of these were then ruthlessly parodied. The satirical habit of mind which typified eighteenth-century England was already in evidence in 1688. Mockery was an invaluable tool when it came to delegitimising the ancient royal line in general and also James in particular. His earnestness when it came to religion was already out of fashion in certain high-born circles. The response of such people was to sneer at his ideas and his newborn son out of existence. If laughter failed, they could always mine a deep seam of anti-Catholicism in the populace.

Against the backdrop of momentous events that month, a massive test of allegiance was unfolding, dividing the nation's elite in two. On the one hand stood subjects like Sarah and John Churchill. They owed their advancement to King James, and they were also indebted to Queen Mary Beatrice. But they belonged to the household of Princess Anne, who, with the coaxing of her great favourite, was emerging as a distinct player in her own right – or possibly Sarah's. Gilbert Burnet, for one, believed that Sarah was Anne's mistress, and not the reverse. Sarah's own words confirm it. 'I could not endure for her to do any thing, which I would not have done in her place,' she wrote of Anne.[8] The Churchills saw themselves as rarities in an increasingly Catholic court. Sarah, in particular, doubted that they could rise much further, and this turned them against their old master. The coveted post of Governor of Portsmouth had gone to James FitzJames, now Duke of Berwick, instead of Churchill. Adherents of the Old Faith had gained lost ground – and any amount of favour shown to them was too much for many people. Resentment brewed in the Churchills' hearts. (Meanwhile, life for Berwick was not so easy as they imagined. King James tried to marry the son he so treasured to Lady Margaret Cavendish, heiress of the Duke of Newcastle. But she sent him packing. No 'papist' and 'bastard' was acceptable to her.[9])

The Churchills' opposite number were Sarah's sister Frances and her husband Richard Talbot, now elevated to Earl of the ancient Gaelic realm of Tyrconnell. The man who had once volunteered to assassinate Oliver Cromwell had just been appointed Lord Deputy of Ireland. Like her husband, Frances Talbot was loyal to James. She was one of the official witnesses to the prince's birth. Tyrconnell's latest act of allegiance had been to warn the king of a Dutch plot to dethrone him. Like Sarah, Frances was a natural politician; like Tyrconnell, she was a strong Catholic, having converted in

France. According to Sarah, her brother-in-law had made efforts to bring her over to the faith that she charged with 'cheats and nonsense'. Tyrconnell was a faithful friend to James, but his Irish policies angered Protestants. He was pushing hard for the liberties of the Catholic majority in Ireland, a group made up of native Irish as well as 'Old English', whose ancestors had arrived in Ireland with the Norman conquerors. Tyrconnell restored to Catholics the right to worship freely and to hold office. He also sought to take back lands recently granted to English and Scottish settlers and restore them to their previous owners. He was therefore hugely distrusted by Protestants. James had been careful to avoid any interference with property in England, and any hint that lands acquired with the Reformation might be in play. Whatever the justice of the Irish situation, Tyrconnell's rapidly advancing redistribution policy had the potential to shake James's rule.[10]

Perceiving that his new coalition and very throne were in jeopardy, James grew more and more distressed. The king's letters to the Princess of Orange grew more urgent. 'Although I know you are a good wife, and ought to be so, yet for the same reason I must believe you will be still as good a daughter to a father that has always loved you so tenderly, and has never done the least thing to make you doubt it.'[11] In October James tried to shore up his position by assembling the Privy Council and compiling forty-one witness statements as to the birth of his son. He invited Anne, who demurred, saying it was unnecessary. In the meantime, she kept up her campaign of rumour-mongering. The facts were immaterial to people who had already decided that England had to be safe from 'Popery', even if it meant disrupting the royal line.

A small group of moguls, known to sympathetic historians as 'the Immortal Seven', had already secretly written to William of Orange asking him to invade England in the name of Protestantism. A plan was afoot moreover to commit the nation to the burgeoning Dutch financial model, which would entail the creation of the Bank of England in the City of London, a national debt and currency reform. As the signatories included a couple of Tories as well as Whigs, William could claim support from both parties. Sarah Churchill asserted that the Prince of Orange was invited to 'oblige King James to keep the laws of this country' – not usurp the throne for himself. In this way, she fended off the appearance of treachery. William was invited only as a kind of regent, since James was 'not to be trusted with the liberties of England.'[12] John Churchill kept in close touch with the

Hague, letting William know through an English envoy that he was ready to usher him in.

On the redolent date of 5 November, William of Orange mounted the largest invasion of England since 1066. His armada rivalled that of William the Conqueror. His 14,000 men came ashore at Torbay just as the English populace were gathering round their annual bonfires to burn Guy Fawkes and the Pope in effigy, chanting 'gunpowder, treason and plot.' To prepare the ground for his invasion, the Prince of Orange drew on the resources of the dissenting community assembled in Holland, their printing presses, in particular. Prominent among William's supporters were Rye House Plot refugees like John Hampden and, indeed, Mary's chaplain, Gilbert 'Tartuffe' Burnet, so called for his great shows of pious virtue. The philosopher John Locke was another Whig exile poised to return in William's wake. They issued a blizzard of anti-'Popery' pamphlets, prints and medals. In fact, it was Hampden who first used the term 'Glorious Revolution'.

Anti-government tracts were read aloud in coffee houses, where Whiggish opinion was formed.[13] (Jacobites tended to congregate in chocolate houses.) A new Bloody Mary was about to rampage through England, the revolutionaries heard. Any day now, went the claim, King James would drop the mask of tolerance and attack the Protestant population. Of particular note was the manifesto Burnet had composed for William laying out 'Five Reasons' for a Dutch invasion. As was customary, much of the blame was laid at the feet of scheming 'evil counsellors', the Jesuit Father Petre in particular, for leading the king astray. (Evelyn maintained that the king's intentions had been 'perverted by Jesuits'.) William referred to Prince James Francis as 'the pretended Prince of Wales' – a term that would stick. He would see that 'a free and lawful Parliament' assembled. James, for his part, promised to call one as soon as William had departed, 'for how is it possible a parliament can be free in all its circumstances, as you petition for, whilst an enemy is in the kingdom?'[14] William was depicted by revolutionary propagandists as tall, handsome and supremely indifferent to becoming king. His Protestantism apparently made him more English than the king himself. He claimed to be coming to the rescue of the nation on behalf of his wife. In reality, William of Orange's chief goal was to mobilise England's considerable resources against his great enemy, France. James, he felt, was much too friendly to Louis XIV. This was his chance to shift the balance of power.

Ultimately, the 'Glorious Revolution' narrative amounted to an ink-cloud shot out to obscure the reality of a coup d'état. Neither was it a bloodless one, especially not in Ireland and Scotland. Before he left Mary in Holland, William told her that if he died in battle, she had his permission to remarry – although he drew the line at a papist. According to Burnet, Mary did not like to hurt her father. And yet she was committed to doing so. 'She had no scruple as to the lawfulness of the design,' he tells us.[15] Anything was permissible when a throne was at stake. With the financial backing of an Amsterdam banker named Francisco Lopes Suasso, who cheerfully loaned him 2 million guilders without collateral, William raised an army and crossed the Channel. 'If thou art victorious, I know thou wilt return them to me,' Lopes Suasso told the Prince of Orange. 'Art thou not victorious, I agree to having lost them.'[16]

Naturally enough, King James was horrified by the news that his nephew had landed at Brixham at the head of 14,000 Dutch and mercenary troops. But it was the conduct of his daughters, and of his long-time protégé John Churchill, that truly broke his spirit. The famously affectionate father hated being pitted against his beloved daughter Mary, who, for the moment, still hung back in the Netherlands. Anne, who had learned from Mary that William planned to invade, was encouraged by the Churchills to make him her ally. Welcoming the interloper with a friendly letter, she made plans to join him. Meanwhile, the valiant Irishman Patrick Sarsfield led troops into a skirmish with Williamite forces in Wincanton, Somerset.[17] At Reading, Sarsfield's clash with the Dutch was undermined by townsfolk frightened by rumours of murderous Irishmen. James did have his champions, but the treachery of close companions like John Churchill robbed the king of the confidence he needed to resist William of Orange. On 24 November the king realised that the young man he had fostered had ridden out of the royal camp with a huge entourage and joined the enemy. Churchill left a letter of self-justification, assuring the king he was moved by only the highest of principles. Prince George followed suit shortly afterwards.

Although certain aides begged the king to fight, he refused. If someone like Churchill, who owed him so much, could abscond, then no one could be trusted. He knew from experience that the fealty of officers is essential, and it seemed to him that the ground was giving way beneath his feet. Nothing was solid. Especially for a man who loved certainty, this was intolerable. Suffering from sleeplessness and nosebleeds, he was loath to risk the lives of troops in such uncertain circumstances.[18] Especially daunting was the prospect of reprising civil war on English soil. James was haunted by that conflict. Those old tensions had re-emerged, but in slightly different form. The king could not help but distrust the heirs of the Roundheads. Ever aware of his father's grim fate, James resolved to stay out of their hands altogether this time. Even if Parliament did not kill him, they would attempt to impose a regency, and he found that repugnant. He would not submit to that.

He ordered that Sarah Churchill be confined to the Cockpit at Whitehall. Once she and Anne learned of their husbands' defections, however, they fled the palace through a back staircase and into the protection of Bishop Compton, who had a hackney cab waiting in the darkness. According to Sarah, Anne would have sooner jumped out of a window than face her father at this time. When the serving-woman discovered Anne's bed had not been slept in, she muddied the waters by screaming, 'The Papists have murdered the Princess!' Soon enough it became clear what had actually occurred. When James learned how thoroughly his cherished daughter had betrayed him, he cried out in pain like a latter-day King Lear, 'God help me! Even my children have forsaken me in my distress.' James would never lay eyes on his Goneril or Regan again.

Even Charles I had not had to endure this species of disappointment. James's father had lost countless old friends in the clash of Royalists and Parliamentarians. His nephew Prince Charles Louis had displayed Roundhead sympathies. But his children had remained true to him. James himself had cut his teeth in his father's service and refused to allow the enemy to use him in any way. In fact, he had first fled captivity in England to stop Parliament trying to make a 'pocket-king' of him. Even in a world ordered around personal loyalty, James stood out. Unfortunately, he often found other people opaque, and was taken unawares when they let him down. He had been a remarkably affectionate, engaged and reliable father to Mary and Anne. And yet, to his humiliation, they had conspired against him and their stepmother. Finally, they had revealed themselves in discarding him. Their mutiny made his other subjects much more inclined to jump ship. Then there was the matter of John Churchill, whom he had kept by him for so long. These treacheries were difficult to swallow.

Others came through for him. The 18-year-old James FitzJames, now Duke of Berwick, was totally reliable. Berwick now headed the troop of Life Guards abandoned by his faithless uncle, Churchill. He had the support of certain Tory men such as Edward Henry Lee, 1st Earl of Lichfield, who had been a constant husband to favourite niece, Charlotte. And the queen was as devoted as ever. Although a large part of the aristocracy turned on him, ordinary soldiers tended to rally behind him. But King James had decided to leave the country, an eccentric move in the eyes of many. When we consider that he felt the ground was crumbling beneath his feet, however, it is more understandable. It was not the Williamite forces that alarmed him, but the treachery, the slipping away, of elites in his own ranks. Ultimately, it was only by leaving the country that King James regained trust in his entourage. His departure compelled people to reveal their true commitments. If they left England and went abroad – as many Cavaliers had done in the 1640s and 1650s – then they must be true. At least in exile, James would be able to depend on those around him. Unfortunately, though, his absence created a power vacuum which would be filled by William and Mary.

James first ensured the safety of his queen and their infant prince. He arranged their escape to France on 18 December. (As for his mistress Catherine Sedley, she remained in England. Her long-time lover had ensured she would receive income from lands.) Mary Beatrice and tiny James Francis were accompanied by William Herbert, Marquis of Powis, one of the Five Lords whom Titus Oates had landed in the Tower. Powis's courageous wife Elizabeth was also on hand to act as governess. A few days later and with William's full knowledge, James attempted to follow them. Famously, he heaved the Great Seal into the Thames as he rode out of the capital. More indignities were in store for the beleaguered king. Once again, he was fleeing his native country in disguise. This time, instead of female attire, he wore a short black wig and a patch on his upper lip. James boarded a small vessel on the Kentish coast and waited for the tide to turn. Some seamen, looking for priests, boarded and detained him. Practically strip-searching him, they confiscated an enamelled gold crucifix containing a sliver of the True Cross, one of the king's most prized possessions. The mariners did not at first understand what manner of being was tangled in their net. Assuming he was a Jesuit, they brought him back to London, seeking a reward. Once James was recognised, they veered to claiming that they had been 'guarding him from harm'.[19] The Tories among the populace lit bonfires to celebrate the king's return and acclaimed him. James was moved by this. At the same time, he knew from long experience that popular sentiment is fickle and could not bear the uncertainty. He feared that he was reliving his father's last days. With Dutch soldiers posted all around his lodgings, he suspected that he would be murdered outright or sent to the

Tower, never to emerge. William pushed James to depart a second time, imprisoning the royal envoy Lord Feversham and sending a messenger to rouse the king in the dead of night. James, harried and stressed, wrote a letter explaining his decision. It was to be published after his departure. And then he was gone. Happily, the gallant Berwick was in his entourage. Father and son shared a narrow cabin on the boat to France. They had a rueful laugh over the captain's struggles to prepare their modest meal of bacon in a damaged pan. Berwick's company was a great relief to James.[20] As ever, he was at ease in straitened circumstances. At least he was in faithful company.

On Christmas Day the exiled king and his little company heard mass at Ambleteuse, near Calais. Once it became clear that the king had truly left London, Princess Anne and Sarah Churchill, cheerfully sporting orange ribbons, appropriated one of James's grandest carriages and rolled off to the theatre. Meanwhile, Whiggish London mobs were attacking any and all Catholic chapels, including that of the Spanish ambassador, throughout the town. A shaken James voyaged to Versailles, where he was welcomed by Louis XIV. History was once again showing its tendency to rhyme. The first cousins had been close since the late 1640s, when the Stuarts had last been forced into exile. Charles II had mostly favoured France over Holland. James too favoured France, although he had tried to carve out a contrasting religious policy. Fortunately, Louis welcomed the deposed king and his English, Scottish and Irish followers. Protestants were gathered in along with Catholics, although Louis stipulated that they would have to practise privately. The French king offered his cousin a generous pension and the use of a château he already knew well from a previous exile. James was housed at St Germain-en-Laye, a few miles from the Sun King's extraordinary new palace. St Germain-en-Laye, which had been Louis XIV's main residence from 1666–1682, was not large enough to accommodate all the members of this court-in-exile. Many followers had to obtain homes nearby. It was the beginning of a distinct Jacobite community, one which would develop over generations.[21]

The letter King James wrote to his people, dated 22 December 1688, was considered by the Lords when they assembled at Westminster on Christmas Eve. William of Orange, he indicates, had 'casted the greatest aspersion upon me that malice could invent in the clause of it which concerns my son.' He shows an awareness of the techniques employed to de-legitimise him and his line. The Prince of Orange had 'by all arts taken such pains to make me appear black as hell to my own people as well as to all the world besides.' This had produced the 'great defection in the army' that had so dismayed him. 'I was born free and desire to continue so,' he writes. 'I have ventured my life for the good and honour of my country on several occasions, and am as free to do it again (as old as I am) to redeem it from the slavery it is like to fall under.' After all, the country had just been invaded by a foreign power, even if Mary was providing a fig-leaf. The king concludes by once again emphasising liberty of conscience. Nothing, he argues, was so likely to produce a great and flourishing nation. 'Some of our neighbours dread it,' he adds.[22] James hoped that his people would come to their senses and restore him, as they had his brother.

The rover king's Tory brother-in-law, Henry Hyde, 2nd Earl of Clarendon, moved that the letter be read to the assembly, and the Earl of Lindsay seconded him. After debate the Lords voted the motion down, effectively suppressing James's communication to the English people. When the Convention Parliament later debated a pronouncement that James had vacated the throne, Clarendon opposed it; he was now a Jacobite. He was among those who refused to take an oath to the new regime. Dutch troops were stationed in the chamber when the assembly voted to make William and Mary joint monarchs. The vote passed the Commons, but was held up in the Lords. The final vote was close: 55 to 41 against James.[23] As a result, just as King James and his predecessors had always feared, the English monarchy now became in effect elective. Parliament next gave William his heart's desire by declaring war on France.

The Churchills had rolled out the red carpet for William and Mary. John was rewarded with the title Earl of Marlborough, while Prince George became Duke of Cumberland. Sarah grew more influential than ever. Still, both John and Sarah exhibited great ambivalence about the new order of things. He soon begin hedging his bets, remaining so closely in touch with his former master that he was eventually arrested, suspected of Jacobitism. His wife, meanwhile, corresponded with her Jacobite sister Frances. Sarah was full of complaints about England's new king and queen, accusing various people of 'ingratitude', and turning Anne against her sister. When Mary arrived at Whitehall on 13 February, Sarah accused her of treating the palace like a hotel and generally failing to show proper regret at having deposed her own father. 'She ran about it, looking into every closet and conveniency, and turning up quilts of beds, just as people do at an inn.'[24] Sarah was not alone in this opinion. Many other people thought that Mary's behaviour lacked the proper gravity. William of Orange may have been at fault here, as he had advised his wife to seem serene, as though nothing should seem amiss in their conduct. In any case, she struck the wrong note. As John Evelyn remarked, 'It was believed that they both, especially the Princesse, would have shewed some (seeming) reluctancy at least, of assuming her Father's Crowne & made some Apologie, testifying her regret … which would have shewed … that there was no intention of deposing the King, but of Succouring the Nation. But nothing of this appeared, she came into Whitehall as to a Wedding, riant & jolly.' Then, Evelyn noted, Mary sat down in her stepmother's chair '& played at Basset, just as her predecessor used to do.'[25] It was all rather sordid.

Mary failed to put the sort of dignified and flattering gloss on the revolution that would absolve James's subjects of betrayal. 'For whatever necessity there was of disposing of King James,' Sarah opined, 'he was still her father, who had been so lately driven from that chamber. She should have at least have looked pensive at so melancholy a reverse of his fortune.'[26]

On 13 February William and Mary appeared at the Banqueting House, the scene of their grandfather's execution and their uncle's Restoration, to sign the declaration that cast James aside and made them joint monarchs. Parliament had decided that by withdrawing, King James had effectively abdicated – never mind that his letter of explanation had been suppressed.[27] A commemorative medal was struck. It showed Jove (William) flinging a thunderbolt at Phaeton (James), who had flown his chariot too close to the sun. Sarah Churchill, for one, failed to see such glory in her new ruler. She had come up with another unpleasant nickname for him. Not content with whispering 'Caliban' behind his back, she now dubbed him 'the Dutch abortion' as well. Sarah sniped continually about the new settlement, which she perceived as unfair to Anne. William and Mary were joint monarchs, much as Mary I and Philip of Spain had been. In the latter case, however, not only was the Dutch Stadtholder crowned alongside his English wife, but he would also rule. William was adamant that he had not, as he said, 'gone over to England to be his wife's gentleman usher.' Unlike her Tudor predecessor, this Mary had no objection. 'My opinion has ever been that women should not meddle in government,' she stated.[28] She further agreed that her husband would reign over the Three Kingdoms for life. If Mary died first, William would remain monarch. Anne would have to wait until he expired to assume the throne, and that was providing that William and Mary produced no children. In part because of this, the two sisters fell out spectacularly, remaining at odds for the remainder of Mary's life. So corroded was this relationship that their usurped father became concerned about it.

Sacred monarchy had never truly recovered from the execution of Charles I. With William of Orange, it suffered further erosion. William himself was impatient with much of the ceremony surrounding English kingship. A strict Calvinist from a quasi-republican land, he rolled his eyes at the prospect of anointment. The Bishop of London performed the joint crowning of William and Mary because the Archbishop of Canterbury, William Sancroft, numbered among a growing group known as the 'Non-jurors'. These were men and women who refused to take an oath to the new rulers. Ironically, Sancroft was the most prominent among the clerics who had refused to have James's Declaration of Liberty of Conscience read aloud in parish churches. Although his protest had helped to bring James down, he still considered the man to be king. Archbishop Sancroft was a man of principled stands. He had crowned James and Mary Beatrice; he could not bring himself to crown his usurpers. That would make a mockery of oaths, he believed. Five of the other seven bishops followed suit, as did 400 clergymen. Sancroft would lose his position, and go on to contribute to the 'Non-juring Schism' by consecrating Nonjuring Anglican bishops. A number of courtiers followed suit. For example, Heneage Finch and his poetess wife Anne abjured the oath, lost their positions and were forced into internal exile.

William III oversaw a disenchantment of the English monarchy. His camp's mocking attacks on James's aura of legitimacy helped depose that king, but also weakened the institution. William broke with tradition, refusing for instance to 'touch for the King's Evil'. The afflicted waited in vain for the monarch to lay hands on them and distribute gold 'angel' coins. In most respects, his style of kingship pleased the Whiggish community that he had sheltered in the Netherlands. They were now back in force. Along with them came a crowd of Dutch bankers, merchants and courtiers: a new ethos. John Locke's political philosophy informed the 1689 Bill of Rights. The document confirmed Parliamentary sovereignty and a newly contractual view of government. It was also wildly anti-Catholic. In defiance of James, Parliament signed off on a Locke-inspired toleration policy which excluded the Old Faith altogether. All dissenting groups *except* Catholics would now be permitted to practise freely. The revolutionaries rejected the idea that Catholicism could co-exist with reformers, an arrangement that had been trialled in Maryland until neighbouring Puritans put a violent stop to it. For the first time, Catholics were explicitly banned from coming to the throne. Further, no monarch would be permitted to marry into the Old Faith. The right to bear arms was codified, its purpose to arm Protestants exclusively in case of a 'popish' uprising.

King James's dream of a wide-ranging toleration was dead and 'Monarchy itself ... grievously plumed'.[29] His new dissident coalition was shattered. The Tories, his former supporters, had retained their church's position but sacrificed their defining principle of legitimist monarchy. Many retained strongly Jacobite sympathies. In return for their sacrifice, they spent a century in the shade. For the Whigs would dominate eighteenth-century politics.

Chapter 15

The Jacobite Peerage

> We believe in God that was crowned with thorns. Shall we abide to tread on nothing but roses?
>
> James II and VII, *Meditations*

The Churchills had let James down in spectacular fashion, but the Talbots stood by him. Tyrconnell wrote to his old comrade from his viceregal court at Dublin Castle. There the beautiful Frances was vicereine, outdoing her sister and rival, Sarah. Tyrconnell encouraged the fugitive Stuart king to join them there. In Scotland there was spirited resistance from John Graham of Claverhouse ('Bonnie Dundee'), who raised the Stuart standard and fought Williamite forces. Ultimately, though, the revolutionary regime had prevailed in Scotland, and a 'giddy multitude and enthusiasticall mob' destroyed James's newly restored abbey church at Holyrood.[1] The Melfort brothers and other Scottish Jacobites fled to Saint-Germain. But Ireland was a different story. 'You may possess a kingdom of your own, with all plentifull of all things for human life,' Tyrconnell urged his master at St Germain-en-Laye.[2] Ireland was a much smaller and more modest realm than England, but the vast majority of the population were Jacobite; the Irish Parliament would rally behind the true king. James had the allegiance of the native Irish and the highly influential Old English. He also commanded a shard of the Church of Ireland – although the remainder of the Protestant minority were fiercely Williamite, particularly in Ulster. Catholics and Protestants alike were vigilant, both groups having experienced all-out massacres in living memory. Ireland was perilous politically. But if the Stuart king came there, he might use it as a base to win back his lost dominions. Mary Beatrice and James Francis would be safe at their St Germain-en-Laye haven. Both King James and Louis XIV were clothed in violet, mourning the death of their niece, Marie Louise of Orléans, Queen of Spain. Mary

Beatrice's melancholy-tinged elegance was winning much admiration in France. Many courtiers familiar from home – English, Scottish and Irish-- were assembling around her. The denizens of Versailles were attracted to the new court forming at the nearby château.[3] Confident he was leaving his family in good hands, King James departed. Passing through Paris, he visited an English convent, where he touched for the King's Evil. He also visited the Chaillot nunnery his mother had founded; her heart was enshrined there. James then set sail for Ireland, landing at Kinsale in March 1689. At Cork he was welcomed by his old comrade-in-arms, Dick Talbot. One of James's first acts in Ireland was to raise him from Earl to Duke of Tyrconnell. Together, on 3 April, they made a triumphal entrance into Dublin. James II and VII was the first English monarch to visit Ireland since Richard II in 1399. As the Stuarts had commanded the hearts of the majority since at least the civil wars, he was made welcome.

He remained for over a year. Presiding over the Irish Parliament, the king tried to parse various sympathies. Nationality and religion intersected in an increasingly complex fashion. James was passionately Catholic, but also a deeply patriotic Englishman – so much so that he could not help cheering English soldiers and seamen, even when they were arrayed against his cause. (After all, he had personally built up England's army and navy.) He wanted to advance liberties for the Irish majority, but at the same time he desired to protect the interests of English and Scottish Protestant groups in Ireland. Moreover, he had to consider how his policies would play out in England and Scotland. Some grumbled at it. 'He is too English for him to agree to anything which could displease the English,' wrote d'Avaux, the French ambassador to the Jacobite court in Ireland.[4]

Unsurprisingly, James's presence in Ireland greatly disturbed England's new rulers. William was not especially keen to fight this question out in person, preferring to concentrate on battling France. Having received appeals from the Scots-Irish Presbyterians, however, he decided it was necessary to sail west. Skirmishes had been kicking off between Protestant militia and the Irish Army, loyal to James. When campaigning weather returned, the Prince of Orange landed in Ireland with 15,000 soldiers, with Danish and Huguenot regiments in addition to the Dutch ones.[5] John Churchill, now Earl of Marlborough, was left in charge of the English Army. He was also supposed to advise Mary. She rejected the appointment: 'I can neither trust or esteem him,' she informed William. Departing for

Ireland, Marlborough campaigned effectively to cut off Jacobite supply lines. Through the looking-glass was his nephew Berwick, fighting hard on his father's behalf. As for King James himself, his old decisiveness had ebbed away, and he got bogged down in detail.[6] That series of personal betrayals in England had weakened and disoriented him.

'The War of the Two Kings' would change Ireland forever. Its consequences are still felt today, particularly in Northern Ireland. The Jacobites faltered, losing the Battle of the Boyne. Tyrconnell urged King James to elude capture, for he would not be safe in enemy hands. James retreated. A probably apocryphal tale has him reaching the home of Frances, now Duchess of Tyrconnell, and remarking to her, 'Your countrymen, Madam, can run well.' 'Not quite so well as your Majesty,' she is supposed to have replied, 'for I see that you have won the race.'[7] By this time, Tyrconnell wanted to make peace with William in exchange for Catholic rights. The French commander, St Ruhe, died in action at the Battle of Augrim, as did thousands of others. After an ample meal with compatriots in Limerick, Tyrconnell suffered a fatal stroke. Another Irish champion who had long been loyal to James was Patrick Sarsfield, 1st Earl of Lucan. He was for battling on, and many still hoped that the French would come in greater numbers to support him. The peace, when it came through the Treaty of Limerick, entailed protections for Catholics, but the new Protestant-dominated Irish Parliament made short work of those as the 1690s rolled on. The Old Faith was methodically suppressed, the lands were confiscated once more, and civil rights were rolled back. Tyrconnell's properties were lost when he was attainted, as were those of so many other Jacobites. Frances departed Ireland for St Germain-en-Laye, taking her daughters and 40,000 gold coins. There she was appointed Lady of the Bedchamber to Mary Beatrice, mirroring her sister's position with Anne. With much of the Jacobite elite dead, suppressed or in exile, Ireland was now governed exclusively by representatives of a 6 per cent minority. The very people who expressed horror at the idea of a Catholic king ruling a Protestant majority happily endorsed the inverse for Ireland. The bitterly disappointed Irish Catholics longed for deliverance.[8]

The crushing of their cause killed roughly 10,000 people from all causes and sent some 40,000 Irish Jacobites into France. Of confiscated lands, 72 per cent belonged to them.[9] This exodus, the storied 'Flight of the Wild Geese', was a great loss to Catholic culture in Ireland because it gutted the elite that might have served to resist and rebuild after the war. However, it was a boon to the Jacobite network 'over the water', a Three Kingdoms community that was taking shape around St Germain-en-Laye. Catholics predominated there, but Anglicans and various Nonconformists joined the court as well. A delegation of Quakers were among the many visitors. Louis XIV's strict policy meant that reformers, forbidden to build churches, had to worship privately. James knew how valuable these Protestants were to the cause. He rewarded all of his followers as best he could. A select group received titles, but they came without the actual properties in question. Those were contingent upon future Jacobite success. Concrete political power – land, income, seats in Parliament – had to be won back. But at least the Jacobite peers had a stake in the fight. The king was also able to reward supporters with household appointments.[10]

While in Ireland and mindful of his mortality, James had drafted a letter of governing advice for the little Prince of Wales. In it James stresses the traditional view that a king is father to his people, protecting the lower orders from the powerful. He therefore underlines the importance of retaining sovereignty. Unless the monarch be 'secure in his privileges,' he argues, 'the people cannot be at ease.' The religious settlement remains foremost in his mind. He urges his son to ensure toleration through a law. Once again, he indicates respect for individual conscience. Using a vivid image, the king repeats the principle that there can be no compulsion in religious matters: 'Our Lord whipped people out of the Temple,' James writes, 'but He never commanded any to be whipped into it.' To bring people to the Old Faith, 'only gentleness, instruction, and good example should be used.' It is a private message consistent with his public declarations.

In order to be able to govern his kingdoms, the prince has to learn to govern himself. James discusses his own Achilles heel, and that of his brother – 'the forbidden love of women'. This is to be avoided. Lust is a vice 'fatal to great men', who have more opportunities to indulge it, 'particularly in peacetime'. Even King David, 'who though a man after God's own heart', had fallen prey to adultery and then murder, he points out. James also alludes to Henry II of England, a great philanderer punished by the rebellion of his four sons. James believed that personal frailty had prevented him from course-correcting Henry VIII, that Bluebeard who had employed such 'indirect and unchristian ways to have successors'. As James saw it, his own flaws gave him insight into Henry, but he had not expiated his sin sufficiently to solve the problems that his predecessor had created. Clearly, the king thought that the rebellion of his daughters was a punishment. Still, he had an heir. He hoped that Prince James Francis Edward could succeed where his father had faltered. 'Let no vice get mastery of you,' he tells the boy, for 'they carry their stings with them.' One should also be wary of hedonistic courtiers who drag others down with them. Ultimately, however, James takes the blame for his own conduct. 'I let myself go too much to the love of women,' he admits simply.

As for practical matters, he further counsels the prince to 'study the trade of the nation ... do everything to increase it lawfully ... and preserve the mastery of the seas, for without it England cannot be safe.' A good king should avoid initiating wars, he adds.

Moving on to the question of Scotland, James makes it clear that he opposes fusing that country with England. He endorses the Three Kingdoms model for the British Isles: three discrete parliaments under one monarch. Scotland should continue to be governed by a de facto viceroy in consultation with the local assembly. The lords and gentry are friends to the monarchy. James echoes Charles II in preferring Episcopalians to Presbyterians. 'Enthusiasts' and 'conventiclers' are 'of so extravagant an opinion that they can never agree amongst themselves.' Highland clans are trustworthy – except the Campbells. (At the time of writing, the clans were under pressure to take an oath to William. One outcome was the Glencoe Massacre.) Turning to Ireland, James offers a balanced view. His son should 'take care of the old natives', meaning chiefly the indigenous Irish but also the Old English; they have suffered greatly in the wars. On the other hand, the monarch should strive to 'wean them off their hatred of the English,' for example, by educating the heads of families. He defends the Irish plantations as a means of improving estates, arguing that the English and Scots have fostered wholesome and thriving farmland 'wheresoever they have settled.'[11]

James had suffered great misfortune and upheaval, but in the last decade of his life, he found considerable fulfilment at St Germain-en-Laye. Family and devotional life made up for painful disappointments. Mary and Anne had betrayed him when Mary Beatrice gave birth to a son, threatening their places in the succession. But that son made him proud. 'Blackbird', who grew up tall like both parents, was a considerate and intelligent young man. Much care was given to his education as a prince and future king. His life at court was if anything more structured by ceremony than it would have been in England, since court etiquette gave form to the chaos of exile.[12] James Francis had no memory of his native land, yet he grew into an Englishman. He revered his parents and hero-worshipped his grown-up half-brother Berwick, who, with his father's permission, accepted a commission in the French army and had a distinguished military career. James Francis also had his half-brother Henry FitzJames, Duke of Albemarle, to look up to. The little prince had boys his age around him as well. He had his cousin, James Radclyffe, 3rd Earl of Derwentwater, as a playmate. The devoted Derwentwater grew up to become a legendary Jacobite hero. Together they were initiated into the warrior caste.

Another great blessing was in store for King James. In 1692 Mary Beatrice gave birth to a healthy baby girl, Louisa Maria Teresa. She was christened in honour of her godfather, Louis XIV. Her godmother was the second Duchess of Orléans, known as 'Madame Palatine'. On the verge of 60, James had a new daughter to cherish. Because the king believed that God had sent her 'to comfort them in their distress,' she became known as 'La Consolatrice'.[13] Louisa Maria's sweetness was like a healing balm to her parents. 'The Princess Over the Water' grew into a lovely young lady, slender, her face a long oval, with rich brown hair and large dark eyes. She looked very much like Prince James Francis. Louisa Maria expressed a strong sense of duty to the members of the Jacobite milieu, people who had sacrificed so much for her family and the larger legitimist cause. Her governess, Countess Middleton, was the wife of Charles, 2nd Earl of Middleton and Jacobite 1st Earl of Monmouth. Louisa Maria was tutored by an English priest, Father Constable, in Latin, history and religion. She paid for many other young girls of the community, Protestant as well as Catholic, to be educated also. The Princess Royal danced well and loved the operas performed at the château's splendid theatre and at Versailles. A painting by court portraitist Alexis Simon-Belle shows Louisa Maria led along hand in hand by her brother, who appears in the guise of a guardian angel. Her birth gave the lie to English subjects who had insisted that Queen Mary Beatrice was infertile – for those who had ears to hear, at any rate. Louisa Maria's existence should have chased the changeling tale away. And yet, because it was politically useful, it lingered on.

A loving daughter, Louisa Maria played Cordelia to her half-sisters' Goneril and Regan. She and Princess Anne began exchanging letters. This was just as well for Anne, for she and Mary were no longer on speaking terms. Until recently, writes Sarah Churchill, the sisters had been 'united in one common cause against a father on account of religion'.[14] Having disposed of that father, they fell to fighting one another. They squabbled over rights to the Cockpit and other lodgings; they disagreed over finances. Anne continued to object to William being sovereign for life, as he had displaced her in the succession. She had conspired to dethrone her own father and half-brother, yet had little to show for it. Another difficulty was William's persistent rudeness to Anne's husband, Prince George of Denmark, whom he considered to be a blockhead. As for Anne, he thought her fat and silly. William and Mary thoroughly distrusted Anne's beloved servants, John and Sarah Churchill, now Earl and Countess of Marlborough. John remained in touch with King James; in fact, he had written to beg his pardon. The spectre of illegitimacy haunted the court of William and Mary. Many complained that he surrounded himself with Dutch followers, and many subjects were charged with Jacobitism. One day at Whitehall, Mary came across the daughter of an accused Protestant Jacobite, Lord Preston, admiring a portrait of King James. When Mary asked what she was doing, the young lady replied: 'I am reflecting how hard it is that my father should be put to death for loving your father.'[15]

Another lady suspected of Jacobitism was Sarah's own favourite, the witty and secretive Barbara Berkeley, née Villiers, Lady Fitzhardinge. (A coded portrait by Sir Godfrey Kneller shows the two friends playing cards. Barbara holds the nine of diamonds, aka 'the curse of Scotland'.) Marlborough was directly accused of Jacobitism and imprisoned in the Tower. The now-married Arabella visited her brother there. Most likely, he had merely been hedging his bets in case of a second Stuart restoration. He had betrayed one master, and might easily betray another. The new queen therefore ordered Princess Anne to dismiss her beloved Sarah. Anne was defiant. Instead of banishing her, 'Mrs Morely' took 'Mrs Freeman' on a trip to Bath. There the princess imbibed the waters for fertility, perhaps her greatest struggle in life. The queen ordered the Mayor of Bath not to receive Anne. Furthermore, the minister at St James's chapel was 'forbid to lay the text upon her cushion, or take any more notice of her than other people.'[16] Until she submitted, the next in line to the throne would enjoy no special signs of favour. 'How this conduct to a sister could suit the character of a devout queen, I am at a loss to know,' huffed Sarah, whose fortunes were in the balance. 'Sure never anybody was so used by a sister!' Anne fretted that 'dear Mrs. Freeman ... looked tonight as if she had the spleen.'

Not only did Mary fall out with Anne over Sarah, but she grew even colder towards James when word reached her that the Duke of Berwick was involved in a plot to kill William of Orange. The two sisters were still on terrible terms when, in 1696, Mary came down with smallpox and died at the age of 32. Some Jacobites saw this as a judgement on Mary for dishonouring her father. One offered a mock epitaph: 'Here ends, notwithstanding her specious pretences,/the undutiful child of the kindest of princes./Well, here let her lie, for by this time she knows/What it is such a father and king to depose.' Another was more succinct: 'Between vice and virtue she parted her life,/she was too bad a daughter and too good a wife.'[17]

The husband in question was devastated by Mary's death. King James too was saddened at the finality of this loss. Now there was no chance for reconciliation. His relationship with Mary had been terribly damaged by the events of recent years. But Anne was beginning to write her father 'conciliatory letters',[18] and he had plenty of family around him. 4-year-old Louisa Maria brightened his life. Also, he had been joined at St Germain-en-Laye by Henrietta and Arabella FitzJames, his daughters by Arabella Churchill. That discarded mistress kept herself aloof from James's cause. She started a new family with that distant cousin, a Whig-minded fellow named Charles Godfrey, who was among the first defectors to William of Orange. Arabella reserved expressions of open scorn for her former lover until after he had been usurped. In contrast to their mother, the four FitzJames offspring were all devout Catholics and firm Jacobites. Berwick went from strength to strength militarily, and would go on marry Patrick Sarsfield's graceful widow, Honora Burke, Countess of Lucan, in the chapel at St Germain-en-Laye. Henry FitzJames, Duke of Albemarle, was named Lord Grand Prior of the newly reformed English chapter of the Knights of Malta. He wed Marie-Gabrielle d'Audibert, Comtesse de Lussan. Arabella took the name Dame Ignatia when she became a Benedictine nun; Queen Mary Beatrice attended the ceremony. And Henrietta, who was treated as a princess at St Germain-en-Laye, would go on to marry twice. James had many grandchildren.

The woman who had supplanted Arabella in James's affections was better disposed towards him. He had left Catherine Sedley, Countess of Dorchester, financially secure, although Parliament tried to withdraw her income after the revolution. She went before them, successfully defending herself, and married the Earl of Portmore in 1696. William settled a pension on her. Catherine opined that both kings were civil to her, even if the queen used her badly. The newly installed Mary had refused to receive her father's long-time mistress, turning her back in blatant disdain. Catherine shot back rapid-fire: 'I beg your Majesty to remember that, if I broke one of the commandments with your father, you broke another, and what I did was more natural.'[19] There was no denying that Catherine Sedley had committed adultery with James over years – the fruit of their affair, little Catherine, had been acknowledged by him with a coat of arms. Mary, however, had thoroughly dishonoured him. A faithless daughter had no claim to the moral high ground.

James suffered sly barbs from the worldlier sort of Versailles courtier. A French cleric, playing on Henry IV's famous comment on his own conversion ('Paris is worth a mass'), quipped that James had 'lost three kingdoms for a mass.' The English ambassador hinted that the aging James resembled Don Quixote. (Later English Jacobites cheerfully acknowledged the Quixotic element in their cause by forming the Order Del Toboso.[20]) On the other hand, the king's increasing asceticism as he aged won respect from the devout. He lived like a lay monk, often retreating to the Cistercian Abbey of La Trappe.[21] The abbey had been founded by a godson of Cardinal Richelieu named Armand-Jean Bouthillier de Rancé, a revert after James's own heart. As a priest, de Rancé had lived a worldly existence of feasting, fox-hunting and lovemaking until the 1657 death of his mistress effected a sea-change in him. He then embraced a penitential way of life shaped by silence, isolation, self-denial, prayer, a sparing diet and hard manual labour – work which permitted the abbey to sustain itself. De Rancé became James's spiritual advisor. 'Until I met you,' wrote the king-in-exile to the abbot, 'I had not renounced the world.'

Like Charles I before him, James II and VII approached death as a penitent. As a young man he had run wild in the spirit of Charles II's court, justifying it as defiance of the regicidal Puritans. He had fully inhabited the Don Juan role, leading many young ladies astray with him. In a sense his chief frailty was the key to his conversion and defining policy, because it had enabled him to see into Henry VIII's heart. He could see what made him tick. James had turned away from 'the forbidden love of women' – but too late and at first without total conviction. Now he was full of regret.

James believed that God had denied him the throne because of his sins. He hoped that, by expiating them, he could make the restoration of the Stuart line possible. One day, he hoped, his beloved child James Francis Edward would be king of England, Scotland and Ireland, a monarch in the fullest sense. James sought to use his traditional powers to implement an updated religious settlement that respected liberty of conscience, and he wanted his son to do the same. The Stuart vision for the Three Kingdoms, with three national parliaments under one monarch, would arguably have balanced local concerns more successfully and perhaps retained the loyalty of Ireland and Scotland.

James experienced ill health for some time. He was sent to take the waters at Bourbonnais, the place where he himself had sent Arabella Churchill to give birth to their first son. Then, like his brother, King James suffered a stroke, and would not long survive it. For a few weeks he struggled on. In his company was a Nonjuring Anglican, Denis Granville, Dean of Durham, who had become a great friend in exile. On 2 September 1701, he fainted at mass. He was put to bed, where he made his final confession and had the Last Rites. He forgave William and his other enemies. His tearful family gathered around him. He said goodbye to James Francis Edward. When the family tried to lead young Prince James away, the 13-year-old clung to his father. 'Keep the faith against all things and all men,' the king urged him.[22] In his words of farewell to 9-year-old Louisa Maria, he paid tribute to Queen Mary Beatrice: 'Adieu, my dear child. Serve your Creator in the days of your youth. Consider virtue as the greatest ornament of your sex. Follow close to the pattern of it, your mother, who has been, no less than myself, over-clouded with calumny. But time, the mother of truth, will I hope make her virtues shine as bright as the sun.' It was an inspired tribute to the graceful woman who had held tight to him through the vicissitudes of fortune. James died on 16 September, and Louis XIV made sure that he was buried with great honours. He was mourned by the Jacobite community in exile and across the English Channel. His death was greatly regretted by William Penn, who continued to insist that 'Friend James' had been a sincere pioneer of religious toleration: a true English patriot. The king's tomb attracted streams of pilgrims, and so many miracles were reported that a cause for sainthood was opened. The great rover had come home at last.

Select Bibliography

'Apology of Colonel Joseph Bampfield', section 92. http://cryptiana.web.fc2.com/code/jamesii.htm

Aubrey, John, *Brief Lives,* Clarendon Press, 1898

Behn, Aphra, *The Rover, or The Banish'd Cavaliers,* ed. Diane Maybank, Oxford UP, 2007

Belloc, Hilaire, *James the Second,* Faber & Gwyer, 1928

- *Monarchy: a Study of Louis XIV,* Cassell & Co., 1938

Buranelli, Vincent, *William Penn and James II,* American Philosophical Society, 15 February 1960

Burnet, Gilbert, *History of his Own Times,* 6 vols., 1833

Callow, John, *The King in Exile: James II, Warrior, King and Saint 1689–1701,* Sutton, 2004

Capp, Bernard, '"The Door of Hope Re-opened": the Fifth Monarchy, King Charles and King Jesus', *Journal of Religious History*, 32, 2008

Cartwright, Julia Mary (Mrs Henry Ady), *Madame: A Life of Henrietta of England,* Seeley & Co., 1894

Cavendish, Margaret, *The Blazing World and Other Writings*, ed. Kate Lilley, Penguin, 2004

Cavendish, William, Duke of Newcastle, *An English 'Prince': Newcastle's Machiavellian Political Guide to Charles II*, ed. Gloria Italiano Anzilotti, Giardini, 1988

Charles II, 'Declaration of Breda', 4 April 1660

Chesterton, Gilbert Keith, *A Short History of England,* John Lane, 1917

Churchill, Sarah, *An Account of the Conduct of the Dowager Duchess of Marlborough,* James Bettenham, 1742

Churchill, Winston, *Marlborough: His Life and Times,* [vols] G.G. Harrap, 1933

Coote, Stephen, *Royal Survivor: A Life of Charles II,* St. Martin's Press, 2000

Corp, Edward, *A Court in Exile: the Stuarts in France, 1689–1718,* Cambridge UP, 2004

Select Bibliography

Coulombe, Charles, 'The Forgotten Canonisation Cause of King James II', *Catholic Herald,* 5 March 2019

Cromwell, Oliver, *Speeches and Letters,* ed. Thomas Carlyle, Chapman & Hall, 1895

Cruickshanks, Eveline, *The Glorious Revolution,* Macmillan, 2000

Cunningham, Peter, *The Story of Nell Gwyn,* Henry B. Wheatley, 1892

'A Deep Sigh Breath'd Through the Lodgings at White-hall,' John Barlow, 1642

Dryden, John, *Collected Works,* Legare Street Press, 2022

Halkett, Anne, *The Autobiography of Anne, Lady Halkett,* ed. John Gough Nicholls, Nicholls and Sons, 1875

Hamilton, Anthony, *Memoirs of the Comte de Gramont,* trans. Horace Walpole, Folio Society, 1965

Henslowe, J.R., *Anne Hyde, Duchess of York,* T. Werner Laurie, 1915

Herman, Eleanor, *Sex with Kings: 500 Years of Adultery, Power, Rivalry and Revenge,* HarperCollins, 2004

Hill, Christopher, *The World Turned Upside-down,* Penguin, 1972

Hyde, Edward, Duke of Clarendon, *History of the Rebellion,* 8 vols., Clarendon Press, 1826

James II, 'Declaration of Indulgence of James II, 4 April 1687', jacobite.ca/documents/16870404.htm

- 'Instructions of King James II and VII to his Son', jacobite.ca/documents/instructions.htm

- 'Letter of James II to Parliament, 22 December 1688', jacobite.ca/documents/16881222a.htm

Jameson, Anna, *Memoirs of the Beauties of the Court of Charles II,* Henry G. Bohn, 1861

Lake, Edward, *The Diary of Doctor Edward Lake,* Camden Society, 1846

Leech, Peter, 'Music and Musicians at the Catholic Chapel of James II at Whitehall', *Early Music,* Vol. 39 No. 3

Life of James the Second, King of England, & cetera, 2 vols., ed. James Stanier Clarke, Longman et al., 1816

Lisle, Leanda de, *The White King: Charles I, Traitor, Murderer, Martyr,* Chatto & Windus, 2018

Melville, Louis, *The Windsor Beauties: Memoirs of the Ladies of the Court of Charles II,* Victorian Heritage Press, 2005

Memoirs of James II, His Campaigns as Duke of York, 1652–1660, ed. A. Lytton Sells, Indiana UP, 1962

Memoirs of the Lives and Actions of James and William, Dukes of Hamilton, ed. Gilbert Burnet, J. Grover, 1677

Macauley, Charles Babington, *The History of England, from the Accession of James II,* Longmans, Green & Co., 1886

Miller, John, *James II: A Study in Kingship,* Methuen, 1978; 1989

Mortimer, Ian, *A Time Traveller's Guide to Restoration Britain 1660–1700,* Vintage, 2017

Norrington, Ruth, ed., *My Dearest Minette: Letters Between Charles II and his Sister, the Duchesse d'Orléans,* Peter Owen, 1996

Pearce, Dominic, *Henrietta Maria: the Betrayed Queen,* Amberley, 2015

Pepys, Samuel, *Diary,* https://www.pepysdiary.com

Pittock, Murray G.H., *Jacobitism,* St. Martin's Press, 1998

Plowden, Alison, *Henrietta Maria: Charles I's Indomitable Queen,* Sutton, 2001

- *The Stuart Princesses,* Sutton, 1996

Porter, Linda, *Royal Renegades: the Children of Charles I and the English Civil Wars,* Pan Books, 2016

- *Mistresses: Sex and Scandal at the Court of Charles II,* Picador, 2020

Sachse, William L. 'The Mob and the Revolution of 1688', *Journal of British Studies,* 4: November 1964

'Some Familiar Letters of Charles II and James, Duke of York to their Daughter and Niece, Lady Charlotte Fitzroy', ed. Arthur, Harold, Viscount Dillon, *Archaeologia,* Vol 58, Issue 1, 1902

Sowerby, Scott, 'Making Toleration: the Repealers and the Glorious Revolution', Harvard Historical Society: 181, 8 March 2013

Starkie, Andrew, 'A Lost Cause? The Cause for Canonization of King James II', *Studies in Religion and the Enlightenment,* 2.1. 2019

The Stuart Courts, ed. Eveline Cruickshanks, The History Press, 2000

Tayler, Alistair and Henrietta, *The Old Chevalier: James Francis Stuart,* Cassell & Co., 1934

Thurley, Simon, *Palaces of Revolution: Life, Death and Art at the Stuart Court,* William Collins, 2021

Townsend Wilson, Charles, *James the Second and the Duke of Berwick,* Henry S. King & Co., 1876

Notes

Prologue: Hide and Seek

1. *The Life of James the Second, King of England,* ed. J.S. Clarke (Longman et al, 1816), p. 30
2. John Miller, *James II: A Study in Kingship* (Methuen, 1978;1989), p. 4
3. Anne Halkett, *The Autobiography of Lady Anne Halkett*, ed. John Gough Nicholls (Camden Society, 1875), p. 20
4. Ibid
5. Ibid, p. 22
6. Simon Thurley, *Palaces of Revolution: Life, Death and Art at the Stuart Court* (William Collins, 2021), p. 273
7. John Evelyn, *Diary,* ed. Guy de la Bédoyère (Boydell), p. 70
8. Clarke, *Life of James the Second,* p. 45
9. Clarke, *Life of James the Second,* p. 46
10. Evelyn, *Diary,* p. 68

Chapter 1: From Gold into Iron

1. As quoted in Leanda de Lisle, *The White King: Charles I, Traitor, Murderer, Martyr* (Chatto & Windus, 2018), p. 87
2. Edward Hyde, *The History of the Rebellion of Civil Wars in England* (Clarendon Press, 1826), vol. I, p. 93
3. Simon Thurley, *Palaces of Revolution: Life, Death & Art at the Stuart Court* (William Collins, 2021), p. 166
4. Hyde, 109
5. *The Life of James the Second, King of England,* ed. W.S. Clarke (Longman et al., 1816), p. 727

6. Ibid, p. 2
7. Ibid, p. 2
8. De Lisle, *The White King*, p. 158
9. *Life of James the Second*, pp. 2–3
10. Ibid, 3
11. Ibid, 158
12. Ibid, 163
13. Ibid, 15
14. John Aubrey, *Brief Lives* (Clarendon Press, 1898), p. 297
15. Oliver Cromwell, *Letters and Speeches,* ed. Thomas Carlyle (Chapman & Hall, 1895), vol. I, p. 101
16. G.K. Chesterton, *A Short History of England* (John Lane, 1917), p. xiii
17. 'A Deep Sigh Breath'd Through the Lodgings at White-Hall' (Printed for John Barlow, 1642)
18. De Lisle, p. 176

Chapter 2: A Mirror World

1. Simon Thurley, *Palaces of Revolution: Life, Death & Art at the Stuart Court.* (William Collins, 2021), p. 222
2. Ibid, p. 226
3. Leanda de Lisle, *The White King: Charles I, Traitor, Murderer, Martyr* (Chatto & Windus, 2018), p. 178
4. Thurley, p. 230
5. Margaret Cavendish, *The Blazing World and Other Writings,* ed. Kate Lilley (Penguin, 2004), p. 134
6. Ian Mortimer, *A Time-Traveller's Guide to Restoration Britain* (Vintage, 2017), p. 12
7. *The Stuart Courts,* ed. Eveline Cruickshanks (History Press, 2000; 2009), p. 9
8. *Memoirs of the Lives and Actions of James and William, Dukes of Hamilton,* ed. Gilbert Burnet (J. Grover, 1677), p. 203
9. Dominic Pearce, *Henrietta Maria* (Amberley, 2015), p. 229
10. De Lisle, p. 184
11. *Memoirs of James II: His Campaigns as Duke of York, 1652-1660,* ed. A. Lytton Sells (Indiana UP, 1962), p. 3

12. De Lisle, p. 211
13. Ibid, p. 214
14. John Miller, *James II: A Study in Kingship* (Methuen, 1978), p. 3
15. As quoted in Miller, p. 2
16. As quoted in de Lisle, p. 218
17. *The Life of James II, King of England,* ed. J.S. Clarke (Longman et al., 1816), p. 33
18. 'Apology of Colonel Joseph Bampfield', section 92. http://cryptiana.web.fc2.com/code/jamesii.htm
19. As quoted in de Lisle, p. 224

Chapter 3: The True Eaglet

1. Hilaire Belloc, *James the Second* (Faber & Gwyer, 1928), p. 63
2. *The Churchman*, vol. 46, p. 52
3. *An English 'Prince': Newcastle's Machiavellian Political Guide to Charles II,* ed. G.I. Anzilotti (Giardini 1998), pp. 167–8
4. As quoted in Alison Plowden, *Henrietta Maria: Charles I's Indomitable Queen* (Sutton, 2001), p. 261
5. *The Memoirs of James II: His Campaigns as Duke of York 1652-1660,* ed. A. Lytton Sells (Indiana UP, 1962), pp. 4–5
6. Plowden, p. 281
7. Simon Thurley, *Palaces of Revolution: Life, Death & Art at the Stuart Court* (William Collins, 2021), p. 267
8. *The Life of James the Second, King of England,* ed. J.S. Clarke (Longman et al., 1816), p. 47
9. Thurley, p. 275
10. John Miller, *James II: A Study in Kingship* (Methuen, 1978; 1989), p. 14
11. *Life of James the Second*, p. 50
12. Pearce, p. 268
13. *Memoir of James II,* p. 59
14. John Evelyn, *Correspondence,* ed. William Bray (Henry G. Bohn, 1859), vol. iv, p. 344
15. *Life of James the Second*, p. 55
16. As quoted in Miller, p. 16
17. *Life of James the Second*, p. 159

18. Belloc, p. 74
19. *Memoirs of James II: His Campaigns as Duke of York, 1652-1660*, ed. A. Lytton Sells (Indiana UP, 1962), p. 6
20. *Life of James the Second*, p. 210
21. Ibid, p. 125
22. Ibid, p. 219
23. Ibid, p. 52
24. Stephen Coote, *Royal Survivor: A Life of Charles II*, (St. Martin's Press, 2000), pp. 108-121
25. Julia Cartwright Ady, *Madame: A Life of Henrietta of England* (Seeley & Co., 1894), p. 19
26. *Life of James the Second*, p. 158
27. Hilaire Belloc, *Monarchy: A Study of Louis XIV* (Arouca, 1938), p. 37
28. Miller, p. 17
29. Cartwright Ady, p. 28
30. Miller, p. 180
31. Ibid, p. 8
32. Cartwright Ady, p. 36
33. Miller, p. 15
34. Cartwright Ady, p. 25
35. *Life of James the Second*, p. 273
36. Ibid, p. 272
37. Ibid, p. 435
38. Ibid, p. 277

Chapter 4: The Rover

1. *The Life of James the Second, King of England*, ed. J.S. Clarke (Longman et al., 1816), p. 277
2. John Miller, *James II: a Study in Kingship* (Methuen, 1978; 1989), p. 8
3. *Life of James the Second*, p. 540
4. Ibid, p. 279
5. Ibid, p. 281
6. Ibid, pp. 285–286
7. Ibid, p. 290
8. Miller, p. 21

9. Ibid
10. *Life of James the Second*, p. 292
11. Alison Plowden, *The Stuart Princesses* (Allan Sutton, 1996), pp. 103–4
12. *Life of James the Second*, p. 327
13. *Life of James the Second*, p. 344
14. Ibid, p. 344
15. Ibid, p. 367
16. Ibid, pp. 375–376
17. *Memoirs of James II: His Campaigns as Duke of York, 1652-1660*, ed. A. Lytton Sells (Indiana UP, 1962) pp. 287–288.
18. *Life of James the Second*, p. 381
19. Hilaire Belloc, *James the Second* (Faber & Gwyer, 1928), p. 23
20. Anthony Hamilton, *Memoirs of the Comte de Gramont*, trans. Horace Walpole (Folio Society, 1965), p. 120
21. *Life of James the Second*, p. 387
22. Ibid, p. 381
23. Belloc, p. 80
24. Samuel Pepys, *Diary*, 7 October 1660
25. Hamilton, pp. 121–122

Chapter 5: The Garland King

1. John Miller, *James II: a Study in Kingship* (Methuen 1978; 1989), p. 23
2. Miller, p. 25
3. Charles II, 'Declaration of Breda', 4 April 1660
4. Miller, p. 25
5. Samuel Pepys, *Diary*, 27 April 1660
6. Ibid, 1 June 1660
7. John Evelyn, *Diary*, ed. Guy de la Bédoyère (Boydell Press, 2004), p. 105
8. Simon Thurley, *Palaces of Revolution: Life, Death & Art at the Stuart Court* (William Collins, 2021), p. 287
9. Linda Porter, *Mistresses: Sex and Scandal at the Court of Charles II* (Pan MacMillan, 2020), p. 45
10. Alison Plowden, *Stuart Princesses* (Alan Sutton, 1996), p. 119
11. Patricia U. Bonomi, 'Edward Hyde, 1st Earl of Clarendon', *Oxford Dictionary of National Biography*

12. Louis Melville, *The Windsor Beauties: Memoirs of the Ladies of the Court of Charles II* (Victorian Heritage Press, 2005), p. 50
13. Andrew Marvell, 'An Historical Poem', *The Complete Works in Verse and Prose,* ed. A.R. Grosart (Fuller, 1872)
14. Pepys, *Diary,* 7 October 1660
15. Plowden, *Henrietta Maria* (Sutton, 2001), p. 304
16. *My Dearest Minette: Letters between Charles II and His Sister, the Duchesse d'Orléans,* ed. Ruth Norrington (Peter Owen, 1996), p. 47
17. Ibid, p. 41
18. Miller, p. 45
19. Pepys, *Diary.* 13 October 1660
20. Anthony Hamilton, *Memoirs of the Comte de Gramont,* trans. Horace Walpole (Folio Society, 1965), p. 71
21. *Life of James the Second, King of England,* ed. J.S. Clarke (Longman et al., 1816) p. 388
22. Evelyn, p. 116
23. Hamilton, p. 124
24. W.A. Speck, 'Mary II', *Oxford Dictionary of National Biography*

Chapter 6: The Best Revenge

1. Bernard Capp, 'The Door of Hope Re-opened', *Journal of Religious History,* 32 (2008), pp. 16-30
2. *Life of James the Second, King of England,* ed. J.S. Clarke (Longman et al, 1816), p. 390
3. Ibid, p. 397
4. Anthony Hamilton, *Memoirs of the Comte de Gramont,* trans. Horace Walpole (Folio Society, 1965), p. 73
5. *Life of James the Second,* p. 399
6. Ibid, p. 400
7. Samuel Pepys, *Diary,* Friday 30 October 1668
8. Hamilton, p. 124
9. Hamilton, p. 126
10. Pepys, Tuesday 2 July 1661
11. Ian Mortimer, *A Time-Traveller's Guide to Restoration Britain* (Vintage, 2017), p. 392

12. Hamilton, p. 129
13. Pepys, Friday 15 May 1663
14. Hamilton, p. 120
15. Ibid, p. 145
16. Pepys, Friday 21 August 1668
17. Hamilton, p. 145
18. Pepys, Wednesday 26 September 1666
19. Ibid, Tuesday 8 January 1666/67
20. Hamilton, p. 146
21. Linda Porter, *Mistresses: Sex and Scandal at the Court of Charles II* (Picador, 2020), pp. 41-42
22. *Life of James the Second*, p. 493
23. Hamilton, p. 231
24. Pepys, Wednesday 31 December 1662
25. Hamilton, p. 106
26. Ibid, p. 140
27. Pepys, Monday 3 November 1662

Chapter 7: Apocalypse

1. Anthony Hamilton, *Memoirs of the Comte de Gramont*, trans. Horace Walpole (Folio Society, 1965), p. 272
2. Ibid, p. 214 ff
3. Charles Townsend Wilson, *James the Second and the Duke of Berwick* (Henry S. King & Co., 1876), p. 2
4. Sarah Churchill, *An Account of the Conduct of the Dowager Duchess of Marlborough* (James Bettenham, 1742), p. 51
5. Hamilton, p. 216
6. John Evelyn, *Diary*, ed. Guy de la Bédoyère (Boydell Press, 2004), p. 164
7. John Miller, *James II: a Study in Kingship* (Methuen 1978; 1989) p. 47
8. *Life of James the Second, King of England*, ed. J.S. Clarke (Longman et al., 1816), p. 487
9. *Memoirs of James II: His Campaigns as Duke of York, 1652-1660,* ed. A. Lytton Sells (Indiana UP, 1962), p. 7
10. Hilaire Belloc, *James the Second* (Faber & Gwyer, 1928), p. 30

11. Ian Mortimer, *A Time-Traveller's Guide to Restoration Britain* (Vintage, 2017), p. 303
12. Evelyn, *Diary*, ed. Guy de la Bédoyère (Boydell Press, 2004), p. 147
13. Pepys, *Diary*, Thursday 14 September 1665
14. Pepys, Sunday 2 September 1666
15. Evelyn, pp. 155–6
16. *London Gazette*, 3-10 September 1666
17. Evelyn, p. 156
18. Miller, p. 51
19. Evelyn, p. 154 ff
20. Pepys, Friday 21 June 1667
21. *Life of James the Second*, p. 430
22. Ibid, p. 432
23. Ibid, p. 438
24. Miller, p. 52

Chapter 8: Reconciliation

1. John Miller, *James II: A Study in Kingship* (Methuen 1978; 1989), p. 57
2. *The Life of James the Second, King of England*, ed. J.S. Clarke (Longman et al., 1816), p. 630
3. G.K. Chesterton, *A Short History of England* (Chatto & Windus, 1920), p. 147 ff; p. 175 ff
4. 'Instructions of King James II and VII to his Son', *http://jacobite.ca/documents/instructions.htm*
5. *Life of James the Second*, p. 630
6. Ibid, p. 440
7. Samuel Pepys, *Diary*, Wednesday 15 April 1668
8. Anne Hyde's declaration is transcribed in J.R. Henslowe, *Anne Hyde, Duchess of York* (T. Werner Laurie, 1915), p. 252
9. Hilaire Belloc, *James the Second* (Faber & Gwyer, 1928), p. 126
10. Alison Plowden, *Henrietta Maria: Charles I's Indomitable Queen* (Sutton, 2001), p. 295
11. Miller, p. 58
12. Paul Seaward, 'Charles II', *Oxford Dictionary of National Biography*

13. John Evelyn, *Diary*, ed. Guy de la Bédoyère (Boydell & Brewer, 2004), p. 197
14. Dominic Pearce, *Henrietta Maria: the Betrayed Queen* (Amberley, 2015), p. 297
15. *Life of James the Second*, p. 445
16. *My Dearest Minette: Letters between Charles II and His Sister,* ed. Ruth Norrington (Peter Owen, 1996), p. 183 ff.
17. John Miller, *Henriette Anne, Oxford Dictionary of National Biography*
18. *Life of James the Second*, p. 442
19. Julia Cartwright Ady, *Madame: A Life of Henrietta of England* (Seeley & Co., 1894), p. 310
20. Alison Plowden, *The Stuart Princesses* (Alan Sutton, 1996), p. 164
21. *Life of James the Second*, p. 451
22. Evelyn, p. 175
23. *Life of James the Second*, p. 443
24. Plowden, p. 165
25. Cartwright Ady, p. 358
26. Clarke, p. 451
27. Pepys, *Diary*, Wednesday 12 September 1664
28. Anne Hyde, 'Declaration' in Henslowe, p. 252
29. As quoted in Miller, p. 71
30. J.R. Henslowe, *Anne Hyde,* p. 287
31. *Life of James the Second*, p. 452

Chapter 9: Numerous Charms

1. John Miller, *James II: A Study in Kingship* (Methuen 1978;1989), p. 71
2. Ibid, p. 72
3. Ibid, p. 78
4. *Life of James the Second, King of England*, ed. J.S. Clarke (Longman et al., 1816), p. 484
5. Ibid, p. 483
6. Miller, p. 73
7. *Life of James the Second*, p. 485
8. Ibid, p. 455
9. Miller, p. 74

10. Alison Plowden, *The Stuart Princesses* (Alan Sutton, 1996), p. 173
11. John Callow, 'Arabella Churchill', *Oxford Dictionary of National Biography*
12. Miller, p. 59
13. Peter Cunningham, *The Story of Nell Gwyn* (Hutchinson & Co., 1892), p. 210
14. *Life of James the Second*, p. 438
15. Eveline Cruickshanks, *The Glorious Revolution* (Macmillan, 2000), p. 11
16. *Life of James the Second*, p. 493
17. Ibid, p. 437
18. Miller, p. 50
19. Ibid, p. 56

Chapter 10: The Duke's Company

1. Winston S. Churchill, *Marlborough: His Life and Times* (G.G. Harrap, 1933), vol. I, p. 44
2. Charles Townsend Wilson, *James the Second and the Duke of Berwick* (Henry S. King & Co., 1876), p. 1
3. Churchill, p. 60
4. Peter Cunningham, *The Story of Nell Gwyn* (Hutchinson & Co., 1892), p. 183
5. Samuel Pepys, *Diary*, Friday 2 April, 1669
6. Alison Plowden, *Stuart Princesses* (Alan Sutton, 1996), p. 173
7. *Life of James the Second, King of England*, ed. J.S. Clarke (Longman et al., 1816), p. 502
8. Plowden, p. 50
9. *Life of James the Second*, p. 510
10. Plowden, p. 173
11. John Miller, *James II: A Study in Kingship* (Methuen 1978; 1989), p. 84
12. Edward Lake, *Diary of Doctor Edward Lake* (Camden Society, 1846), p. 10
13. Ibid, p. 9
14. Plowden, p. 179
15. Cunningham, p. 208
16. Aphra Behn, *The Rover; or, the Banish'd Cavaliers*, ed. Diane Maybank (Oxford UP, 2007), I.ii.121–122

17. Cunningham, p. 182
18. Christopher Hill, *The World Turned Upside-down* (Penguin, 1972), p. 174 ff
19. Samuel Pepys, *Diary*, Monday 11 January, 1663/4
20. Pepys, *Diary*, Sunday 29 December, 1667
21. Miller, p. 156
22. 'Quaker Colonies: Penn's "Holy Experiment"', YouTube, *Justine Brown's Bookshelf*, 09/04/2021. https://www.youtube.com/watch?v=PUItyVanjPs&list=PLibD5jJAAM-vvoz9VCf_sL8i7ZFugNfBe
23. David Hackett-Fischer, *Albion's Seed.* Oxford UP, 1989, p. 189 ff.
24. For more on the 'Holy Experiment', read William Penn, *The Frame of Government of the Province of Pennsilvania in America* (A. Sowles, 1682)
25. See Scott Sowerby, *Making Toleration: the Repealers and the Glorious Revolution.* Harvard UP, 2013.

Chapter 11: Fountain of Impudence

1. Charles Townsend Wilson, *James the Second and the Duke of Berwick* (Henry S. King & Co., 1876), p. 68
2. Andrew Barclay, 'Catharine [sic] Sedley, Countess of Dorchester', *Oxford Dictionary of National Biography*
3. Ibid
4. Townsend Wilson, p. 68
5. Winston S. Churchill, *Marlborough: His Life and Times*, ed. H.S. Commager (Charles Scribner & Sons, 1933; 1968), p. 20 ff
6. Linda Porter, *Mistresses: Sex and Scandal at the Court of Charles II* (Picador, 2020), p. 74
7. Thomas Babington Macauley, *The History of England, from the Accession of James II* (Longmans, Green & Co., 1886), vol. II, p. 185
8. Anthony Hamilton, *Memoirs of the Comte de Gramont*, trans. Horace Walpole (Folio Society, 1965), p. 172
9. *Life of James the Second, King of England*, ed. J.S. Clarke (Longman et al., 1816), p. 488
10. Eveline Cruickshanks, *The Glorious Revolution* (MacMillan, 2000), p. 8
11. *Life of James the Second*, p. 515

12. Ibid, p. 529
13. John Miller, *James II: A Study in Kingship* (Methuen 1978; 1989), p. 487
14. Cruickshanks, p. 9
15. *Life of James the Second*, p. 534
16. John Evelyn, *Diary*, ed. Guy de la Bédoyère (Boydell & Brewer, 2004), p. 225
17. *Life of James the Second*, p. 523
18. Cruickshanks, p. 12 ff
19. Peter Cunningham, *The Story of Nell Gwyn* (Henry B. Wheatley & Co., 1892), p. 201
20. Cruickshanks, p. 10
21. Miller, p. 87
22. Evelyn, p. 226
23. Clarke, p. 531
24. Hilaire Belloc, *James the Second* (Faber & Gwyer, 1928), p. 169
25. Miller, p. 94
26. *Life of James the Second*, p. 562
27. For more on Sir Jeffrey Hudson, see Nick Page, *Lord Minimus: the Extraordinary Adventures of Britain's Smallest Man* (HarperCollins, 2001)
28. *Life of James the Second*, p. 560
29. Ibid, p. 540
30. Ibid, pp. 536–7
31. Ibid, p. 530
32. Alison Plowden, *Stuart Princesses* (Alan Sutton, 1996), p. 184
33. *Life of James the Second*, p. 552
34. Ibid, p. 566
35. Miller, p. 100
36. Evelyn, p. 228
37. *Life of James the Second*, p. 559
38. Ibid, p. 550

Chapter 12: The High Road

1. John Miller, *James II: A Study in Kingship* (Methuen 1978; 1989), p. 101
2. Ibid, p. 107

3. Hugh Ouston, '"From Thames to Tweed Departed": the Court of James, Duke of York in Scotland 1679–82', *The Stuart Courts,* ed. Eveline Cruickshanks (The History Press, 2000; 2009), p. 270
4. Ibid, p. 267
5. See 'Some Familiar Letters of Charles II and James, Duke of York to Their Daughter and Niece, Lady Charlotte Fitzroy', ed. Harold Arthur, Viscount Dillon (Cambridge UP, 1902; 2011)
6. Ouston, p. 271
7. Alison Plowden, *The Stuart Princesses* (Alan Sutton, 1996), p. 187
8. John Evelyn, *Diary*, ed. Guy de la Bédoyère (Boydell & Brewer, 2004), p. 262
9. *Life of James the Second, King of England*, ed. J.S. Clarke (Longman et al., 1816), p. 580
10. Ibid, p. 670
11. Ibid, p. 579
12. Eveline Cruickshanks, *The Glorious Revolution* (MacMillan, 2000), p. 10 ff
13. 'Speech of Charles II to the 1681 Oxford Parliament', https://www.british-history.ac.uk/commons-hist-proceedings/vol2/pp101-164#h3-0002
14. *Life of James the Second*, p. 620
15. Ibid, p. 730
16. Ibid, p. 690
17. Evelyn, p. 259
18. *Life of James the Second*, p. 740
19. Cruickshanks, p. 14
20. *Life of James the Second*, p. 552
21. Ibid, p. 745
22. Miller, p. 117
23. Plowden, p. 188
24. Evelyn, p. 262
25. W.A. Speck, 'Prince George of Denmark', *Oxford Dictionary of National Biography*
26. Sarah Churchill, *An Account of the Conduct of the Dowager Duchess of Marlborough* (James Bettenham, 1742), p. 13
27. Charles Townsend Wilson, *James the Second and the Duke of Berwick* (Henry S. King & Co., 1876), p. 2

28. Hilaire Belloc, *James the Second*, (Faber & Gwyer, 1928), p. 179
29. Peter Cunningham, *The Story of Nell Gwyn* (Henry B. Wheatley & Co., 1892), p. 241

Chapter 13: A King of England Too

1. John Evelyn, *Diary*, ed. Guy de la Bédoyère (Boydell & Brewer, 2004), p. 275
2. Eveline Cruickshanks, *The Glorious Revolution* (Macmillan, 2000), p. 17
3. Lorraine Madway, 'The Coronation of Charles II', *The Stuart Courts,* ed. Eveline Cruickshanks (The History Press, 2000; 2009), p. 143
4. Susan Abernethy, 'The Coronation of Mary Beatrice of Modena, Queen of England', *The Freelance History Writer.* thefreelancehistorywriter.com. 23 April 2021
5. Hilaire Belloc, *Monarchy: A Study of Louis XIV* (Arouca Press, 1938; 2022), p. xli
6. *The Life of James the Second, King of England,* ed. J.S. Clarke (Longman et al., 1816), p. 656
7. Evelyn, p. 283
8. Simon Thurley, *Palaces of Revolution: Life, Death and Art at the Stuart Court* (HarperCollins, 2021), p. 365
9. Evelyn, p. 277
10. Peter Leech, 'Music and Musicians in the Catholic Chapel of James II at Whitehall', *Early Music.* Vol. 39, no. 3, 2011, pp. 379–400
11. J.P. Kenyon, *Robert Spencer, Second Earl of Sunderland 1641–1701* (Gregg Revivals, 1992), p. 129
12. Cruickshanks, p. 16
13. Ibid, pp. 15–16
14. Charles Townsend Wilson, *James the Second and the Duke of Berwick* (Henry S. King & Co., 1876), p. 7
15. Samuel Pepys, *Diary*, Wednesday 16 July 1665
16. Evelyn, p. 287
17. Townsend Wilson, p. 15
18. Evelyn, p. 298
19. Murray G.H. Pittock, *Jacobitism* (St. Martin's Press, 1998), p. 14
20. John Miller, *James II: A Study in Kingship* (Methuen 1978; 1989), p. 168

21. Cruickshanks, p. 19
22. 'Declaration of Indulgence of James II, April 4, 1687', jacobite.ca/documents/16870404.htm
23. Cruickshanks, p. 17
24. Scott Sowerby, 'Making Toleration: the Repealers and the Glorious Revolution'. Harvard Historical Society: 181. 8 March 2013, p. 10
25. Alison Plowden, *The Stuart Princesses* (Alan Sutton, 1996), p. 191
26. Plowden, p. 192
27. Sarah Churchill, *An Account of the Conduct of the Dowager Duchess of Marlborough* (James Bettenham, 1742), p. 20
28. Plowden, p. 193

Chapter 14: Another Exile

1. John Evelyn, *Diary*, ed. Guy de la Bédoyère (Boydell & Brewer, 2004), p. 310
2. Alison Plowden, *The Stuart Princesses* (Alan Sutton, 1996), p. 195
3. As quoted in David Green, *Queen Anne* (Collins, 1970), p. 43
4. John Miller, *James II: A Study in Kingship* (Methuen 1978; 1989), p. 186
5. Plowden, p. 195
6. Alistair and Henrietta Tayler, *The Old Chevalier* (Cassell & Co., 1934), p. 18
7. Ibid, p. 17
8. Sarah Churchill, *An Account of the Dowager Duchess of Marlborough* (James Bettenham, 1742), p. 112
9. Charles Townsend Wilson, *James the Second and the Duke of Berwick* (Henry S. King & Co., 1876), p. 37
10. Eveline Cruickshanks, *The Glorious Revolution* (Macmillan, 2000), p. 55
11. Plowden, p. 197
12. Churchill, p. 21
13. 'Whig Propaganda and the "Glorious Revolution"'. YouTube. *Justine Brown's Bookshelf*. 3/09/2020. https://www.youtube.com/watch?v=c1iyEcVJYnU&list=PLibD5jJAAM-v5wTQHw5C0aXyItWSZFylm&index=8
14. Townsend Wilson, p. 89

15. W.A. Speck, 'Mary II', *Oxford Dictionary of National Biography*
16. David B. Green, 'The Banker Who Helped William of Orange Conquer England Dies', *Haaretz*. 22 April 2015
17. Cruickshanks, p. 29
18. Miller, p. 202
19. Ibid, p. 206
20. Townsend Wilson, p. 109
21. Murray G.H. Pittock, *Jacobitism* (St. Martin's Press, 1998), p. 25
22. 'Letter of King James II and VII to Parliament, 22 December 1688', jacobite.ca/documents/16881222a.htm
23. Cruickshanks, p. 39
24. Churchill, p. 25
25. Evelyn, p. 320
26. Churchill, p. 26
27. Townsend Wilson, p. 14
28. Speck, 'Mary II'
29. *The Life of James the Second, King of England,* ed. J.S. Clarke (Longman et al., 1816), p. 693

Chapter 15: The Jacobite Peerage

1. Simon Thurley, *Palaces of Revolution: Life, Death, & Art at the Stuart Court* (William Collins, 2021), p. 365
2. James McGuire, 'Richard Talbot', *Irish Dictionary of National Biography*
3. Charles Townsend Wilson, *James the Second and the Duke of Berwick* (Henry S. King & Co., 1876), p. 112
4. John Miller, *James II: A Study in Kingship* (Methuen 1978; 1989), p. 224
5. Eveline Cruickshanks, *The Glorious Revolution,* (Macmillan, 2000), p. 56
6. Ibid, p. 55
7. Deirdre Bryan, 'Frances Talbot', *Irish Dictionary of National Biography*
8. Cruickshanks, p. 58
9. Ibid, p. 59
10. See Nathalie Genet-Rouffiac, 'The Jacobite Court in Exile and the Stuart Papers'. *State Papers Online: the Stuart and Cumberland Papers from the Royal Archives, Windsor Castle* (Cengage Learning EMEA Ltd., 2018)

Notes

11. 'Instructions of King James II and VII to His Son', jacobite.ca
12. Edward Corp, 'The Jacobite Court at St. Germain-en-Laye', *The Stuart Courts,* ed. Eveline Cruickshanks (The History Press, 2000; 2009), p. 242
13. John Callow, *The King in Exile: James II, Warrior, King, and Saint, 1689–1701* (Sutton, 2004), p. 203
14. Sarah Churchill, *An Account of the Conduct of the Dowager Duchess of Marlborough* (James Bettenham, 1742), p. 24
15. W.A. Speck, 'Mary II', *Oxford Dictionary of National Biography*
16. Churchill, p. 100
17. Speck, 'Mary II'
18. Alison Plowden, *The Stuart Princesses* (Alan Sutton, 1996), p. 209
19. Andrew Barclay, 'Catharine [*sic*] Sedley, *suo jure* countess of Dorchester', *Oxford Dictionary of National Biography*
20. '"Tilting at Windmills": the Order del Toboso as a Jacobite Social Network', in eds. Monod, Pittock and Szechi, *Loyalty and Identity: Jacobites at Home and Abroad* (Basingstoke, 2010), pp. 243–264
21. Andrew Starkie, 'A Lost Cause? The Cause for the Canonization of King James II', *Studies in Religion and the Enlightenment.* 2019 1:2, pp. 6–9
22. Hilaire Belloc, *James the Second* (Faber & Gwyer, 1928), p. 282

Index

Anne, Princess, 77, 94, 95, 102, 107, 108, 109, 110, 111, 118, 125, 126, 127, 130, 131–132, 137, 138, 142, 146, 147, 150, 151, 152, 153–154, 155, 156, 158, 159, 161, 162, 163, 164, 168, 170, 171, 172, 173
Anne of Denmark, 4, 141
Apsley, Frances, 109, 111
Arundell, Henry, 3rd Baron Arundell of Wardour, 92, 123
Ashley-Cooper, Anthony, 7th Earl of Shaftesbury, 100, 103, 119, 121, 123, 127, 133, 135, 136, 137
Astley, Sir Jacob, 10

Bacon, Sir Francis, 115
Bampfield, Joseph, Colonel, viii–ix, 24, 39, 83
Barillon, Paul d'Amancourt, Marquis de Branges, 106, 111
Barry, Elizabeth, 69, 112
Bedingfeld, Father Thomas, 120, 123
Behn, Aphra, 69, 106, 112, 123, 128, 142, 154
Belasyse or Bellasis, John, 1st Lord Belasyse, 97, 123
Belasyse, née Armine, Lady Susan, 97

Bennet, Sir Henry, 39
Berkeley, née Villiers, Barbara, Lady Fitzhardinge, 172
Berkeley, Charles, 1st Earl of Falmouth, 39, 43, 45, 61, 80–81
Berkeley, Sir John, 38, 39, 40, 41, 42, 43, 49
Berry Godfrey, Sir Edmund, 120, 121
Betterton, Thomas, 68, 107
Blagge, Margaret, 95, 108
Boleyn, Anne, 59, 71, 72, 77, 87
Booth, Sir George, 47
Boy the poodle, 10
Bruce, Sir William, 130, 131
Burnet, Gilbert, Bishop, 102, 120, 151, 155, 157, 158
Burke, Honora, Countess of Lucan, 173
Butler, James, 1st Duke of Ormond, 29, 41, 54, 75, 125

Campbell, Archibald, 9th Earl of Argyll, 145
Carliss, William, Colonel, 35
Carnegie, Lady Anne, 67–68
Carnegie, Robert, 3rd Earl of Southesk, 67–68
Catherine of Aragon, 87, 105

Catherine of Braganza, 72, 77, 79, 92, 98, 109, 111, 120, 122, 132, 139, 141, 145, 154
Cavendish, née Lucas, Margaret, Duchess of Newcastle, 16, 56, 107
Cavendish, William, 1st Duke of Newcastle, 5, 8, 16, 27, 56
Charles I
    imprisonment, vii
    directs James's escape, vii–viii
    death, x
    as young father and husband, 1–4
    as art collector, 3
    Personal Rule, 6–7
    agrees to the execution of Strafford, 7
    retreats from London, 8
    First English Civil War, 8–19
    letters discovered, 20
    leaves Oxford court, 21
    imprisonment, 23, 24, 25
    prepares for death, 26
    as martyr, 57, 58
    as husband, 88
    shadow of, 112, 125, 134, 159, 164, 174
Charles II
    joins James in Holland, ix–x
    childhood, 4
    First English Civil War, 10, 12–19
    leaves Oxford court, 20
    spends time in Jersey, 23, 29
    in Scotland, 30–1
    fights Cromwell, 32
    escape after Worcester, 34–6
    on the Continent, 38ff
    welcomes James to Bruges, 41
    love affairs in exile, 49–50
    Restoration, 53–60
    promises liberty of conscience, 54
    patron of theatre, 68–9
    puts James in charge of fire-fighting, 81
    character, 88
    religious sensibility, 90
    Treaty of Dover, 92–4
    forbids James to marry another commoner, 97
    issues Declaration of Indulgence, 100
    meets Nell Gwyn, 102–3
    marries his niece Mary to William of Orange, 108–9
    worries about James's future, 113
    dealings with Quakers, 114–15
    'Popish Plot', 120–26
    draws the line with Parliament, 134
    confronts Rye House Plot, 136–38
    conversion and death, 139–40
Charles Louis, Prince Elector Palatine, 8, 159
Christina, Queen of Sweden, 38, 89, 143
Churchill, Arabella, 76, 77–9, 83, 102, 106, 117, 118, 173
Churchill, John, 1st Duke of Marlborough, 79, 80, 106, 107, 118, 119, 127, 130, 132, 135, 138, 145, 155, 156, 158, 161, 162, 167–8, 172

Churchill, née Jennings, Sarah, 109, 110, 111, 118, 132, 138, 150, 151, 155, 156–7, 159, 162, 163, 172, 173
Churchill, Sir Winston, 78, 106
Claudia Felicitas, Archduchess of Austria, 98
Clement X, Pope, 98, 99
Coleman, Edward, 120–1, 128
Compton, George, Bishop 109
Coningsby, Juliana, 35
Corelli, Arcangelo, 143
Coventry, Sir William, 72, 80, 84
Crofts, James *see* Scott, James, 1st Duke of Monmouth
Crofts, William, 1st Baron Crofts of Saxham, 49, 73
Cromwell, Oliver, 11, 20, 21, 25, 29, 30, 31, 32, 36, 38, 39, 41, 42, 43, 44, 45, 46, 48, 50, 54, 55, 66, 68, 73, 78, 87, 113, 129, 141, 155
Cromwell, Richard, 46, 48, 50
Cromwell, Thomas, 11, 87

Darnley, Lady Catherine, 138
Davenant, Sir William, 68
Denham, Sir John, 58, 71, 72, 73
Denham, née Brooke, Lady Margaret, 70–1, 72, 73
Digby, George, 2nd Earl of Bristol, 8, 9, 42–3
Dobson, William, 17
Dryden, John, 65, 69, 71, 80, 82, 131, 137, 143
Duppa, Bishop Brian, 5, 22
de Duras, Louis, 2nd Earl of Feversham, 145, 161

Edward VI, 87
Elizabeth I, 5, 9, 29, 35, 87, 124
Elizabeth, Princess (sister), vii–viii, ix, 7, 14, 15, 16, 23, 24, 25, 26, 30, 107
Elizabeth of Bohemia, 1
Elizabeth Charlotte, Madame Palatine, later Duchess of Orléans, 171
d'Este, née Martinozzi, Laura, Duchess of Modena, 98, 101, 133
d'Este, Mary Beatrice (Mary of Modena), Queen of England, 98, 99, 100, 101, 102, 103, 108, 109, 111, 112, 117, 118, 122, 125, 127, 130, 131, 133, 138, 141, 143, 144, 146, 147, 150, 151, 152, 153, 160, 166, 167, 170, 171, 175
Evelyn, John, x, 32, 46, 57–8, 62, 72, 79, 81, 82, 83, 90, 93, 95, 97, 121, 123, 128, 135, 137, 140, 142, 143, 146, 153, 157, 163

Fairfax, Mary, Duchess of Buckingham, 39, 56, 70
Fairfax, Sir Thomas, vii, 20, 21, 39, 51, 56
Ferguson, Robert, 145
Filmer, Sir Robert, 105, 119
Finch, née Kingsmill, Anne, Countess of Winchelsea, 164
Finch, Heneage, 5th Earl of Winchelsea, 164
FitzJames, Lady Arabella, 78, 102, 118, 173

Index

FitzJames, Lady Henrietta, 78, 118, 146, 173
FitzJames, Henry, 1st Duke of Albemarle, 78, 106, 118, 138, 146, 171, 173
FitzJames, James, 1st Duke of Berwick, 78, 106, 118, 138, 146, 155, 159, 168, 171, 173
Fitzroy, Lady Charlotte, 72, 127, 131, 159
Foxe, George, 114

Gascar, Henri, 80
Gaunt, Elizabeth, 136
George of Denmark, Prince, 132, 137, 138, 158, 162, 172
Gibbons, Grinling, 68, 143
Gibson, Richard, 3, 95, 107
Giffard, Father Bonaventure, 144
Godolphin, Sidney, 153
Godfrey, Charles, 118, 173
Graham of Claverhouse, John, 1st Viscount Dundee, 166
de Gramont, Philibert, Count, 37, 42, 75
Granville, Denis, Dean of Durham, 175
Grossi, Francesco aka Siface, 143–4
Guidi, Alberto, 143
Gwyn, Nell, 69, 102–3, 112, 122, 139, 140

Halkett, Lady Anne, viii
Hall, Jacob, 79
Hamilton, Lady Anne, 73
Hamilton, Anthony, 62, 63, 65, 69–70, 74, 118

Hamilton, Elizabeth, later Comtesse de Gramont, 75
Harrison, Thomas, Major-General 62, 64
Harvey, Sir William, 5, 10
Hay, Lucy, Countess of Carlisle, 22
Henrietta of England, vii, 19, 23, 37, 61, 63, 65, 70, 73, 90–4
Henriette Anne, Princess, *see* Henrietta of England
Henrietta Maria, ix, x, 1–4, 5–6, 12, 13, 14, 15 16, 17, 19, 23, 28, 29, 32, 34, 36, 37, 38, 44, 51, 59, 61, 62, 63, 65, 88, 89, 90–1, 93, 95, 141
Henry IV of France, 174
Henry VIII, 5, 11, 71, 86–7, 100, 105, 124, 142, 144, 148, 169–170, 174
Henry, Duke of Gloucester, vii, viii, 1, 7, 15, 16, 23, 24, 25, 26, 27, 30, 36, 41, 44, 45, 55, 56, 60, 63
Herbert, née Somerset, Elizabeth, Marchioness of Powis, 124, 160
Herbert, William, 1st Marquess of Powis, 123, 160
Heylyn, Peter, 86–7, 88, 89, 95, 151
Hobbes, Thomas, 119
Hooker, Richard, 26, 88
Hotham, Sir John, 8–9
Howard, Katherine, 23
Howard, Philip, Cardinal, 120
Hubert, Robert, 82
Huddleston, Father John, 35, 139
Hudson, Sir Jeffrey, 3, 6, 12, 19, 89, 124–5

Hyde, Anne, Duchess of York, 44,
    47, 48–9, 50, 51, 52, 55, 58,
    59–61, 62, 66, 69, 70, 77–80,
    89–90, 95–7, 103, 111, 162
Hyde, Edward, 1st Earl of
    Clarendon, 2, 8, 10, 23, 24,
    28, 44, 46, 49, 51, 54, 59, 61,
    79–80, 83–5
Hyde, née Backhouse, Flower, 138
Hyde, Henry, 2nd Earl of
    Clarendon, 96, 162
Hyde, Laurence, 1st Earl of
    Rochester, 96, 134

Innocent XI, Pope, 111
Isabella, Princess, 111, 125, 130,
    132–3, 147

James, Duke of Cambridge,
    70, 85
James, Duke of York, *see* James II
    and VII
James I and VI, 5, 131, 141
James II and VII
    escape as a youth, vii–x
    birth and childhood;
        education, 1–5
    receives the Order of the
        Garter, 7
    First English Civil War, 8–19
    in Oxford, 13–22
    view of parents, 20–1
    negotiates with Roundheads, 21
    Parliament's prisoner, 22–4
    first exile, 26–8
    enjoys Jersey, 29
    returns to Holland, 31

fights for the French king, 32–8
dispute over household, 38–40
fights for Spain, 44–6
falls in love with Anne Hyde,
    48–9
joy at the Restoration, 56–9
puts down Fifth Monarchists,
    64–5
runs the Admiralty, 65–6
as Restoration rake, 66–70
as patron of the arts, 68–69
leads the fleet against the
    Dutch, 80
fights the Fire of London, 81
conversion to Catholicism,
    87–90
urged to remarry, 97–8
resigns as Lord High
    Admiral, 100
character as compared to
    Charles II, 104–5
obliged to accept Mary and
    William's marriage, 109
enjoys *The Rover*, 112
commitment to religious
    freedom, 113
friendship with William Penn,
    113–16
exiled to Flanders, 125
sent to Scotland, 128
on freedom of conscience, 142,
    149–150
learns of his betrayal, 158
sends his wife and child to
    France, 160
goes to Ireland, 167
death, 175

Index

James Francis Edward, Prince of Wales, 153, 154, 157, 160, 166, 169, 170, 171, 175
Jermyn, Harry, 34, 38, 39, 43, 44, 45, 48, 52, 61
Jermyn, Henry, 1st Earl of St Albans, 19, 24, 28, 38, 42
John José of Austria, Don, 44
Jones, Inigo, 4, 5, 68, 130
Jonson, Ben, 4, 68

Ketch, Jack, 145
de Kéroualle, Louise, Duchess of Portsmouth, 118, 122, 127, 134, 138, 139, 140
Killigrew, Thomas, 69
Kneller, Sir Godfrey, 154, 172

Lambert, John, Major-General, 47, 51, 55
Lane, Jane, 35, 36, 44
Laud, William, Archbishop, 1, 2, 5, 20, 26
Lee, Edward, 1st Earl of Lichfield, 127, 159
Lely, Sir Peter, 25, 70, 75, 77, 97, 107
Locke, John, 119, 136, 142, 157, 164, 165
Lockhart, Sir William, 41, 45
Lopes Suasso, Francisco, 158
Louisa Maria Teresa, Princess, 171, 172, 173, 175
Louis XIV, 21, 32, 46, 37, 38, 91, 92, 93, 99, 110, 111, 121, 122, 132, 134, 148, 157, 161, 166, 169, 171, 175
Louise Hollandine of the Palatinate, Princess, 10, 89
Lovelace, Richard, 13, 17, 25
Lully, Jean-Baptiste, 37

Makin, Bathsua, 16, 107
Marie d'Orléans-Longueville, 36
Marvell, Andrew, 59, 60, 77, 81, 83
Mary I, 2, 123, 124, 142, 143, 144, 148, 157, 163
Mary of Modena, *see* d'Este, Mary Beatrice
Mary, Princess of Orange (daughter), 70, 77, 94, 102, 107, 108, 109–11, 123, 126, 135, 136, 149, 150, 151, 156, 158, 159, 160, 162, 163, 164, 167, 170, 171, 172, 173, 174
Mary, Princess of Orange (sister) ix, 1, 3, 7, 8, 15, 25, 28, 30, 31, 36, 42, 43, 44, 46, 48, 51, 55, 56, 60, 61, 63
Mary, Queen of Scots, 29, 70, 110, 131, 138, 147
Maurice of the Palatinate, ix, 14, 21, 36
Mayerne, Theodore, 19
Mazarin, Jules, Cardinal, 21, 32, 34, 38, 41, 62, 98
de Mesmes, Jean-Antoine, Comte d'Avaux, 167
Middleton, née Brudenell, Lady Catherine, 171
Middleton, Charles, 2nd Earl of Middleton, 171
Modena, Duchess of, *see* d'Este, née Martinozzi, Laura

Monck, George, 1st Duke of Albemarle, 50, 51, 53, 54, 56, 82, 130
Monck, Nicholas, 51, 53, 54
Montagu, Walter, 6, 37
Montecuccoli, Vittoria Davia, Countess of Almond, 99
Mordaunt, Henry, 2nd Lord Peterborough, 98, 99, 101, 127
Mordaunt, née O'Brien, Penelope, 99

Oates, Titus, 119, 120, 121, 123, 125, 127, 128, 133, 135, 160
d'Orléans, Anne-Marie Louise, 36
d'Orléans-Longueville, Marie, 36
Osborne, Thomas, 1st Earl of Danby, 108, 120

Palmer, née Villiers, Barbara, Lady Castlemaine and Duchess of Cleveland, 50, 58, 70, 71, 72, 73, 74, 79, 83, 85, 88, 91, 100, 103, 106, 118, 127
Penn, William, Admiral, 57, 114–15
Penn, William, 57, 113–16, 136, 137, 140, 149, 175
Pepys, Samuel, 53–4, 55, 57, 59–60, 62, 64, 68, 69, 70, 71, 72, 74, 75, 76, 81, 83, 94, 101, 102, 107, 114, 128, 146
Percy, Algernon, 10th Earl of Northumberland, vii, viii, 15, 21, 22, 23, 24, 26
Petre, Father Edward, 139, 151, 157
Petre, William, 4th Baron Petre, 123

Petty, Sir William, 148
Philippe d'Orléans, 61, 63, 91, 93, 94
Philip II of Spain, 163
Plunkett, Archbishop St Oliver, 125
Price, Goditha, 67, 71
Prynne, William, 6, 10, 68
Purcell, Henry, 141, 143

Radcliffe, Sir George, 21–2, 40
de Rancé, Armand Jean de Bouthillier, 174
Reynolds, John, General, 44–5
Robinson, Luke, 55
Rupert of the Rhine, Prince, ix, 4, 8, 10, 12, 14, 18, 20, 21, 36, 61, 80, 93, 100, 133

de Saint-Ruhe, Charles Chalmot, General, 168
Sancroft, William, Archbishop of Canterbury, 164
Sarsfield, Patrick, 1st Earl of Lucan, 158, 168, 173
Scott, Anne, Duchess of Buccleuch, 74, 137, 145
Scott, James, 1st Duke of Monmouth, 49, 73, 74, 77, 80, 103, 104, 105, 108, 110, 123, 125, 127, 128, 136–7, 139, 144, 145–6, 151
Sedley, Catherine, later Countess of Dorchester, 117, 118, 135, 138, 144, 146, 160, 173–4
Sedley, Sir Charles, 117
Seymour, Edward, 1st Duke of Somerset, 87
Seymour, Jane, 87

Index

Seymour, William, 1st Marquess of Hertford, 7
Sidney, Algernon, 136
Simon-Belle, Alexis, 171
Smith, James, 143
Stanhope, née Butler, Elizabeth, Countess of Chesterfield, 75, 76, 77
Stanhope, Philip, 2nd Earl of Chesterfield, 75, 76
Stewart, Frances, Duchess of Richmond, 77, 78, 102

Talbot, née Jennings, Frances, Duchess of Tyrconnell, 118, 155, 162, 166, 168
Talbot, Father Peter, 53, 125
Talbot, Richard, Duke of Tyrconnell, 43, 53, 67–8, 75, 118, 155–6, 166, 167, 168
Thurloe, John, 39, 47
de la Tour d'Auvergne, Henri, Vicomte Turenne, 26, 33, 37, 42, 43, 45, 46, 47, 89, 93

Urban VIII, Pope, 2

Van Dyck, Sir Anthony, 1, 3, 17, 25, 70
Venner, Thomas, 64–5
Villiers, Anne, Lady Dalkeith, 19, 23, 28, 38, 39, 91
Villiers, Betty, 112
Villiers, née Howard, Lady Frances, 95
Villiers, George, 1st Duke of Buckingham, 2, 3
Villiers, George, 2nd Duke of Buckingham, 4, 18–19, 22, 29, 30, 35, 39, 50, 56, 61, 73, 74, 79, 85, 91, 92, 93, 94, 103, 121, 143
Vitali, Giovanni Battista, 141

Walter, Lucy, x, 49, 73, 74, 104
Wentworth, Henrietta, 108, 137, 144, 145
Wentworth, Thomas, 1st Earl of Strafford, 7, 22, 84
de Wet, Jacob, 131
William of Orange, 31, 60, 63, 91, 93, 108, 109–11, 112, 126, 132, 135, 136, 137, 144, 145, 149, 154, 156, 157, 158, 161, 162, 163, 164, 167, 172, 173, 175
Williams, Sir William, 149
Wilmot, Henry, 1st Earl of Rochester, 35, 36
Wilmot, John, 2nd Earl of Rochester, 69, 73, 76, 102, 104, 112, 117, 134
Wren, Christopher, 82, 142, 143
Wright, John Michael, 85, 130